THE NAVARRE BIBLE

Romans and Galatians

NOW AVAILABLE
IN THE ENGLISH EDITION
St Matthew's Gospel
St Mark's Gospel
St Luke's Gospel (with index to the four Gospels)
St John's Gospel
Acts of the Apostles
St Paul's Epistles to the Romans and the Galatians

FORTHCOMING
St Paul's Epistles to the Corinthians
St Paul's Epistles to the Thessalonians,
and Pastoral Epistles
St Paul's Captivity Epistles
Epistle to the Hebrews
Catholic Epistles
Revelation

THE NAVARRE BIBLE
St Paul's Epistles
to the Romans and the Galatians

in the Revised Standard Version and New Vulgate
with a commentary by the Faculty of Theology,
University of Navarre

FOUR COURTS PRESS

Original title: *Sagrada Biblia: VI. Epístolas de San Pablo
a los Romanos y los Gálatas*.
Quotations from Vatican II documents
are based on the translation in *Vatican Council II:
The Conciliar and Post Conciliar Documents*,
ed. A. Flannery, OP (Dublin 1981).

Nihil obstat: Stephen J. Greene, *censor deputatus*.
Imprimi potest: Desmond, Archbishop of Dublin, 2 November 1989.

Typeset by Gilbert Gough Typesetting, Dublin
and designed by Jarlath Hayes,
this book is published by Four Courts Press,
Kill Lane, Blackrock, Co. Dublin, Ireland.

BRITISH LIBRARY CATALOGUING IN PUBLICATION DATA
[Bible. N.T. Epistles of Paul. *English. Revised Standard.*]
The Navarre Bible: St Paul's Epistles to the Romans and to the Galatians
1. Bible. N.T. Romans. Commentaries   2. Bible N.T. Galatians
I. Universidad de Navarra. *Faculty of Theology*
227'.107

ISBN 1-85182-056-6
ISBN 1-85182-055-8 Pbk

Printed and bound in Great Britain by
Richard Clay Ltd, Bungay, Suffolk.

Contents

Preface

In providing both undergraduate and postgraduate education, and in the research it carries out, a university is ultimately an institution at the service of society. It was with this service in mind that the theology faculty of the University of Navarre embarked on the project of preparing a translation and commentary of the Bible accessible to a wide readership — a project entrusted to it by the apostolic zeal of the University's founder and first chancellor, Monsignor Josemaría Escrivá de Balaguer.

Monsignor Escrivá did not live to see the publication of the first volume, the Gospel according to St Matthew; but he must, from heaven, continue to bless and promote our work, for the volumes published since 1976 have been well received and widely read.

This edition of the Bible avoids many scholarly questions, discussion of which would over-extend the text and would be of no assistance to the immense majority of readers; these questions are avoided, but they have been taken into account.

The Spanish edition contains a new Spanish translation made from the original texts, always taking note of the Church's official Latin text, which is now that of the New Vulgate, a revision of the venerable Latin Vulgate of St Jerome: on 25 April 1979 Pope John Paul II, by the Apostolic Constitution *Scripturarum thesaurus*, promulgated the typical edition of the New Vulgate as the new official text; this is the Latin version published in this edition. For the English edition of this book we consider ourselves fortunate in having the Revised Standard Version as the translation of Scripture and wish to record our appreciation for permission to use that text, an integral part of which are the RSV notes, which are indicated by superior *letters*.

The introductions and notes have been prepared on the basis of the same criteria. In the notes (which are the most characteristic feature of this Bible, at least in its English version), along with scriptural and ascetical explanations we have sought to offer a general exposition of Christian doctrine — not of course a systematic exposition, for we follow the thread of the scriptural text.[1] We have also tried to explain and connect certain biblical passages by reference

1 This essay is one of a series of introductory essays in different volumes of the Navarre Bible; taken together these essays (which do not necessarily refer to the particular volumes in which they appear) form a short general introduction to Sacred Scripture. The following such essays have been published in Spanish to date and have appeared or will appear, in the English edition,

to others, conscious that Sacred Scripture is ultimately one single entity; but, to avoid tiring the reader, most of the cross-references etc. are given in the form of marginal notes (the marginal notes in this edition are, then, those of the Navarre Bible, not the RSV). The commentaries contained in the notes are the result of looking up thousands of sources (sometimes reflected in explicit references given in our text) — documents of the Magisterium, exegesis by Fathers and Doctors of the Church, works by important spiritual writers (usually saints, of every period) and writings of the founder of our University. It would have been impertinent of us to comment on the Sacred Bible using our own expertise alone. Besides, a basic principle of exegesis is that Scripture should be interpreted in the context of Sacred Tradition and under the guidance of the Magisterium.

From the very beginning of our work our system has been to entrust each volume to a committee which then works as a team. However, the general editor of this edition takes ultimate responsibility for what it contains.

It is our pleasant duty to express our gratitude to the present chancellor of the University of Navarre, Monsignor Alvaro del Portillo y Diez de Sollano, for his continued support and encouragement, and for reminding us of the good our work can do for the Church and for souls.

"Since Sacred Scripture must be read and interpreted with its divine authorship in mind,"[2] we pray to the Holy Spirit to help us in our work and to help our readers derive spiritual benefit from it. We also pray Mary, our Mother, Seat of Wisdom, and St Joseph, our Father and Lord, to intercede that this sowing of the Word of God may produce holiness of life in the souls of many Christians.

---

in these volumes: in *St Mark*: "General Introduction to the Bible"; "Introduction to the Books of the New Testament"; "Introduction to the Holy Gospels"; and "The Dates in the Life of our Lord Jesus Christ"; in *Acts*: "The History of the Text of the New Testament"; in *Corinthians*: "The Divine Inspiration of the Bible"; in *Romans and Galatians*: "Introduction to the Epistles of St Paul"; in *Captivity Epistles*: "The Canon of the Bible"; in *Hebrews*: "The Interpretation of Sacred Scripture and the Senses of the Bible"; "Divine Worship in the Old Testament"; in *Thessalonians*: "The Veracity of Sacred Scripture".

2 Vatican Council II, Dogm. Const. *Dei Verbum*, 12.

Abbreviations and Sources

1. BOOKS OF SACRED SCRIPTURE

Acts	Acts of the Apostles	2 Kings	2 Kings
Amos	Amos	Lam	Lamentations
Bar	Baruch	Lev	Leviticus
1 Chron	1 Chronicles	Lk	Luke
2 Chron	2 Chronicles	1 Mac	1 Maccabees
Col	Colossians	2 Mac	2 Maccabees
1 Cor	1 Corinthians	Mal	Malachi
2 Cor	2 Corinthians	Mic	Micah
Dan	Daniel	Mk	Mark
Deut	Deuteronomy	Mt	Matthew
Eccles	Ecclesiastes (Qohelet)	Nah	Nahum
Esther	Esther	Neh	Nehemiah
Eph	Ephesians	Num	Numbers
Ex	Exodus	Obad	Obadiah
Ezek	Ezekiel	1 Pet	1 Peter
Ezra	Ezra	2 Pet	2 Peter
Gal	Galatians	Phil	Philippians
Gen	Genesis	Philem	Philemon
Hab	Habakkuk	Ps	Psalms
Hag	Haggai	Prov	Proverbs
Heb	Hebrews	Rev	Revelation (Apocalypse)
Hos	Hosea	Rom	Romans
Is	Isaiah	Ruth	Ruth
Jas	James	1 Sam	1 Samuel
Jer	Jeremiah	2 Sam	2 Samuel
Jn	John	Sir	Sirach (Ecclesiasticus)
1 Jn	1 John	Song	Song of Solomon
2 Jn	2 John	1 Thess	1 Thessalonians
3 Jn	3 John	2 Thess	2 Thessalonians
Job	Job	1 Tim	1 Timothy
Joel	Joel	2 Tim	2 Timothy
Jon	Jonah	Tit	Titus
Josh	Joshua	Tob	Tobit
Jud	Judith	Wis	Wisdom
Jude	Jude	Zech	Zechariah
Judg	Judges	Zeph	Zephaniah
1 Kings	1 Kings		

2. OTHER SOURCES REFERRED TO

Alphonsus Mary Liguori, St
  The love of Jesus Christ reduced to practice
Ambrose, St
  De sacramentis
  Expositio Evangelii secundum Lucam

Anselm, St
  Prayers and Meditations
Augustine, St
  The City of God
  Confessions

Augustine, St
De bono viduitatis
De dono perseverantiae
De spiritu et littera
De Trinitate
Enarrationes in Psalmos
Enchiridion
Expositio Epistulae ad Galatas
In Epistulam Ioannis ad Parthos
In Ioannis Evangelium tractatus
Letters
Sermons
Bernard, St
De fallacia et brevitate vitae
Bernal, Salvador
Monsignor J. Escrivá de Balaguer
Constantinople, Third Council of
Definitio de duabus in Christo voluntatibus et operationibus, sess. XVIII
Escrivá de Balaguer, J.
Christ is passing by (followed by section no.)
Conversations (do.)
Friends of God (do.)
Holy Rosary
Homily on Loyalty to the Church
The Way
The Way of the Cross
Eusebius of Caesarea
Ecclesiastical History
Francis de Sales, St
Introduction to the Devout Life
Gregory the Great, St
In Ezechielem homiliae
Gregory Nazianzen, St
Sermons
Irenaeus, St
Against heresies
Jerome, St
Commentarium in Epistulam ad Galatas
Homily to neophytes on Psalm 41
John of Avila, St
Audi, filia
Lecciones sobre la Epístola a los Gálatas
Sermons
John Chrysostom, St
De coemeterio et de cruce
Homilies on the Epistle to the Romans
Homilies on the Gospel of St Matthew
Second homily in praise of St Paul
John Paul II
Address (on date given)
Apos. Exhort. *Catechesi tradendae*, 16 October 1979)
Enc. *Dives in misericordia*, 30 November 1980
Enc. *Redemptor hominis*, 4 March 1979
Homily (on date given)

John XXIII
Enc. *Ad Petri Cathedram*, 29 June 1959
Leo XIII
Enc. *Diuturnum illud*, 29 June 1881
Enc. *Divinum illius munus*, 9 May 1897
Enc. *Immortale Dei*, 1 November 1885
Enc. *Libertas praestantissimum*, 20 June 1888
Enc. *Quod apostolicis*, 28 December 1878
Letter to Diognetus (second century)
Luis de Granada
Guide to Sinners
Introducción al símbolo de la fe
Orange, Second Council of
Doctrina de gratia
Origen
In Leviticum homiliae
Paul VI
Address (on date given)
Apos. Exhort. *Evangelii nuntiandi*, 8 December 1975
Creed of the People of God, 30 June 1968
Pius V, St
Catechism of the Council of Trent for Parish Priests
Pius XII
Address (on date given)
Enc. *Humani generis*, 12 August 1950
Enc. *Mediator Dei*, 20 November 1947
Pliny the Younger
Letters
Pseudo-Ambrose
Commentarium in Epistulam ad Romanos
Pseudo-Dionysius
De divinis nominibus
Quierzy, Council of
Doctrina de libero arbitrio hominis et de praedestinatione
Missale Romanum ex decreto sacrosancti oecumenici concilii Vaticani II instauratum auctoritatae Pauli PP. VI promulgatum, editio typica altera (Vatican City, 1975)
Sacred Congregation for the Doctrine of the Faith
Instruction on Infant Baptism, 20 October 1980
Seneca
Consolatio ad Helviam
Suetonius
Life of Claudius
Teresa of Avila, St
Book of Foundations
Life
Thomas Aquinas, St
Exposition on the two commandments of love and the ten commandments of the Law
Summa theologiae

Super Epistulam ad Galatas lectura
Super Epistulam ad Romanos expositio
Trent, Council of
   Decree *De peccato originali, sess. V*
   Decree *De iustificatione, sess. VI*
Valence, Third Council of
   Doctrina de praedestinatione
Vatican, First Council of the
   Dogm. Const. *Dei Filius*

Vatican, Second Council of the
   Decl. *Dignitatis humanae*
   Decree *Ad gentes*
   Decree *Presbyterorum ordinis*
   Decree *Unitatis redintegratio*
   Dogm. Const. *Dei Verbum*
   Dogm. Const. *Lumen gentium*
   Past. Const. *Gaudium et spes*

3. OTHER ABBREVIATIONS

A.D.	after Christ	e.g.	*exempli gratia*, for example
ad loc.	*ad locum*, commentary on this passage	Enc.	Encyclical
		f	and following (*pl.* ff)
Adhort.	Exhortation	*ibid.*	*ibidem*, in the same place
Apost.	apostolic	*in loc.*	*in locum*, commentary on this passage
B.C.	before Christ		
can.	canon	*loc.*	*locum*, place or passage
chap.	chapter	n.	number (*pl.* nn.)
cf.	*confer*, compare	OT	Old Testament
Const.	Constitution	p.	page (*pl.* pp.)
Decl.	Declaration	*pl.*	plural
Dz-Sch	Denzinger-Schönmetzer, *Enchiridion Symbolorum*	par.	and parallel passages
		Past.	Pastoral
Dogm.	Dogmatic	sess.	session
EB	*Enchiridion Biblicum*	v.	verse (*pl.* vv.)

Introduction to
the Epistles of St Paul

THE LIFE OF ST PAUL

SOURCES

We know more about St Paul's life than about that of any other Apostle – even St Peter or St John – thanks to the information to be found in his Epistles and in St Luke's Acts of the Apostles; yet it is not possible to construct a complete biography of Paul from these sources, for the simple reason that they were not written with a biographical or autobiographical purpose in mind. However, by using the Epistles and Acts we can identify the main features of his personality – which comes across very directly in the Epistles – and the general outline of his life (with some gaps) from his youth up to the time he was martyred.

HIS YOUTH AND UPBRINGING AS A HELLENISTIC JEW

He was born in Tarsus (cf. Acts 21:39; 22:3), the capital of Cicilia, a busy commercial city and a cultural centre of some prominence. He was brought up there and returned to the city a number of times even after his conversion to Christianity (cf. Acts 9:30; 11:25; Gal 1:21). He belonged to the tribe of Benjamin and was a zealous Pharisee (cf. Phil 3:5; Acts 23:6). In his letters he calls himself Paul (*Paûlos*), but prior to his conversion he seems to have preferred to be known as Saul (*Shaúl*): it was quite common for Jews living in Roman territories to use two names – Latin or Greek, and Hebrew. In Acts he calls himself Saul up to Acts 13:9; and from then on, Paul. His early education in Tarsus was along traditional lines, typical of a Jewish boy living in a Greek-speaking province of the Empire. His letters show him to be utterly at home in the Greek *koiné*, the oral and written *lingua franca*: he has a great mastery of this language but does not use academic turns of phrase. As a young man he seems to have been keen on athletics, as suggested by his use of the language of the Games to illustrate his spiritual teaching.[1] He also acquired a broad general culture – literary (cf. Acts 17:28) and philosophical[2] – as also

---

1   Cf. Rom 9:16; 1 Cor 9:24-27; 2 Cor 4:7-9; Gal 2:2; Eph 4:12-14; Phil 2:16; 1 Tim 4:7; 2 Tim 4:7-8; Heb 2:1-2; Acts 13:25; 20:24; etc.
2   Cf. Rom 1:20-23; 1 Cor 2:2, 11-15; Gal 4:4; Eph 1:23; Col 2:9; 1 Tim 6:4-5; etc.

familiarity with the main religions of the pagan world;[3] but places and scenery and monuments do not seem to have interested him, despite the fact that he was much travelled.

In addition to this Hellenistic and humanistic training, he also received a specifically Jewish education, going to Jerusalem when still very young, probably to be trained as a rabbi; he attended the school of Gamaliel (cf. Acts 22:3), one of the most prominent rabbis of the time and an enthusiastic Pharisee (cf. Gal 1:14). He probably began to study Hebrew, the religious language of the Jews, while still in Tarsus, and became steeped in that language during his period in Jerusalem, as well as mastering the Aramaic dialect of Palestine (cf. Acts 21:40; 22:2). In line with rabbinical custom, St Paul learned and worked at a trade: he became a tentmaker[4] (*skenopoiós*) – a term which can also cover subordinate jobs, such as harness-making and canvas-making.

During his rabbinical studies in Jerusalem, probably shortly after the death of our Lord, we find him a committed persecutor of Christians (cf. Acts 7:58; 8:1; 9:1; 22:20) and the initiator of the spread of that persecution to the Jewish quarter of Damascus.[5]

HIS CONVERSION AND EARLY YEARS AS A CHRISTIAN

However, as he was approaching that city, armed with the High Priest's authority to arrest Christians, the risen Lord appeared to him; this vision, and the influence of grace, brought about Saul's conversion; there and then he realized that he had been completely in the wrong (cf. Acts 9:1-9; 22:5-11; 26:9-18). This instantaneous conversion (cf. Phil 3:12), which the Apostle later described as radically changing his life (cf. 1 Tim 1:13), was caused by his being directly called by Jesus; Paul was taken completely by surprise and was always convinced that this calling came from God.[6]

Immediately after this experience on the road, Saul was brought to Damascus, where he was spoken to by Ananias, who had received a vision telling him of Saul's vocation (cf. Acts 9:10-19). Saul recovered his sight (he had been blinded by the vision) and was baptized (cf. Acts 9:18-19), and he immediately set about preaching God's mercy and bearing witness that Jesus, who had truly appeared to him on the road to Damascus, was the Messiah and Son of God (cf. Acts 9:20-22; Gal 1:15-17). A short time after this, Saul withdrew to Arabia (most likely the south-west of present-day Syria) and later returned to Damascus (cf. Gal 1:15-17), where he received further instruction in the Christian faith and again bore witness to the risen Christ. As a result, the Jews began to persecute him until he eventually had to go into hiding and escape from the city by night, the disciples letting him down in a basket from a window in the walls (cf. Acts 9:23-25).

3 Cf. Acts 17:17; 1 Cor 6:12; Col 2:8-10; 1 Tim 4:7; 2 Tim 4:3-4; etc.
4 Cf. Acts 18:3; 20:34; 1 Cor 4:12; 1 Thess 2:9.
5 Cf Acts 9:1-2; 26:9-11; 1 Cor 15:9; Gal 1:13-14; 1 Tim 1:13.
6 Cf. Gal 1:15; Rom 1:1; 1 Cor 1:1; 15:9-10.

He then made his way to Jerusalem, where, thanks to the good offices of St Peter and St Barnabas, he was welcomed by the Christian community, who at first were suspicious of their former persecutor (cf. Gal 1:18; Acts 19:26-28). Disputes with Jews once again put his life at risk (cf. Acts 9:29) and his new Christian brethren brought him to Caesarea, where he took ship for his native Tarsus (cf. Acts 9:30). From there he went on to other cities in Cilicia and Syria where he spent four or five years, bearing witness to his Christian faith (cf. Gal 1:21-24) and encouraged all the time by Barnabas (Acts 11:25-26). This period ended with a further visit by Paul and Barnabas to Jerusalem to bring the Christians of Judea monies collected to relieve their needs (cf. Acts 11:27-30).

THE GREAT MISSIONARY JOURNEYS

St Luke provides us (in Acts 13:1 - 21:16) with the broad outline of the years which follow, years of intense missionary work. St Paul's apostolic base was Antioch in Syria; he started out from there and gravitated back there, except after his third and last journey, when he headed for Jerusalem. The last main stage in his life begins in Jerusalem.

First journey The basic information about this journey is contained in Acts 13:1 - 14:28. By direct inspiration of the Holy Spirit, Barnabas and Paul set out to spread the Gospel (cf. Acts 13:1-4), accompanied by John Mark, then a young man. They preached in a number of cities in Cyprus (cf. Acts 13:4-12) and then went back to the mainland to visit Pamphylia, Pisidia and Lycaonia (in the south-west of present-day Turkey); there also they preached in quite a number of towns and in most cases eventually met with violent opposition from Jews settled there. In Lystra, after rejecting divine honours, Paul was stoned at the instigation of Jews who had come from Iconium and Antioch of Pisidia (where Paul had given a very memorable speech to Jews and converts to Judaism; cf. Acts 13:16-43). They then made their way back to Syrian Antioch, and there we witness the first clash with Judaizing Christians, who had come from Jerusalem and were insisting that Christians of pagan background observe the Mosaic Law (cf. Acts 15:1-2).

The Antiochene Christians decided to send Paul and Barnabas to Jerusalem, to consult with the Apostles on the matter (cf. Acts 15:2-3). These, in what is known as the Council of Jerusalem, determined that Christians were under no obligation whatever to observe the ritual, disciplinary and other precepts of the Mosaic Law (cf. Acts 15:4-29).

Second journey Our basic source of information about this journey is Acts 15:36 - 18:22. Paul and Barnabas decided to leave Antioch to visit the churches founded during their first missionary journey (cf. Acts 15:36), but they fell out over whether to keep Mark with them (cf. Acts 15:37-39). Barnabas, with Mark, went off to Cyprus (cf. Acts 15:39), while Paul, with Silas as his assistant, toured the churches of Syria and Cilicia (cf. Acts 15:40-41). In Lystra they were joined by Timothy (cf. Acts 16:1-3). They then went on into Phrygia and Galatia, where they founded new Christian communities (cf. Acts 16:4-8). In Troas Paul had the vision of the Macedonian in a dream (cf. Acts 16:9-10) and as a result crossed over into Europe, where the first cities he visited were Neapolis and Philippi (cf. Acts 16:11-15). At Philippi Paul and Silas were beaten with rods and imprisoned (cf. Acts 16:16-24) but were then set free through a miracle (cf. Acts 16:25-40). They moved on to Thessalonica (cf. Acts 17:1-9) and Beroea (cf. Acts 17:10-14). Silas and Timothy stayed on in Beroea (cf. Acts 17:14), while Paul, in the company of some recent converts, went on to Athens (cf. Acts 17:15), where he preached to Jews in the synagogue and to pagans in the Areopagus (cf. Acts 17:16-33). He then moved to Corinth (cf. Acts 18:1), where he founded a church and spent a year and a half ministering to it, eventually leaving because of opposition from certain Jews (cf. Acts 18:2-18). He set out for Antioch, accompanied as far as Ephesus by Aquila and Priscilla, a recently converted married couple (cf. Acts 18:19-21). At Ephesus he embarked for Caesarea in Palestine, "went up and greeted the church" (Acts 18:22) – which must refer to Jerusalem – and then made his way back to Antioch.

Third journey Once again Acts (18:23 - 21:16) is our main source of information but now, additionally, we can glean a good deal from Paul's own letters. After staying for a while in Antioch in Syria, the Apostle visited the churches in Galatia and Phrygia, "strengthening all the disciples" (Acts 18:23). He spent three years in Ephesus, during which time he laid the foundations of that important local church (cf. Acts 19:1-20). From Ephesus the Gospel spread to Colossae, Laodicea and Hierapolis (cf. Col 1:7; 2:1; 4:13-14), and Paul went once to Corinth to see to the church there (cf. 2 Cor 12:14; 13:1-2). The riot of the silversmiths caused him to leave Ephesus, and he then travelled again through Macedonia and Achaia, accompanied by a number of disciples (cf. Acts 20:1-4).

Embarking at Philippi, he set out for Jerusalem, his last visit there as far as we can tell. He stopped off in Troas, Mitylene and Samos, and in Miletus (cf. Acts 20:5-15), where he called a meeting of the elders of Ephesus and gave them one of his most memorable addresses (cf. Acts 20:17-38). He then went by boat to Cos, Rhodes and Patara, and from there went directly to Tyre in Phoenicia, coming in sight of Cyprus and leaving it on his left (cf. Acts 21:1-3). He stayed in Tyre to spend a few days with the disciples of that city, and they gathered on the beach for prayer (cf. Acts 21:4-5). Once again he took ship, called in at Ptolemais and finally reached Caesarea, where the disciples pleaded with him not to go to Jerusalem, because of Agabus' prophecy that Paul would be imprisoned (cf. Acts 21:6-14); but the Apostle was determined to go up to the Holy City, and some disciples went with him (cf. Acts 21:15-16).

The brethren, the elders and St James gave Paul and his companions a warm welcome. He told them all about the wonders God had been working among the Gentiles, and about the many people who had joined the Church (cf. Acts 21:17-26). Some Jews in the city then created an uproar over Paul and would have lynched him had it not been for the intervention of the tribune and his cohort; Paul was arrested, but the tribune gave him permission to address the crowd (cf. Acts 21:27-40). Paul gave a very moving speech (cf. Acts 22:1-21), which was interrupted by shouting (cf. Acts 21:27-40). Unable to discover what all the row was about, the tribune gave orders for Paul to be cross-examined by scourging – a frightful Roman form of torture – to make him confess; but Paul claimed his rights as a Roman citizen and the tribune withdrew his order (cf. Acts 22:22-29). Once more the tribune tried to discover the reason for the Jewish opposition to Paul by calling a meeting of the Sanhedrin and having Paul appear before it; Paul managed himself very well, but soon after this a plot was made to kill him, from which he was saved by being sent under heavy guard to Caesarea (cf. Acts 22:30 - 23:32).

There Paul was examined by Antonius Felix, the governor, who kept him confined for two years under military guard, and shortly after the arrival of a new governor, Festus, Paul felt obliged to "appeal to Caesar" in order to avoid being handed over to the Jewish authorities (cf. Acts 23:33 - 25:11). The result was that he was sent to Rome by sea, in the custody of a centurion (cf. Acts 25:12 - 27:2).

St Luke gives a detailed account of events of this voyage – storm, shipwreck, and refuge on Malta – and of the rest of the journey to Rome (cf. Acts 27:3 - 28:15). Once Paul reached Rome he was placed under the supervision of a soldier in a type of house-arrest (cf. Acts 28:16) which allowed him to receive visitors without restriction (cf. Acts 28:17-28). He spent two years in this situation, preaching the Gospel unhindered to those who came to see him (cf. Acts 28:30-31). At this point the narrative of Acts comes to an end. After these two years, the charges against Paul must have been dropped due to his accusers failing to appear or to present a written indictment; so that around the spring of 63 he was set free.

THE LAST PERIOD OF HIS LIFE

The Acts of the Apostles do not cover the period after Paul's first imprisonment in Rome, so the only information we have has to be gleaned from the Apostle's own personal letters (1 and 2 Timothy, and Titus) and certain references contained in the traditions preserved in Christian writings (Pope St Clement's first epistle, dating from the end of the first century) and the Muratorian Canon (c. 180).

It is probable that very soon after being set free Paul went ahead with his long-cherished plan of preaching the Gospel in Spain (cf. Rom 15:24, 28), as this seems to be confirmed by 1 Clem 5:7, the Muratorian Canon, lines 38-39, and certain local traditions, such as that of Tarragona. This would have been a short visit, lasting no more than a year (around 63-64), with him then going back to Asia Minor. It is not possible to reconstruct these journeys. The only thing we know is that he did return to Ephesus and from there went into Macedonia. He also visited Crete (cf. Tit 1:5), Corinth and Miletus (cf. 2 Tim 4:19-20).

It is possible that he was arrested in Troas (cf. 2 Tim 4:13) and underwent trial at Ephesus (cf. 2 Tim 4:14-18). Around the autumn of 66 he was once again a prisoner in Rome (cf. 2 Tim 4:9-21), from where he did what he could for the churches (cf. 2 Tim 4:11). He was not to be set free again, but suffered martyrdom; the tradition is that he was beheaded near Tre Fontane, in Aquae Salviae, almost certainly in the year 67.

ESTABLISHING DATES IN ST PAUL'S LIFE

We do know a number of exact or very close dates: St Luke is very helpful in this regard, and certain episodes in Paul's life can be connected up with data available from secular history; there is also the information which can be extracted from Paul's own letters. All these sources allow us to establish fairly accurate dates for other less well-dated events – with a margin for error of not more than five years. This allows us to suggest the following chronological table (a hyphen between two dates means the event falls somewhere between the two; an oblique line indicates that one or other year applies, depending on the dating system used).

A.D.	Event or activity
7-12	Born in Tarsus, Cicilia.
Later than 30	In Jerusalem doing rabbinical studies.
34/36	Is called to the Christian faith. Stays in Damascus and then withdraws to the desert of Arabia.
37/39	First visit to the Apostles in Jerusalem.
43-44	In Tarsus.
44/45	In Antioch, Syria.
Spring 45 - Spring 49	First missionary journey.
49-50	Council of Jerusalem. The incident at Antioch.
End of 49 or beginning of 50, until the autumn of 52	Second missionary journey.
50-52	1 and 2 Thessalonians (Corinth).

A.D.	Event or activity
Spring 53 - spring 58	Third missionary journey.
Autumn 54 - spring 57	In Ephesus.
54	Epistle to the Galatians (Ephesus?).
Spring 57	1 Corinthians (Ephesus).
57	Visits Corinth.
Summer 57	Travels to Macedonia.
Autumn 57	2 Corinthians (Macedonia).
Spring 57-58	Corinth. Epistle to the Romans (Corinth).
Easter 58	In Philippi.
Pentecost 58	Arrested in Jerusalem.
58-60	Imprisoned in Caesarea.
Autumn 60 - spring 61	Travels by sea to Rome.
Spring 61 - spring 63	First Roman imprisonment.
62/54-57	Epistle to the Philippians (Rome) (Ephesus?).
62	Epistles to Philemon and to the Colossians (Rome).
End of 62 or early 63	Epistle to the Ephesians (Rome).
63-64	Travels to Spain (?).
64-67	Travels to Asia Minor, Crete and Macedonia.
65	1 Timothy. Epistle to Titus (Macedonia).
64-66	Epistle to the Hebrews (Rome?, Athens?).
66-67	2 Timothy (Rome).
66-67	Second Roman imprisonment and death by martyrdom.

THE EPISTLES OF ST PAUL

From the very beginning Christian tradition has recognized St Paul as the author of fourteen of the twenty-one epistles in the New Testament. This makes him the most prolific New Testament writer, in terms of number of items, although

St John has the greatest range of type of writing (Gospel, Book of Revelation and three Epistles), and St Luke, with just two books, his Gospel and Acts, is first in terms of length.

In the classical world letters took two forms – ordinary "letters" as such, dealing with family, commercial, administrative and other such matters; and "epistles" properly so called, a type of treatise or essay on some particular subject, addressed to some important personage, or some friend or relative. St Paul's writings are both epistle and letter: they are letters, because they retain a familiar tone, with personal greetings, recommendations of people, etc; and epistles, in that they contain teachings, in a more or less elaborate form. In any event they are inspired writings, a source of Christian revelation, of permanent relevance to the Church even though they often deal with matters arising in the day-to-day affairs of the infant churches.

The order in which St Paul's epistles are given in most Bibles is quite artificial. Usually the letters addressed to the various communities are given first and then those to particular individuals. Within these groups the order tends to follow the length of the document and the frequency of its use in Christian writings, with the exception of the Epistle to the Hebrews, which is usually put at the very end. In other words, the epistles are not arranged in chronological order; but we will discuss them in that order here, in order to give a better idea of the way the Apostle's teaching developed.

THE LETTERS TO THE THESSALONIANS

All scholars, ancient and modern, are agreed that St Paul's first two letters were 1 and 2 Thessalonians, written in Corinth in the years 50-52. It has been suggested that possibly, but less probably, the Epistle to the Galatians was written before these, in which case it should be dated around 49. The two Letters to the Thessalonians contain St Paul's teaching on certain matters raised by the Christians of Thessalonica, who would have been converted to Christianity only some months earlier, during the first phase of Paul's second missionary journey. These matters all have to do with the *parousía*, or second coming of Christ, and the resurrection of the dead: the neophytes of Thessalonica were none too clear on these subjects, which caused them considerable worry. The Apostle does not know when these events will take place, because this has not been revealed (cf. Acts 1:6-8; Mt 24:36; Mk 13:32), and stresses the need to be spiritually vigilant, as our Lord teaches,[7] so that we be always found ready whenever he does come. A particular difficulty concerns the "man of lawlessness" (2 Thess 2:3-12), the "Antichrist"; again, nothing definite is known about when he will appear. The Thessalonians should not be worried about these matters, nor be wasting their time trying to work out when they will come to pass; what they should be doing is living holy lives and taking their everyday work seriously; he even says, "If any one will not work, let him not eat" (2 Thess 3:10).

7   Cf. Mt 24:37 - 25:30; Mk 13:33-37; Lk 21:34-36.

The Epistles to the Thessalonians, written some twenty years after the death of our Lord, are almost certainly the two oldest writings in the New Testament (which contains St Matthew's Gospel only in its later, Greek, redaction); not only do they contain perennial teaching: they tell us about the hearts and minds of those recently converted first Christians and about their community, which was one of the very first churches founded by St Paul on the continent of Europe.

THE "GREAT EPISTLES"

This is the general description given to Galatians, 1 and 2 Corinthians, and Romans, all written during the third missionary journey (spring 53 to spring 58). No one now disputes their Pauline authorship. It is quite clear that they are fully consistent with one another as regards doctrine, style and outlook, and are stamped with St Paul's strong personality.

Galatians This is usually dated 54 or 55, during the Apostle's long sojourn in Ephesus. As we have already said, a few scholars do not reject the possibility of his having written this letter in Antioch in Syria, in the year 49, shortly before the apostolic Council of Jerusalem. It has also been suggested that it may have been written as late as 57, on the grounds that the teaching it contains is similar to that of Romans and that it may even have been a first draft of Romans.

The main theme of the letter has to do with Christians' freedom as regards the observance of the complex prescriptions of the Mosaic Law and the elaborations of the same in the traditions of the scribes. It all has to do with the dispute with some Christians of Jewish background who regarded these observances as necessary for salvation and who were pressurizing the faithful of Galatia to adhere to this interpretation. St Paul makes it absolutely clear that Christians are completely free to do whatever they want in this regard; in fact, five years earlier, at the Council of Jerusalem, he had brought the matter up and obtained a definitive ruling on it. This dispute with "Judaizers" gives the Apostle an opportunity to expound the redemptive value of Christ's Passion: Christians are inserted into Christ's salvific action through faith and Baptism, with absolute independence of the Old Law, which has been superseded in this new stage of salvation.

Corinthians St Paul wrote his first epistle to the Corinthians in Ephesus in the spring of 57. The riot of the silversmiths forced him to leave the city in a hurry, and from Macedonia, in the autumn of the same year, he wrote the second letter to the Corinthians. At that time, Corinth, located on the isthmus of the same name, with two ports, one on the Aegean and the other on the Ionian Sea, was one of the foremost commercial cities in the Mediterranean, frequented by trading ships of all nations. It had a very cosmopolitan population, with religions of every sort, but was also notorious for its moral decadence. One of its aberrations had to do with the worship of Aphrodite and the thousand "priestesses" dedicated to the goddess, who practised so-called "sacred prostitution". This and the prevalence of other kinds of immorality must have meant that the young church in Corinth had to operate in a difficult environment; but divine Providence showered graces and charisms on that cosmopolitan church.

The first epistle to the Corinthians is very important from an historical as well as a doctrinal point of view. One of the first subjects the Apostle takes up is that of the unity of the Church and of Christians; he does so in the context of certain divisions which had arisen among those recent converts. He stresses the need for all to be at one, the danger of letting oneself be led by merely human preferences, and the obedience the Corinthians owe him as an Apostle and as their father in faith. He speaks out against certain moral abuses tolerated by the community – for example, a case of incest, where a man was continuing to live with his step-mother (not so unusual in that society) – and he explains marriage and virginity in passages which provide basic Christian principles on these subjects (chap. 7). A delicate point at this time had to do with whether it was lawful or not to eat the meat of animals which had been sacrificed to idols, which was sold in the market as a matter of course. St Paul recommends to the Corinthians not to create problems of conscience for themselves, but to make sure they did not cause scandal (chaps. 8-10). Important subjects dealt with in the Epistle include the Eucharist – its institution at the Last Supper, the real presence of Christ in the eucharistic species and rules concerning the celebration of the Eucharist, as also the fraternal meal or *agápe* which was held along with it (chap. 11) – and the Resurrection of Christ and of the dead (chap. 15). In discussing these subjects the Apostle gives a series of guidelines about how to discern and channel the many charisms with which the Holy Spirit – as we have said – was endowing the church of Corinth.

In the second epistle, in the course of defending his own authority, Paul delineates the main features of the office of apostle, to which Christ personally called him, making him one of the Twelve. In these pages he pours out his heart and shows his love for his children in the faith, his strength of spirit and his sense of his own responsibility as an Apostle. As we have indicated in the chronology of his life, it can be taken as certain that he wrote this letter in the autumn of the year 57, from some city in Macedonia very soon (not much more than a month) before he actually visited Corinth again, in the winter of 57 to 59.

Romans Both letters to the Corinthians proved very effective; the church had become spiritually healthy and fervent. All the indications were that the grace of the Spirit was also working well in the other local churches the Apostle had founded. In view of this, Paul began to plan an apostolic journey to Spain, combining this with an extended stay in Rome, where a considerable number of Christians were now established. Prior to this, however, he wanted to go to Jerusalem to bring the faithful of Palestine, who were in a very impoverished state, the proceeds of a considerable collection made on their behalf; this palpable sign of the charity of brethren in other countries would be a consolation to the mother church of Jerusalem. To prepare the ground for his stay in Rome, Paul now wrote his great Epistle to the Romans, from Corinth, in the early months of 58. This letter, Paul's longest, has also been regarded as his most important. In it he deals with key aspects of the teaching and redemptive work of Christ, extending and deepening what he had said in Galatians (which letter, as we have said, may be regarded as a first draft of Romans).

The letter begins with a long greeting, full of theological interest, and then proceeds to give a vision of unredeemed mankind, alienated and hostile to God after the fall of Adam. It surveys the moral degeneration of the Gentiles and the similar sins of the Jews, concluding that all men are in absolute need of redemption by Christ, to obtain God's forgiveness and grace. To understand this epistle one needs to notice what it says about four key notions – sin, death, the flesh and the Law. We will examine these in some detail in the section on "The 'Theology' of St Paul" below. Man in his unredeemed state is subject to these four forces and can be freed from them only by the Redemption wrought by Christ Jesus: salvation comes only from Christ our Lord, and we appropriate it by means of faith, which is a free gift from God and not the result of our own efforts or "works". Once we do open ourselves to faith, and through Baptism are inserted into Christ, we can and should do good, that is, practise virtue, through the Holy Spirit who dwells within us, completing the work of justification effected by Christ, sanctifying us and making us adoptive sons and daughters of the Father. And so we change from being enemies of God to being his friends; from being in a state of unredemption we move into a state of grace, a new level of creation, shot through with the hope of attaining the glory of the children of God.

In the second part of the epistle St Paul applies this teaching to the way in which the person who has embraced faith in Christ should live his or her life: he spells out what faith demands in terms of moral conduct, what "life in the Spirit" entails, and he gives us practical advice on how to make one's way in the world, a world as yet unredeemed, which must be led to salvation.

The Epistle to the Romans marks the high point of God's revelation given us in the Apostle's letters; in his other letters he develops certain aspects of the theology already sketched out in Romans.

THE CAPTIVITY EPISTLES

In the late spring of 58 Paul reached Jerusalem. During the feast of Pentecost he was arrested as a result of the machinations of the Jewish authorities. He was taken, under heavy armed guard to Caesarea, where he later appeared before a Roman tribunal – and appealed to Caesar. Shipwrecked en route to Rome, he eventually arrived there and was held under house arrest for probably two years, from 61 to the spring of 63, when his case went by default. During this first Roman captivity he wrote the letter to Philemon, Colossians,

Ephesians and, most likely, Philippians: for this reason these are usually referred to as "the captivity letters".

Philemon No one disputes the Pauline authorship of this short letter, sent to Philemon, a Christian, to have him welcome Onesimus, a former slave of Philemon's, who had run away and taken refuge in Rome, where he became a Christian. Paul feels that the best thing for Onesimus to do is to return to his master's house: both are now brothers in the Lord. St Paul does not discuss the abolition of slavery – which would have been unthinkable in that culture – but his teaching apropos of this particular case actually undermines the very basis of the institution of slavery by making it quite clear that all men are radically equal.

Philippians The subject-matter and thrust of this letter is quite different from that of Colossians and Ephesians; for this reason, some scholars are of the view that, although it was written in prison, the imprisonment was not Paul's first Roman imprisonment but rather an earlier one, possibly in Ephesus, at some point during the Apostle's stay in that city in the period 54-57. Some scholars argue against a Pauline authorship but they have no solid ground for doing so. The difference in subject-matter and approach as compared with Colossians and Ephesians can be explained by the particular circumstances of the faithful in Philippi: the Christian community in that city was made up mainly of retired legionaries, who had been assigned lands and employment by a grateful Empire. Twenty years earlier Philippi had been given the privilege of *ius italicum*, with the title *Colonia Iulia Augusta Philippensis*. Retired army men had settled there with their families; their military training and experience had bred in them a sense of discipline, loyalty and dedication. St Paul had great affection for these people, with their unshakeable faith and their generous response to its demands (cf. his remarks about their financial contributions: Phil 4:18). The letter contains a number of terms which have a military ring to them, and its tone is cheerful and serene, even though it contains references to the difficulties which imprisonment meant for Paul.

The most important doctrinal passage in the epistle is what is called the "Christological hymn" (Phil 2:6-11), quite possibly a hymn with which they were already familiar, transcribed by the Apostle with some little glosses of his own; it sings of Christ humbling himself by his incarnation, life and death, and then of how his humanity was exalted in heaven after the Resurrection.

Colossians From earliest times the Pauline authorship of this letter was acknowledged in the Church, but in the nineteenth century some scholars began to question this, with respect to the whole letter or parts of it. These doubts stemmed from the degree to which the teaching in Colossians is more developed than that in earlier epistles and from the new vocabulary it uses. However, these objections seem insufficient to reject the traditional attribution of the entire epistle to Paul.

The Christian community at Colossae had been founded not by Paul but by his disciple Epaphras, and in fact it was Epaphras who reported to Paul, around the year 62, when he was under house arrest in Rome, about doctrinal matters which were worrying the Colossians. It is now thought that the Christians at Colossae had been affected by early instances of Persian and Mesopotamian Gnosticism, imported via Jewish travellers. Gnostic teaching began to spread in the countries of the Roman Empire around the middle or early part of the first century A.D., promoted sometimes by certain Jews and sometimes by people interested in Hellenist philosophy or religion.

The main feature of Gnosticism was its dualistic notion of God, of man and of the world: two opposite principles, good and evil, spirit and matter, provided the key to understanding everything. Gnosticism projected itself as the highest form of Wisdom, superior to all other religions, Christianity included; these it regarded as providing inadequate explanations, useful only to the unlearned. At Colossae early Gnostic influences seemingly sought to show the compatibility of Christianity with Gnosticism: Gnostics regarded Christ, because he was man, as on a lower level than angelic powers; these were purer, for being entirely spiritual; Christ would be an *aeon*, an intermediary between God (the Spirit) and matter.

Doctrinal confusion of this type led St Paul – inspired by God – to outline clearly and vigorously certain central points of faith to which the Colossians should adhere, rejecting these foreign notions. He deals in great depth with basic aspects of the mystery of Christ's being (Christology) – his infinite superiority over all creatures, whether they be called angels or powers or be given some other name. The Apostle makes some very profound statements, such as when he says that in Christ "the whole fulness of deity dwells bodily" (Col 2:9), the doctrinal content of which is equivalent to St John's "the Word became flesh and dwelt among us" (Jn 1:14). Thus, what we find in Colossians are new terms which were being used by Hellenist Gnostics, but which Paul uses for the purposes of argument and with new meanings or shades of meaning. Essentially what he explores is the truth that Jesus Christ is eternal God, who on assuming a human nature does not cease to be God; therefore, he is first among all created beings and is superior to them.

In addition to developing doctrine on this subject, Paul also deals with moral and disciplinary matters such as the duties of husband and wife and slave and master, and gives advice about the practice of Christian virtues.

Ephesians Christian tradition has acknowledged St Paul as the author of the epistle to the Ephesians. However, since the 1860s some biblical scholars have questioned this attribution, or questioned whether certain parts of the letter are by Paul. Their arguments are more or less on the same lines as those used against the Pauline authorship of Colossians. However, there is as yet insufficient basis for rejecting the traditional attribution; the doctrinal and literary characteristics of Ephesians still seem to support the view that Paul was its author.

25

Ephesians marks a climax in St Paul's spiritual and doctrinal discussion of the mystery of Christ's nature and personality; the meaning of Redemption; and the theology of the Church. Definitely written towards the end of the year 62, or the beginning of 63, this letter is a kind of second version, a very free redaction, of the letter to the Colossians, written a few months earlier. Ephesians deals with the same subjects but it deals with them in greater depth, more calmly and against a broader background. The so-called "Colossae crisis" was also the external circumstance which led the Apostle to write this other letter, addressed to the churches located in the western coastal region of Asia Minor, where Ephesus was the main city. Paul wanted to ensure that the kind of doctrinal confusion Colossae had experienced would not spread to these churches. The biblical and extra-biblical data available to us suggest that Paul was taking issue with Hellenistic Gnostic notions about the material world being ruled by powers intermediary between God and men, powers which in their different ways actually intervene in human affairs. Countering these ideas, in the course of this epistle, and in various ways, he teaches that Christ Jesus is the head of all creation; he is the absolute Lord of heavenly as well as earthly creatures, and their Saviour; nothing is outside the scope of his lordship.

Ephesians 1:3-14 is an elaborate hymn or canticle, located as a kind of overture to the whole epistle, which sings the praises of God's design to save mankind through Christ. All created beings, which on account of sin have become unconnected from one another and from God, are now, through the Redemption wrought by Christ, once more united to one another and to God, who has established the incarnate Christ, now in glory, as the Head over all things.

Starting from reflection on communities or local churches, Ephesians proceeds to explore the very nature of the Church, its unbreakable unity, its Christ-given mission to be his "body", his "fulness", his spotless bride, the unique instrument devised by him to apply to mankind the salvation he brought through his Death and Resurrection.

As usual the Apostle draws practical moral and ascetical conclusions from his theology: all the faithful should be one in charity, for they form "one body" with Christ, a body whose soul is the Holy Spirit. The duties of spouses, of parents and children, masters and servants, derive from this fact, for they all receive the life-giving influence of the Head, Christ Jesus.

THE PASTORAL EPISTLES

Since the eighteenth century the three letters addressed to Timothy (two letters) and Titus, prominent disciples and helpers of St Paul, have been given the general title of "pastoral letters". The first letter to Timothy must have been written towards the end of the year 65, possibly from Macedonia. And the letter to Titus also would have a date and place close to it, possibly also the end of 65 and from Macedonia. St Paul was enjoying freedom at the time of writing these letters, whereas the second letter to Timothy was written during his last imprisonment, certainly from Rome and shortly before his martyrdom – which means it should be dated 66 or 67. The three letters were written to guide and help these two disciples in their work as Paul's assistants in the pastoral government of various churches.

Church tradition has always held that St Paul was the author of these letters. From the nineteenth century onwards, many rationalist and liberal Protestant scholars questioned or rejected this attribution, mainly on the grounds that it is impossible to envisage that the notions of apostolic succession and tradition, sacred ordination by the laying-on of hands, and some kind of church hierarchy and discipline, could have emerged as early as during the Apostle's lifetime. Such concepts, which appear in the letters, although in an underdeveloped form, are things which these critics cannot accept as being articulated at such an early stage of the Church. But in fact, as the Pontifical Biblical Commission stated,[8] there are no sound arguments against Pauline authorship of the pastoral epistles: the objections referred to are based on a priori attitudes as to how and when the Church's structure took shape.

St Paul always rejected the oppression implied by slavish, literal fulfilment of the Mosaic Law and the way the Jews interpreted that law. But this does not mean that the content of the natural moral law – specified in the Law of Moses – can ever be superseded or that Christian society and Christian churches can be anarchic, that is, devoid of any system of government.

Ever since his first letter to the Corinthians in the year 57, St Paul can be seen to be concerned about ecclesial order and discipline. However, the hierarchical system of Church government described by St Paul in the pastoral epistles was still in the process of taking shape: as yet no precise vocabulary had been devised to designate and distinguish the role and ministry of bishops and priests, but the letters do reveal a distinction between the order of bishops and priests and the order of deacons. The differences in terminological precision noticeable between this group of letters, for example, and the letters of St Ignatius of Antioch (*d.* 107) is enormous. Clearly referring to an already existing institution, St Ignatius speaks of residential bishops with monarchical authority and jurisdiction over priests, who act by authority delegated by the bishops. Therefore, one must recognize that on this point the pastoral letters are clearly very early writings and are consistent with the years 65-67, the last years of Paul's life.

In these letters Paul's main concern is the consolidation of those churches already founded, in the government of which he is being helped by Titus and Timothy, two very faithful and competent disciples. In them we can notice St Paul's typical ability to move directly from deep theological concepts (such as in 1 Tim 3:16; Tit 2:11-14; 3:3-7; 2 Tim 2:8-9) to practical advice, and he has a lot to say about how Christians should conduct themselves in their various communities and in civil society and how they should achieve holiness and attract others to the faith through their example and virtue.

8   Cf. *Reply* of 12 June 1913: *EB*, 407-410; *AAS* 5 (1913) 292-293.

This is the only Pauline epistle which carries no opening salutation or address, although it does include a few words of farewell at the end. From the beginning of the fourth century onwards all the churches attributed it to St Paul. Prior to then it was generally accepted in the East as being by St Paul, but in the West there was much less unanimity. These doubts were based on its obvious difference in style, syntax and vocabulary from the other letters attributed to St Paul: Hebrews is written in a very pure, elegant Greek which is in contrast to the free, vigorous Greek of St Paul. However, its underlying style and its thought are consistent with what we are used to in St Paul. From very early on two solutions have been proposed to explain these differences. One is that this letter, unlike the others, was not dictated by Paul but was composed by a secretary, obviously a very cultured one, who wrote the epistle in his own style, using ideas which the Apostle wanted to communicate to his immediate readership.[9] The other solution is that St Paul dictated the letter in Hebrew or Aramaic but that this primitive redaction was very soon lost, leaving the Church with this early, elegant translation into Greek, which version found its way into the Canon of Scripture; in which case it had the same career as the Gospel of St Matthew.

The title "to the Hebrews" was added to the epistle later – but still in very early times, as extant documents show; it is a highly appropriate title. The great majority of commentators are agreed in seeing the letter as being addressed in the first instance to a group of Christians of Jewish origin, a group, furthermore, in which convert priests and Levites of the Temple of Jerusalem were numerous or at least very influential. After their conversion they would of course have been excluded from taking part in priestly rites in the Temple and would have found themselves without any occupation or means of support. At certain times they may have felt somewhat depressed and have hankered for the splendour of the liturgical rites of the Temple. St Paul would have written to them to give them reassurance in the faith, arguing, very much in the rabbinical style, that the ancient sacrifices of the Temple, and the Temple itself, were no more than a figure, a foreshadowing, of the unique, true Sacrifice of Christ, the real Temple and High Priest. These new Christians should base their life on the faith in Christ to which they have been converted and on the hope that, just as the ancient people of Israel made their way through the desert, suffering many setbacks but always helped by God's power, so these Christians – and all Christians who would follow them – should make their pilgrim way on earth until they reach the glory of heaven: this hope should help them sustain persecution and the loss of their precious position, where they had prestige and were supported by their fellow Jews.

The Apostle used the situation of these Christians to develop doctrine about

---

9   Cf. Pontifical Biblical Commission, *Reply* of 24 June 1914: *EB*, 411-413; *AAS* 6 (1914) 417f. The authorship of Hebrews is discussed at somewhat greater length in *The Navarre Bible: Epistle to the Hebrews* (forthcoming).

the Priesthood and Sacrifice of Christ, which is what makes this such an important New Testament text. The epistle was clearly written from Italy (cf. Heb 13:24), probably from Rome, around the year 65.

INTRODUCTION TO
THE "THEOLOGY" OF ST PAUL

The ordinary Christian reader may experience a certain difficulty in understanding the letters of St Paul. In fact, the second letter of St Peter adverts to this: "And count the forbearance of our Lord as salvation. So also our beloved brother Paul wrote to you according to the wisdom given him, speaking of this as he does in all his letters. There are some things in them hard to understand, which the ignorant and unstable twist to their own destruction, as they do the other scriptures" (2 Pet 3:15-16). Our Lord revealed supernatural truths to the crowds, and even to his disciples, using simple language full of comparisons and parables taken from ordinary life. Except for a few pages of the Gospel – mainly in St John – Jesus' teachings seem to be quite accessible, at least at first glance; but the Apostle's letters, which are addressed to people who have already received initial Christian instruction, very often use a language which is much more difficult than that of Jesus. For this reason we here provide a short introduction to the "theology" of St Paul, which surveys the basic ideas underlying the teaching revealed in St Paul's letters and which should help the reader to understand them better.

It should be pointed out that in what follows we are not following a chronological order (which was the way we introduced the epistles themselves); instead we are going to look at the legacy of St Paul, ranging back and forth over the whole corpus of his letters.

HUMAN LIFE WITHOUT CHRIST

God made Paul see particularly clearly the tragedy of man-without-Christ – a life in which man was subject to the slaveries of sin, of the flesh and of death, and, in the case of Jews, slavery to the Law as interpreted by the rabbis of their time. This situation of unredeemed man applies to everyone who, in any period of history, whether before or after Christ, does not open his heart to the freedom which Christ gained for us (cf. Gal 4:31).

1. *Sin* One basic underlying theme in the revealed teaching of St Paul is that Christ's achievement, Christianity, means redemption, liberation from sin. Sin is a predominant factor in life-without-Christ, in the life of unredeemed man. For Paul, sin is a palpable fact, which consists, above all, in disobedience, in rebellion against God's majesty, against his will, against his moral law; this rebellion has installed man in a state of enmity towards God – a wretched

situation, leading to eternal death. An examination of the situation of the world and human history, and contemplation of Sacred Scripture (the Old Testament) demonstrate that "all [both Gentiles and Jews] have sinned and fall short of the glory of God" (Rom 3:23). Were it not for the presence of Christ, man would be submerged in most extreme pessimism, "so that every mouth may be stopped, and the whole world may be held accountable to God" (Rom 3:19). Paul sees this so clearly that he presents sin as a force which tyrannizes over man and has done so ever since the sin of Adam (cf. Rom 5:12, 21).

Of course, Paul's personalization of sin must not be taken literally as meaning that sin is a created entity, an evil spirit which exists as a person. What he means by sin is the situation in which man finds himself and from which he cannot escape by his own efforts; man, on his own, is unredeemable, impotent and enslaved; there is no way out for him, despite the fact that he has intellect, free will and freedom of choice (cf. Rom 7:7-25). This state of sinfulness is something quite obvious to Paul, and he describes it using all kinds of images and literary expressions designed to thrust home his point.

2. *The flesh* In the Old Testament the world "flesh" is used not only to describe human tissue but man's entire body and particularly his lower self including his senses, instincts, emotions, passions etc. – everything which is material and impermanent as distinct from the higher faculties of the human spirit. This is the sense given to the word by St Paul also. Following on original sin, all these lower elements in man are in a state of rebellion; his higher faculties – intellect and will – no longer wield the authority they should have over his base instincts etc. This "flesh" has thus become the ally of sin in its war against the spirit, like a kind of fifth column which sin uses to draw the entire person in the direction of evil.[10] Sin and flesh are not one and the same thing,[11] but sin finds an accomplice in that lower part of man – "the flesh", in the broad sense given the word in the Old Testament and in St Paul.

3. *Death* Sin, with the complicity of the flesh, draws the entire person towards enmity with God, misfortune, infirmity, and in the last analysis *death*: "Therefore as sin came into the world through one man [Adam] *and death through sin*, and so death spread to all men because all men sinned . . ." (Rom 5:12). Death is punishment for sin (cf. Rom 6:23). To summarize: man without Christ is a slave of sin, betrayed by the flesh and inescapably destined to die, for "while we were living in the *flesh*, our *sinful* passions, aroused by *the law*, were at work in our members to bear fruit for *death*" (Rom 7:5).

Finally, man's sin has had dire effects also on the irrational world: "the creation was subjected to futility, not of its own will but by the will of him who subjected it in hope; because the creation itself will be set free from its bondage to decay [. . .]; the whole creation has been groaning in travail together until now" (Rom 8:20, 22).

10 Cf. Gal 5:16-21, 24; Rom 6:19; 7:14-24; 8:3-4; 13:14.
11 Cf. Rom 6:12-14; 12:1; 2 Cor 4:10-11.

4. *The Law* In Rom 7:5 we have just seen a fourth element that leads to sin – the Law. It is the Jews to whom this directly applies, but indirectly it affects all men. How is it possible for the Law of God to become another ally of sin, tempting man to commit sinful acts, when that Law is something essentially good and holy? The answer is that although the Law does point the way to good, it does not contain the grace man needs to prevent him from doing evil; it leaves man in his carnal (= "flesh") state. This happens also with every kind of law, even with the natural moral law which is impressed on every person's conscience (cf. Rom 2:15; 1:21). Every law tells us what is sinful, but that is all it does (cf. Rom 3:20); and because we are so informed, our violation of law becomes a formal violation of the will of God.

We should not lose sight of the historical context in which St Paul is speaking: Jews boasted about their righteousness to Gentiles and even to God; they thought that they were keeping the Law, whereas in fact all they were doing was performing certain external actions and rites and their hearts were devoid of charity and mercy. They considered God, whom they cast in the role of a mere judge, as duty-bound to recognize and reward the good deeds they did by their own efforts: they, not God, were their own liberators. Some of the Christian converts from Judaism had not shed these inherited notions: they thought the Mosaic Law was what saved them, and they tried to impose this idea on other Christians of Gentile background and have them, too, conform to the Law. Paul could see how wrong they were: what they were in effect saying was that man is made good and righteous by his own efforts, thereby emptying God's work of redemption of any real value; they had not understood the basics of the Christian faith.

St Paul – or, rather, God through St Paul – entered the fray against these "Judaizers", and won, thereby liberating the early Church (and later Christians) from the worst and most persistent kind of error. Christians in every generation need to remember that they can never be saved by their own efforts; only the grace merited by Christ can bring us to salvation, and to that grace we obtain access through faith; only if we appropriate Christ's redemption can we perform actions which merit eternal life.

5. *Unredeemed mankind* St Paul's teaching is quite clear: man on his own, without Christ, is radically incapable of breaking out of the terrible situation into which he fell as a result of original sin. That sin, compounded by personal sins, holds man in thrall. Sin, dwelling in man's flesh as in a breeding ground, tyrannizes over man in his unredeemed state; he is God's enemy, cut off from eternal life and condemned to suffering and death. Even the Law – whether it be the natural moral law or even the divine-positive law promulgated through Moses – only aggravates the situation, because man cannot live up to it. St Paul does not deny human freedom; man is endowed with intellect and will; but he describes in no uncertain terms the situation in which man finds himself even after receiving the benefit of redemption: "I do not understand my own actions.

For I do not do what I want, but I do the very thing I hate" (Rom 7:15). "So I find it to be a law that when I want to be right, evil lies close at hand. For I delight in the law of God, in my inmost self, but I see in my members another law at war with the law of my mind and making me captive to the law of sin which dwells in my members. Wretched man that I am! Who will deliver me from this body of death?" (Rom 7:21-24).

SALVATION IN CHRIST

The answer to this anguished question is: Christ. "God has done what the law, weakened by the flesh, could not do: sending his own Son in the likeness of sinful flesh and for sin, he condemned sin in the flesh" (Rom 8:3). The Apostle is constantly making this same point, which is crucial to understanding the Redemption: Christ – who is God and Man – is man's Saviour. Paul then goes on to show the sublime mission of the Church and the dignity of redeemed man, who is called to be an adoptive son of God, to share in the very holiness of God *in Christ Jesus.*

1. *The salvific mystery* "Paul's Gospel" ("my Gospel", as he puts it himself: cf. Rom 2:16; 16:25) is primarily a salvific or soteriological message, that is, the revelation and implementation of a plan or design of God to bring salvation to man. To refer to this plan St Paul uses various short formulae, all very similar – the mystery of Christ, the mystery of the Gospel, the mystery of God, the mystery of his will, the mystery of faith, or just "the mystery".

This theme runs right through Paul's letters, at times breaking out exuberantly; as time goes on it develops, achieving its most elaborate formulation in Ephesians. As far as the origination of this theme is concerned, we can say it is peculiar to St Paul. The "mystery" is always basically the same – a divine mission of salvation; embracing all mankind without any discrimination on the grounds of nation or race; a plan conceived by God from all eternity, revealed only now (in the apostolic age) but foretold in the Old Testament; a plan which begins to take effect in this world but which will only be fully effected in the world to come.

This mystery of salvation as described by St Paul has its roots in the Old Testament and, especially, in Jesus' teaching and also in traditional rabbinical doctrine. This does not mean that St Paul, precisely because of the need to defend the "Gospel of Christ" initially against Judaizers and later against Gnostic influences (cf. Colossians), did not probe and formulate in a very vivid, personal style this "mystery", this gospel of his (cf. Gal 1:11-12).

For Paul this "mystery" derives from and is closely linked to God's "Wisdom". The first text in which he talks about this link is 1 Cor 1:17ff, where he contrasts the wisdom of the world with the wisdom of God. The Greeks search eagerly for human wisdom (cf. v. 20), but to God's mind that is only foolishness. What Paul is preaching is a wisdom which, in turn, seems foolishness to Gentiles and is a stumbling-block to Jews – because his wisdom is "Christ crucified" (v. 23). For us Christ himself stands for wisdom; and also for justice, holiness and redemption (v. 30). This divine plan of salvation which Paul preaches is "a secret and hidden wisdom of God" (1 Cor 2:7). The connexion between "mystery" and "wisdom", so deeply rooted in the best biblical tradition, is ever-present in some way or other in Paul's thinking (cf. for example Rom 16:25-26), and becomes most explicit in Colossians and Ephesians. In Colossians St Paul brings in the fundamental concept of reconciliation, a reconciliation of all creation, effected *in* Christ; he cannot get over how wonderful this is (cf. Col 1:27).

This reconciliation reconciles pagans with God, even if they have not conformed to the Mosaic Law, and also Jews, whom the Law itself indicted because they failed to keep it. The Cross of Christ means that the preparatory stage of the Old Testament is at an end, and the new stage of salvation in Christ has arrived (cf. Col 2:13-15).

Already in Colossians the notion of "the mystery" associates the Church with Christ (cf. Col 1:24 - 2:19); the Church is his Body and the instrument he uses to spread salvation; also, from one point of view, it *is* salvation, because in the Church the reconciliation of Jews and Gentiles with each other and with God is effected (cf. Col 1:21-29).

The revelation of "the mystery" in St Paul's letters reaches a conceptual climax in the letter to the Ephesians (cf. for example Eph 1:3-22). In addition to developing the theology of the Church, Ephesians adds the key theme of "recapitulation" in Christ as *head* (*caput*: cf. Eph 1:10) of all creation, heavenly as well as earthly: he is their source and their head; in Christ the original divine order of creation shattered by sin, is restored and enhanced. This recapitulation of all things in Christ is a new focus which Paul gives to salvation. In Ephesians Paul's explanations of the divine plan of salvation and all his teaching about Christ and about the Church are synthesized and perfected.

2. *The divinity of Jesus Christ*   Jesus, then, is the only one capable of carrying out God's plan of salvation; he came into the world to do just this. When St Paul speaks about him, he usually refers to him as "the Lord" or "Christ"; but no sooner does he begin his first epistle than he explains that the Christ Jesus who rose from the dead and who redeems us is the Son of God (cf. 1 Thess 1:10), or, as he will say in a later letter, the Son whom God gave up for us all (cf. Rom 8:32) and whose death reconciled us with God (cf. Rom 5:10).

In all his epistles it comes across quite clearly that Jesus, whom Paul preaches, is the Son of God (cf. 2 Cor 1:19). Christ's divinity and his divine sonship (a natural as distinct from an adoptive sonship) were revealed to Paul on the road to Damascus on the day when God with a blinding light made Paul see his vocation. From that moment on he preached Jesus to be the Son of God (cf. Acts 9:20).

This way of referring to Jesus, although it is not as common as the other names mentioned – "Christ" and "the Lord" –, clearly shows, by a special revelation, that the Son is consubstantial with, one in substance with, the Father. We profess faith in this when we say the Creed, where we affirm that the Son is "of one Being with the Father", that is, he is God. St Paul reserves this name "the Father" to refer to the first person of the Blessed Trinity, and almost always when he speaks of "God" he is referring to the Father, except in Rom 9:5 and Tit 2:13. In those two texts he also calls Jesus "God"; but the divinity of Christ, in St Paul's teaching, does not rely on these texts alone or any other particular passage: it is implicit in all Paul's letters and it was what nourished his faith long before he wrote the letters, ever since, as we said, he met God on the Damascus road.

St Paul goes as far as to say that he lives "by faith in the Son of God, who loved me and gave himself for me" (Gal 2:20); he thereby sets an example for us, for Jesus Christ is "our great God and Saviour . . . who gave himself for us to redeem us from all iniquity" (Tit 2:13), and he is "God over all, blessed for ever" (Rom 9:5).

Jesus is God!, he who exists before all creation, "the first-born of all creation; for in him all things were created, in heaven and on earth . . . all things were created through him and for him. He is before all things, and in him all things hold together" (Col 1:15-17), for "in him the whole fulness of deity dwells bodily" (Col 2:9).

This eternal pre-existence of Christ before being sent into the world, before the world even existed, is further evidence of the divinity of the Son of God, who is the Father's own Son in the proper sense,[12] begotten, not adopted, who "reflects the glory of God and bears the very stamp of his nature" (Heb 1:3), co-eternal with the Father and sent by him, out of love for men, in order to make us sons of God by being made like God's natural Son, through grace.

3. *The Son becomes man*   The mystery of salvation derives entirely from the mercy of God (cf. Rom 15:8-9; 11:32) and the love of God (cf. Rom 5:8). No other reason can explain why the only Son of the heavenly Father became man. The Incarnation demonstrates that man's salvation did not come from a benevolent but strange and distant God; it came in a manner most intimate to man – through the man Jesus, who without ceasing to be God, really took on human existence, with all its limitations, sin excepted, emptying himself in order to do so (cf. Phil 2:7). By becoming man the Son entered our unredeemed, sinful state (cf. 2 Cor 5:21); he voluntarily made himself a sin-offering; he conquered sin "in his body of flesh" (cf. Rom 8:3; Col 1:22), dressed in the nature of a slave, humble and obedient unto death (cf. Phil 2:7-8), "born of woman, born under the law" (Gal 4:4). Thus, through the Incarnation all the elements which held man in bondage – sin, the flesh, death and the Law – were conquered by Christ.

This total victory and liberation was made possible by the fact that Jesus

---

12 Cf. Rom 1:3; 8:3, 32; Gal 4:4; Heb 1:2; 5:8.

Christ is both God and man. St Paul's faith in this dogma is quite unshakeable, and it is something which he expresses again and again in his letters, but it would be tedious to cite them here.

4. *Theology of the Death of Christ*   Nor is it possible to quote all the texts in which Paul refers to the redemptive effects of Christ's death; we shall just give some examples of what he says on this matter. Christ has undergone the punishment which we merited on account of our sins (cf. Rom 4:25; 8:32). We have been ransomed by the shedding of his blood (cf. 1 Cor 6:20; 7:23; Rom 3:24; Col 1:14); Christ's death is the greatest proof of God's love for man (cf. Rom 5:8); it was an offering pleasing to God (cf. Gal 2:20; 1 Cor 11:25; Eph 5:2, 26); it has assuaged God's justifiable anger (cf. Rom 3:25). In 2 Cor 5:21 Paul goes as far as to say , "For our sake he made him [Christ] to be sin who knew no sin, so that in him we might become the righteousness of God."

By taking on human nature Christ became the representative and "head" of all mankind – the "new Adam".[13] When Christ dies on the Cross, we all die with him. "He died for all, that those who live might live no longer for themselves but for him who for their sake died and was raised" (2 Cor 5:15). Christ's death is perfect atonement for sin; but it implies, for that very reason, introduction to a new life in which the relationships between God and man change radically: Christ "was put to death for our trespasses and raised for our justification" (Rom 4:25).

5. *Theology of the Resurrection of Christ*   Like the other Apostles St Paul uses the historical event of the Resurrection of our Lord as the basic proof of the truth of what Jesus did and of what he said about himself. Those who denied Christ found themselves bereft of arguments. Those who falsely accused him at his trial have themselves been accused and found guilty.

St Paul bears witness to the historical fact of the Resurrection of Jesus in chapter 15 of the first letter to the Corinthians and also asserts there that Christ's Resurrection proves our future resurrection to glory. The rite of immersion in the water of Baptism signifies and effects our dying to sin in Christ; the rite of coming out of the water of Baptism signifies and effects our rebirth into the life of grace, and hope in our ultimate glorious resurrection (cf. Rom 6:5-11).

At Christ's Resurrection his human nature began to be glorified and exalted above all created beings: "To this end Christ died and lived again, that he might be Lord both of the dead and of the living."[14] The life of the risen Christ is not the same as the life he gave up on the Cross: he lives as the Son of God in power (cf. Rom 1:4) – and also as man; Christ's human nature, capable of feeling pain, humbled ever since his Incarnation, has moved into a heavenly mode of existence, where it can no longer experience suffering: there it is, joined to his divinity. Christ, from his Incarnation onwards but even more on account of the

13 Cf. 1 Cor 15:20-22; 2 Cor 5:14; Rom 5:14; Col 1:18.
14 Rom 14:9; cf. 1 Cor 15:25; Phil 2:9; Eph 1:20.

merits of his Death and Resurrection, stands for all men as their representative and true head, so complete is his solidarity with mankind. If we keep this idea of solidarity in mind it will be easier for us to see what Christ's Resurrection means for our redemption and justification; this salvific dimension of the Resurrection is always implicit in the Apostle's teaching (cf. for example, the quotation just given from Rom 4:25). Insofar as Christ is the head of those who believe in him we have already been raised in him in some way – our hope of resurrection has dawned – and when he rose we rose in him. As head of the Church Christ's influence extends over all his members, conveying life to them (this teaching, begun in Romans, is something Paul goes on to develop in Colossians and, particularly, Ephesians).

Moreover, through his Spirit the risen Christ is alive in Christians. This life in the Spirit only comes about after the Resurrection, when Christ sent his Spirit to those who adhere to him through faith and Baptism. "You are not in the flesh, you are in the spirit, if the Spirit of God really dwells in you. Any one who does not have the Spirit of Christ does not belong to him. But if Christ is in you, although your bodies are dead because of sin, your spirits are alive because of righteousness" (Rom 8:9-10).

Note: the term "objective" redemption is often used in Catholic teaching to describe the redemptive, salvific action of Christ which took place once and for all during his life on earth, especially through his Passion, Death and Resurrection.

This dimension of the Redemption is effected *in* Christ and *through* Christ and it focusses on all mankind: Christ is the Saviour of all. However, such is God's respect for the dignity of the human person that he leaves full scope for the exercise of individual freedom: he respects this freedom and seeks man's personal, free and therefore meritorious, response. This brings us into the sphere of what is usually referred to as "subjective" redemption, in other words, the application of the salvific merits of Christ to the individual human person – the process of justification and sanctification which takes place *within* each individual, after the original salvific action of the Incarnate Son of God which extends to all without exception. So far in our discussion we have been looking mainly at objective redemption. Now we move on to the sub- jective dimension. St Paul does not make an explicit distinction between the two, but his teaching is consistent with this distinction and many of the things he says envisage these two aspects.

THE CONVERSION OF MAN

1. *The process of justification in the individual person* How can man, domin- ated as he is by the power of sin, enmeshed in the flesh, destined to suffer death, how can he share in the salvation achieved by Christ? How can he move out of this state of unredemption into that of personal redemption? Putting it another way, how does one move from objective to subjective redemption?

The corpus of St Paul's letters provides the following answer: God takes the initiative and "calls" a particular individual by means of Gospel preaching, which brings with it a "grace". If a person accepts the word he is being offered, he makes an "act of faith" with the help of grace and begins to believe – faith is a form of knowledge – in the saving power of the Death and Resurrection of Jesus Christ, a power which operates through faith in the message which preaching brings. The process which normally follows on from this is that the person desires to be baptized and is baptized: Baptism forgives his sins and makes him born again to a new life by union with Christ; he becomes a member of the Church, receives the Holy Spirit and the infused virtues and gifts, and is adopted as a son of God. This whole process is referred to technically as "justification". We shall later examine its final stage, the "sanctification" of the individual person.

Three parts need to be emphasized particularly. First, the initiative in justification lies with God: he gives the initial grace, which is not merited by the person's previous actions: "Those whom he predestined he also called; and those whom he called he also justified; and those whom he justified he also glorified" (Rom 8:30).

Second, God desires the salvation of everyone: "This is good, and it is acceptable in the sight of God our Saviour, who desires all men to be saved" (1 Tim 2:3-4).

Third, although initial grace comes from God and plays the main part in justification, the individual also has a part to play: "But thanks be to God, that you who were once slaves of sin have become obedient from the heart to the standard of teaching to which you were committed, and, having been set free from sin, have become slaves of righteousness" (Rom 6:17-18).

2. *Faith* St Paul speaks so much about faith that his letters provide the groundwork of Christian teaching on this theological virtue, which is the beginning of all the other virtues. Firstly, as we have said, he tells us that faith is a gift from God: "For by grace you have been saved through faith and this is not your own doing, it is the gift of God"(Eph 2:8). Faith does not come from evidence intrinsic in things, but from God's power which accompanies preaching: "Our gospel came to you not only in word, but also in power and in the Holy Spirit" (1 Thess 1:5). "When I came to you, brethren, I did not come proclaiming the testimony [or: mystery] of God in lofty words or wisdom. For I decided to know nothing among you except Jesus Christ and him crucified. . . . My speech and my message were not in plausible words of wisdom, but in demonstration of the Spirit and power, that your faith might not rest in the wisdom of men but in the power of God" (1 Cor 2:1-5).

As regards the person who receives the gift of faith, his or her act in accepting it is always a free act and therefore a meritorious one: it is an act of obedience to an influence direct from God or through the Gospel of Jesus Christ, "through whom we have received grace and apostleship to bring about the obedience of faith for the sake of his name among all the nations" (Rom 1:5).

3. *The content of faith* What has this person to believe, this person who has accepted the gift of faith: in summary, he has to believe in the Gospel (cf. Rom 1:16-17). And what does this involve? "Now I would remind you, brethren, in what terms I preached to you the gospel, which you received, in which you stand, by which you are saved [. . .]. For I delivered to you as of first importance what I also received, that Christ died for our sins in accordance with the scriptures, that he was buried, that he was raised on the third day in accordance with the scriptures, and that he appeared to Cephas, then to the twelve. Then he appeared to more than five hundred brethren at one time, most of whom are still alive, though some have fallen asleep" (1 Cor 15:1-6).

Thus, the person who has accepted the divine gift of faith has to believe not in a personal theory of Paul or anyone else, but in the teaching taught by the Twelve, who witnessed the life, death and resurrection of Christ – that is, in the content of the "articles" of faith which, as we would say now, are summed up in the *Creed*, the "symbol" of faith, whose origins go back to the Apostles. Faith is not an abstract theory about God; it is belief in a God who is active and all-powerful, a God who saves, who has made himself known through his Son Jesus Christ, who has redeemed us through his Death and Resurrection and in whom are fulfilled the ancient promises made to the patriarchs and prophets of the Old Testament.

This belief in the Christian faith is not the same thing as accepting a piece of news (current or dated) which one has checked out – as one might the fact that Julius Caesar conquered Gaul or that a new spaceship has been launched. No: the Gospel is "Good News" which involves each and every one of us. It is as we have said, *obedience* to God's will.[15] It is also complete *trust* in God, who will always be true to his promises (as he has been true to those promises concerning Christ, and those concerning ourselves, up to this point): "the Lord is faithful; he will strengthen you and guard you from evil [or: the evil one]" (2 Thess 3:3). "May the God of peace himself sanctify you wholly; and may your spirit and soul and body be kept sound and blameless at the coming of our Lord Jesus Christ. He who calls you is faithful, and he will do it" (1 Thess 5:23-24).

4. *The demands of faith* The moral degradation to be seen in the permissive society of today gives us an indication of the sort of environment in which the early Christians had to live in the Greco-Roman world; but in many aspects theirs was a more depraved environment, since in ours Christian moral principles still exert some influence. In St Paul's times, when a person – already an adult – who had received the initial grace of faith decided to step into the waters of Baptism, he had to abandon not only his old clothes but all his past life as well, a life typically steeped in sin. When he came up out of the baptismal

15 Cf. 2 Cor 10:5; Rom 1:5; 6:17; 16:26; etc.

waters he really would have been "a new creation" (2 Cor 5:17).

The Apostle gives a pained description of the depraved moral environment in which those first disciples had to make their way: "For this reason God gave them up to dishonourable passions. Their women exchanged natural relations for unnatural, and the men likewise gave up natural relations with women and were consumed with passion for one another, men committing shameless acts with men and receiving in their own persons the due penalty for their error. And since they did not see fit to acknowledge God, God gave them up to a base mind and to improper conduct. They were filled with all manner of wickedness, evil, covetousness, malice. Full of envy, murder, strife, deceit, malignity, they are gossips, slanderers, haters of God, insolent, haughty, boastful, inventors of evil, disobedient to parents, foolish, faithless, heartless, ruthless" (Rom 1:26-31).

Much divine grace was needed – and great generosity on the part of converts – if they were to shed, as they had to, many aspects of their pagan lifestyle. St Paul had to speak quite bluntly to the Corinthians in this connexion: "I wrote to you in my letter not to associate with immoral men; not at all meaning the immoral of this world, or the greedy and robbers, or idolaters, since then you would need to go out of the world. But rather I wrote to you not to associate with any one who bears the name of brother if he is guilty of immorality or greed, or is an idolater, reviler, drunkard, or robber" (1 Cor 5:9-11).

Christian faith, therefore, brings with it certain specific moral demands: "Do you not know that the unrighteous will not inherit the Kingdom of God? Do not be deceived; neither the immoral, nor idolaters, nor adulterers, nor homosexuals, nor thieves, nor the greedy, nor drunkards, nor revilers, nor robbers will inherit the kingdom of God" (1 Cor 6:9-11).

Despite the fact that conversion to Christ involved substantial, difficult moral demands, the early Christians managed to meet these – partly thanks to their personal dispositions, but primarily thanks to the divine life of which they partook. Using St Paul as a guide we shall now see that spiritual phenomenon taking place during the first stage of the Church's history, and how it can be repeated in later stages – including our own time, which somewhat resembles that of the early Christians, at least in the sense that it is one which has regressed towards paganism.

CHRISTIAN LIFE IN CHRIST

Through St Paul, God shows us the sublimity of the state of redemption not as something which belongs to a privileged minority but as the normal situation of every Christian, who is called to achieve a high level of spiritual maturity. Nowhere does Paul suggest two standards of morality – a lower one for the mass of the people of God and a higher one for a select few. He held out the same high ideal, the same spiritual and moral exigencies, to all those early Christians, even those who had been steeped in paganism: "for once you were darkness, but now you are light in the Lord; walk as children of light (for the fruit of light is to be found in all that is good and right and true)" (Eph 5:8-9).

1. *Children of God*   Our Christian faith automatically makes us see ourselves as children of God. By being *in Christ*, by adhering to him through faith, we are made sons and daughters of God: "For those whom he foreknew [all Christians] he [God] also predestined to be conformed to the image of his Son, in order that he might be the first-born among many brethren" (Rom 8:29). This quality of being children of God, although it reaches its perfection only in heaven, is already something very tangible: our faith should make us almost feel it: "But when the time had fully come, God sent forth his Son, born of woman, born under the law, to redeem those who were under the law, so that we might receive adoption as sons. And because you are sons, God has sent the Spirit of his Son into our hearts, crying, 'Abba! Father!' So through God you are no longer a slave but a son, and if a son then an heir" (Gal 4:4-7).

Christian life *in Christ* through grace begins at Baptism, whereby we begin to be "sons of God", that is, his adoptive children, likened to the natural Son of God. "Do you not know that all of us who have been baptized into Christ Jesus were baptized into his death? We were buried therefore with him by baptism into death, so that as Christ was raised from the dead by the glory of the Father, we too might walk in newness of life. For if we have been united with him in a death like his, we shall certainly be united with him in a resurrection like his [. . .]. But if we have died with Christ, we believe that we shall also live with him" (Rom 6:3-5, 8).

St Paul very often points out that the redeemed person's new kind of life is *life-in-Christ*: "Therefore, if any one is in Christ, he is a new creation."[16] However, we should note that when he speaks of "my being in Christ" and of Christ "being in me", he means the same thing; we can see this in the following text: "I have been crucified with Christ; it is no longer I who live, but Christ who lives *in me*" (Gal 2:19-20). Obviously the Apostle is not saying that once a person becomes a Christian he has no life of his own: he means that his life is shaped and inspired by an energy which comes from Christ; Christ is present in the Christian much more positively than the way lovers are in each other's thoughts: Christ's own Spirit – the Holy Spirit – is present in the Christian's soul. This presence of the Holy Spirit also plays its part in making the person a son or daughter of God *in Christ*: "For all who are led by the Spirit of God are sons of God. For you did not receive the spirit of slavery to fall back into fear, but you have received the spirit of sonship. When we cry, 'Abba! Father!' it is the Spirit himself bearing witness with our spirit that we are children of God, and if children, then heirs, heirs of God and fellow heirs of Christ, provided we suffer with him in order that we may also be glorified with him" (Rom 8:14-17).

16 2 Cor 5:17; cf. 1 Cor 1:30; Rom 6:11; etc.

2. *The gift of the Spirit*   We have seen the way "life-in-Christ" is somewhat the same thing as being "sons of God". And also we have seen that this life-in-Christ involves the Christian soul receiving the gift of the Holy Spirit. This happens because at Baptism the believer receives, along with grace and the infused virtues, the Holy Spirit and his gifts: "God's love has been poured into our hearts through the Holy Spirit who has been given to us" (Rom 5:5). The Holy Spirit, which the glorified Son sends on his Father's behalf, abides in the Christian in grace and cooperates with Christ to make him a new creation, to give him new-life-in-Christ and to make him become steadily more like Christ.

It is Jesus Christ who, with his Death and glorious Resurrection, has merited the sending of the Spirit. The Spirit of Jesus, which has been given us, co-operates to make us like unto Christ, so that the Father can recognize in us the image of his only Son and can adopt us as sons in the Son (cf. Rom 8:29- 30).

3. *The value of suffering*   Earlier, in connexion with the Christian's divine sonship, we quoted Rom 8:14-17; the two last verses of that passage link this sonship with suffering: "It is the Spirit himself bearing witness with our spirit that we are children of God [. . .], fellow heirs of Christ, provided we suffer with him in order that we may also be glorified with him" (Rom 8:16-17). St Paul is insistent that this new birth necessarily includes participating in Christ's sufferings: "always carrying in the body the death of Jesus, so that the life of Jesus may also be manifested in our bodies" (2 Cor 4:10-11).

The presence of pain and suffering in mankind is something self-evident. In some way they are unavoidable; yet they are particularly present in the life of the Christian, as they were in the lives of Christ and of the Apostles. However, suffering acquires a new value in the light of faith in Christ: it is a badge of honour, a necessary step towards solidarity with Christ, and an indication that a person already has some degree of union with him: "Henceforth let no man trouble me; for I bear on my body the marks of Jesus" (Gal 6:17).

Hope of reaching heaven helps the Christian to bear suffering joyfully and even to desire it: "So we do not lose heart. Though our outer nature is wasting away, our inner nature is being renewed every day. For this slight momentary affliction is preparing for us an eternal weight of glory beyond all comparison" (2 Cor 4:16-17). During his first imprisonment in Rome the Apostle writes: "Now I rejoice in my sufferings for your sake, and in my flesh I complete what is lacking in Christ's afflictions for the sake of his body, which is the church" (Col 1:24).

What this means is that Christ's sufferings, his Passion, are in some way extended in time, until the end of the world, in Christians who suffer in imitation of Christ and in union with him. Therefore, suffering will continue, it will be like a pledge of future glory, as long as this world lasts; and yet, paradoxical though it be, when the Christian suffers for Christ and the Church he or she actually experiences a deep happiness.

4. *The ascetical struggle* This brings us to the subject of asceticism. "Do you not know that in a race all the runners compete, but only one receives the prize? So run that you may obtain it. Every athlete exercises self-control in all things. They do it to receive a perishable wreath, but we an imperishable. Well, I do not run aimlessly, I do not box as one beating the air; but I pommel my body and subdue it, lest after preaching to others I myself should be disqualified" (1 Cor 9:24-27).

The Christian, in other words, must not rest on his laurels, content with faith and the gift of grace. He has an obligation to make these precious gifts bear fruit: "Working together with him [Christ], then, we entreat you not to accept the grace of God in vain" (2 Cor 6:1). The Christian still has a long way to go: the flesh will keep on trying to regain its lost rights; concupiscence still seethes within him. . . . Therefore, he must be vigilant: "Look carefully then how you walk, not as unwise men but as wise, making the most of the time, because the days are evil" (Eph 5:15-16).

5. *The outcome of love* God's perfect love for us is manifested to us in the entire life of Christ (cf. Heb 10:5-10), who "loved us and gave himself up for us, a fragrant offering and sacrifice to God" (Eph 5:2). St Paul has a deep sense of Christ's love for us, which led him to give up his life: "the life I now live in the flesh I live by faith in the Son of God, who loved me and gave himself for me" (Gal 2:20); "and so by your knowledge this weak man is destroyed, the brother for whom Christ died" (1 Cor 8:11). God's love and Christ's love are poured into us by the Holy Spirit: "God's love has been poured into our hearts through the Holy Spirit who has been given to us",[17] and the Christian has a duty to respond (cf. 1 Cor 8:3; Rom 8:28).

In the last analysis, it is our love of God that keeps us true to the demands of the faith no matter what difficulties we come up against; all the other virtues and charisms are secondary to charity: "If I speak in the tongues of men and of angels, but have not love, I am a noisy gong or a clanging cymbal. And if I have prophetic powers, and understand all mysteries and all knowledge, and if I have faith, so as to remove mountains, but have no love, I am nothing. If I give away all I have, and if I deliver my body to be burned, but have not love, I gain nothing" (1 Cor 13:1-3).

Christ's Cross, however, has two planks – an upright which unites me to God, and a horizontal which unites me to all other men and women, beginning with those who share the same faith: "So then, as we have opportunity, let us do good to all men, and especially to those who are of the household of the faith" (Gal 6:10). The Eucharist is the principal sacrament of love of God and love of neighbour; through it, by communing with the Body of Christ, we become one with him and, in him, with our brethren: "The cup of blessing which we

17 Rom 5:5; cf. 2 Cor 13:13; etc. "Love of God" and "love for God" frequently mean the same thing.

bless, is it not a participation in the blood of Christ? The bread which we break, is it not a participation in the body of Christ? Because there is one bread, we who are many are one body, for we all partake of the one bread" (1 Cor 10:16-17).

Fraternal charity is not just a matter of feeling well-disposed to people; it should be something active and have quite practical expressions; consider, for example, St Paul's instructions "concerning the contribution for the saints [the impoverished Christians of Palestine]: as I directed the churches of Galatia, so you also are to do. On the first day of the week, each of you is to put something aside and store it up, as he may prosper, so that contributions need not be made when I come" (1 Cor 16:1-2).

THE CHURCH

Of all the inspired writers of the New Testament, St Paul is the one who speaks most often about the Church, the one who has gone deepest into its mystery and best explained it. His insight into the mystery of the Church began at the very moment of his conversion, when he heard Jesus identifying himself with Christians: "Saul, Saul, why do you persecute me?" (Acts 9:4). Paul had not been conscious of persecuting Christ, whom he regarded as a dead man: he was persecuting Christians, because they were spreading pernicious ideas. After this first, direct revelation of Christ, Paul received other revelations and had other experiences which further developed his understanding of the mystery of the Church.

Although in his letters of the years 50-60 (1 and 2 Thess, Gal, 1 and 2 Cor, Rom) Paul generally describes as "churches" the Christian communities located in cities or small regions, he always had a concept of the Church as one single entity. His understanding of Baptism shows us the deep solidarity it creates with Christ and with each other (cf. Rom 6:3-5), a solidarity which is strengthened by the graces and gifts of the Spirit: "For by one Spirit we were all baptized into one body" (1 Cor 12:13).

1. *The unity of the Church*   Even at the stage when he was writing the first six letters, Paul had a very clear concept of the unity of the Church (the Church is one entity) and of its unicity (there is no other church). All Christians make up a single body, whose life and unity is caused and nourished by sharing in the eucharistic Body and Blood of Christ: "Because there is one bread, we who are many are one body, for we all partake of the one bread" (1 Cor 10:17). This is why Christians cannot be divided into different groups or classes: " I appeal to you, brethren, by the name of our Lord Jesus Christ, that all of you agree and that there be no dissensions among you, but that you be united in the same mind and the same judgment. For it has been reported to me by Chloe's people that there is quarrelling among you, my brethren. What I mean is that each of you says, 'I belong to Paul', or 'I belong to Apollos', or 'I belong to Cephas', or 'I

43

belong to Christ'. Is Christ divided? Was Paul crucified for you? Or were you baptized in the name of Paul?" (1 Cor 1:10-13).

All Christians, whether they be in Rome, Jerusalem, Corinth, Colossae etc. are brethren, chosen and loved by God, and called to be saints.[18]

This sense of the Church's oneness will deepen for Paul during the years of his first imprisonment in Rome (61-63 A.D.). From then on he tends to use the term "Church" to refer to the universal Church into which God has called Jews and Gentiles, free men and slaves, men and women: ". . . eager to maintain the unity of the Spirit in the bond of peace. There is one body and one Spirit, just as you were called to the one hope that belongs to your call, one Lord, one faith, one baptism, one God and Father of us all, who is above all and through all and in all" (Eph 4:3-6). "For as many of you as were baptized into Christ have put on Christ. There is neither Jew or Greek, there is neither slave nor free, there is neither male nor female; for you are all one in Christ Jesus" (Gal 3:27-28).

2. *The Church, the people of God*   In addition to discovering in Paul's letters, as features of the Church, its unity and the solidarity of Christians with Christ and with one another, we also find the key concept of the Church as the "people of God". Paul arrived at this concept in the first years after his conversion: he could see that the Apostles and first Christians in Jerusalem were acutely conscious of their constituting the true Israel, the Israel promised to the Patriarchs, that is, the holy, chosen, remnant, spoken of by the prophets, and now convoked and established by Jesus Christ. In his Church, as in Jesus' own person, the prophecies of the Old Testament were finding fulfilment.[19] St Paul stresses the fact that pagans who find faith in Christ enter the Church on equal terms with converts from Judaism (cf. Rom 11:5, 17-24): "the Gentiles are fellow heirs, members of the same body, and partakers of the promise in Christ Jesus through the gospel" (Eph 3:6); "for neither circumcision counts for anything, nor uncircumcision, but a new creation" (Gal 6:15).

The last times, the *éschaton*, however long they are to last, have been inaugurated with the first coming of Christ and will end with his second coming or Parousia.[20] In the period between these two comings the Gospel will be preached all over the world and the Church will be growing. This "eschatological" dimension of the Church means that Christians are "wayfarers": the whole Church is, as it were, God's people on the march, waiting for the Lord to come (cf. 1 Cor 16:22), moving onward towards their heavenly, enduring homeland (cf. Heb 3:5-6; 3:16 - 4:11).

3. *The Church, the Body of Christ*   Note: St Paul provides an actual theology of "the body", a theology which gives us the key to understanding the true meaning of Christian asceticism and which shows how different it is from any

18 Cf. 1 Cor 1:2; 16:1-4; 2 Cor 8:9; Rom 1:7; 15:26.
19 Cf. 1 Cor 1:2; 16:1; Rom 1:7; 15:26; Col 3:12; etc.
20 Cf. Gal 3:24; Col 4:5; Eph 5:16; Rom 11:25; 1 Cor 10:11; Rom 8:21; 1 Thess 4:16; 1 Cor 15:22; 2 Thess 2:8; 1 Cor 15:28.

kind of "disincarnated" spirituality, whether of Gnostic, Platonic or other origin. For St Paul "the flesh" and "the body" are different things: the latter merits respect, whereas the former, as we said earlier, he sees as the perishable element in man, the soil on which sin thrives. Hence the Apostle provides no list of sins of the body, but he does list the sins of the flesh (cf. Gal 5:19ff). However, although the body *per se* has a certain dignity, the body of the Christian has an enhanced dignity: it will be changed into a "glorious body" (cf. Phil 3:21), a "spiritual body" (1 Cor 15:44). For this to happen we must first die and our body be resurrected.

In his captivity letters St Paul expounds his teaching on the Church in a more developed form than previously; but this teaching in earlier (the "great") epistles and in later epistles is consistent. In the captivity letters the Church is identified with the "body of Christ". This is not an absolute identity: Christ and the Church cannot be exactly the same thing; perhaps the best way to explain it is to say that the statement "The Church is the body of Christ" can be translated as follows: "The Church is Christ-in-his- body," in the same sort of way as a man's body is a man-in-his-body: It *is* this man in concrete, visible form, not just "part" of this man.[21] The formula "body of Christ" applied to the Church is one which St Paul uses to emphasize the deeply mysterious relationship that exists between the Church and Christ, and it represents his attempt to plumb the deepest level of the Church's personality. In 1 Corinthians and Romans the Apostle begins to formulate this way of understanding the Church, but it is in Colossians and Ephesians that he really develops it.

In Colossians and Ephesians he does not just describe the Church as the Body of Christ; he superimposes on this the image of Christ as Head of the Church: Christ is distinct from the Church, but the Church is joined to him as to its head (cf. Eph 1:22ff; Col 1:18). By saying that Christ is the "head" and the Church the "body", he is not saying that the head is not "part" of the body; the head is being distinguished by reason of its special eminence: the head is the most important part of the body (however, it is incorrect to be speaking here of "parts"). Thus, the Church in relation to Christ is in a subordinate position (cf. Eph 4:15ff). Christ, being the head and principle, is as it were the internal motor of the entire body.

The Christian shares, truly, in the Body of the Lord through eucharistic Communion. In this way all Christians reinforce their membership of the Body of Christ (cf. 1 Cor 12:27) and their relationship to one another (cf. Rom 12:5). This union of each Christian with Christ and with other Christians is a very intimate one;[22] it goes far beyond mere external association: suffering and joy are shared; Christians "edify" each other by the practice of charity and the other virtues: spiritual life flows through the Body in this way.[23]

This union with Christ is what rebuilds lost unity at various levels of creation

21 Cf. Rom 1:24; 6:12; 7:24; 8:10ff; 12:1; etc.
22 Cf. 1 Cor 12:12; Rom 12:5; 1 Cor 12:14-26.
23 Cf. Rom 12:3ff; 1 Cor 12:14ff; Eph 4:1ff.

– the inner unity of the individual, pulled in different directions by his passions (cf. Rom 7:14ff; 8:2, 9); union in marriage: for the married couple, their model is Christ's union with his Church (cf. Eph 5:25-32); unity among mankind: the Holy Spirit makes people children of the same heavenly Father (cf. Eph 4:6); and, very particularly, unity among Christians, who, having one heart and one soul (cf. Acts 4:32), also praise their Father God with one voice (cf. Rom 15:5ff). Finally, this unity is a sign or identifying feature of the one and only Church, united on earth by the very links which join it to Christ (cf. Eph 4:5).

This view of the unity of Christians and of the unity of the Church as the Body of Christ does not conflict with diversity of gifts and graces. Each Christian receives specific graces, which we should faithfully use for the glory of God (cf. Rom 12:6-8; 1 Pet 4:10-11). In the context of this wealth of gifts, a deep unity is produced; that unity and those gifts all derive from the same source, the Spirit (cf. 1 Cor 12:4-11).

4. *The Church, the way for all men to be saved*   In the captivity letters, in line with the teaching first seen in the "great" epistles, St Paul not only declares that Christ, God and Man, is the Saviour of Christians; he also discusses the salvific role of the Body of Christ. To see this one needs look up a number of passages,[24] not all of them referring to the Body of Christ in the same sense: 1 Cor 10:16; 2 Cor 4:10, Col 1:22, 2:17-19, and Eph 2:16 speak of Christ's physical body; whereas Eph 4:11-12, 15-16 seems to refer to the Body of the Church, though this distinction may not always be easy to see. The point is that Christ's physical body, formed in the virginal womb of Mary,[25] the body which died on the Cross and was buried, bore our sins; God has reconciled us in his body of flesh (cf. Col 1:22); Christ was the true paschal lamb (cf. 1 Cor 5:7) and through the sacrifice of his body we were sanctified, once and for all (cf. Heb 10:10). This physical body of Christ, united to the godhead of the Word, was, therefore, the instrument of our salvation.

After its glorification, the physical Body of Christ exists in heaven, but it also is present on earth in the Eucharist (cf. 1 Cor 11:23ff), at the centre of the Church. This eucharistic Body of Christ is also the instrument of salvation and of union of Christians with Christ and with one another. By communion with the Body of Christ, glorious in heaven and present on earth, the Church, which is intimately and actually associated with Christ's Body, to which it is joined and yet from which it is distinct, is also made the instrument of mankind's salvation (cf. Eph 2:14-17; 3:10).

In St Paul's epistles we can even sense the basis of the Church's unity as lying in the Unity of God – and Christian plurality as being rooted in the Trinity of God (cf. Eph 4:4-6, 11-12, 15-16). Through union with Christ the Head, the members of the Church are linked to the Second Person of the Trinity, and through this they share in God's very nature (cf. 2 Cor 3:18; 2 Pet 1:4). Through

24 1 Cor 10:16; 2 Cor 4:10; Col 1:22; 2:17-19; Eph 2:16; 4:11-12, 15-16; etc.
25 Cf. Gal 5:4; Heb 10:5; Lk 1:35, 38; Mt 1:20.

the Son, then, believers attain to union with the Father and with the Holy Spirit, and are intimately involved in the interior life of the Trinity (cf. Eph 2:18; 4:4-6).

Thus, the Body of Christ is also the universal Church.[26] The unity of and the distinction between Christ and the Church are explained by Paul in other ways than in terms of head and body – for example, by the idea of the Church as the Bride of Christ (cf. Eph 5:23-32), where this unity and this distinction are both asserted, and the Church is seen as Christ's instrument for applying salvation to all mankind.

26 Cf. Eph 1:22; 3:10, 21; 5:23-25, 27, 29, 32; Col 1:18, 24.

Introduction to St Paul's Epistles
to the Galatians and the Romans

NOTE

In the general introduction to St Paul's letters we have already looked at the dating and doctrinal content of Romans and Galatians. Here we shall concentrate on the context in which these letters were written, to help the reader understand them better; then we shall go on to examine the structure of each letter.

In the prologue to his *Commentary on St Paul's Epistles* St Thomas Aquinas very succinctly describes the content of these letters when he says that all the teaching revealed therein refers to the "grace of Christ", that is, the fruits of the Redemption, viewed in three ways – as found in Christ himself (cf. Hebrews), as distributed hierarchically (cf. the pastoral epistles) and as found in Christ's mystical Body, the Church (cf. the other epistles). By saying this, Aquinas is treating as one single block Romans, 1 and 2 Corinthians, Galatians, the captivity letters and 1 and 2 Thessalonians. Within this group, Galatians and Romans are particularly akin, dealing as they do with the same subject, though from slightly different angles. Both study grace, that is, justification (= sanctification) effected by faith in Christ and not by the works of the Law. Because they are so similar and complementary we are including Romans and Galatians in the one volume, with a joint introduction.

We shall first look at the context in which they were written, because this helps in understanding certain details and nuances of these letters.

THE CONTEXT IN WHICH THE TWO EPISTLES WERE WRITTEN

1. *Galatians*   The Letter to the Galatians is the first of the so-called "great" epistles of the Apostle of the Gentiles. It was very probably written around the year 54 or 55, although some scholars bring the date forward to 49 and others put it back to 57. Whatever about the exact date, God inspired Paul to write it and to do so at a very providential time, because it provides the best commentary (or, if one prefers, the best introduction) to the decisions of the Council of Jerusalem (cf. Acts 15:23-29). At that gathering the Apostles, with the help of the "elders", or presbyters, of the local church of Jerusalem, and, as they themselves tell us, in union with the Holy Spirit, decided that Christians of Gentile origin were under no obligation to conform to Jewish precepts. This

was an exceptionally important development: the Church was coming to realize the implications of being not a mere part of Judaism but rather a new and different product of God's action in history.[1] It was a new expression of God's redeeming love which through Christ had been grafted on to the ancient trunk of the chosen people.

Despite the decision of the council, the subtle yet profound relationship between the Old and New Covenants was difficult to understand; there was an obvious continuity between the two, and an obvious discontinuity. This difficulty was experienced particularly by those Jews who were hidebound by national and religious traditions, inclined to give more importance to the ancient rites of Israel than to the freedom won by Christ and to the law of grace. It is quite likely that some of these "false brethren" (Gal 2:4), as happened prior to the council of Jerusalem (cf. Acts 15:1, 5), even reached the communities founded by St Paul (cf. Acts 16:6) in the course of his second missionary journey. We do not know exactly who they were, or whether they were individuals or small groups working on their own initiative or part of a wider campaign against Paul; but certainly they constituted an ever-present threat to him and even pressurized the Apostles: in Antioch they were responsible for Simon Peter disguising his "pro-Gentile" conduct (cf. Gal 2:11-14). The incident in question must have occurred shortly after the council and prior to Paul's third missionary journey (winter 52-53). Peter acted in an ambiguous way, cowed by fear of what Judaizers might think: when he first arrived in Antioch he had mixed freely with its many Christians of Gentile background (cf. Acts 11:20-21, 24-26) and without following the rules of the Mosaic Law. Then, when a number of "James' men" came to the city, Peter backtracked and ceased to consort with these Christians, thereby opening the way to divisions in the young church. The newcomers were probably connected with early Jerusalem converts who had been Pharisees or priests (cf. Acts 6:7; 15:5); and they probably used St James' reputation in support of retaining Judaic practices and even requiring others to do the same, despite the line James himself took at the council of Jerusalem (cf. Acts 15:19-21; Jas 1:25; 2:12). Paul saw these people as intruders, "false brethren", seeking to spy on true believers. It is difficult to work out from what Paul says whether these Judaizers were arguing that all Christians *had* to observe the Mosaic Law[2] or, rather, were saying that it was desirable or more perfect to do so, which is what some texts seem to say.[3]

In spite of the decision of the council of Jerusalem, the Judaizers were very active in promoting their ideas; we come across them not only in Galatia but also soon afterwards in Corinth, and later on in Philippi, Colossae, Ephesus

1 Cf. Rom 11:16-18; Jesus had already preached this: cf. Jn 5:39, 45-46; Mt 5:17; 8:11-12; 21:33-43; etc.
2 Cf. Acts 15:5: "But some believers who belonged to the party of the Pharisees rose up, and said, 'It is necessary to circumcise them, and to charge them to keep the law of Moses'." Cf. Acts 15:1.
3 Cf., for example, Gal 4:9-10; 5:2; Phil 3:2-4; etc.

49

and Crete[4] – a threat to St Paul right to the end of his life (cf. 2 Tim 3:5-6).

Their aggressiveness and the thrust of their ideas led the Apostle, under the inspiration of the Holy Spirit, to spell out very clearly the truth about justification through faith and about Christian freedom. He did all that he could to counter circumcision (which Judaizers wanted to impose) with the triumph of Christ's Cross (cf. Gal 5:2-3; 5:11; 6:12): "For neither circumcision counts for anything, nor uncircumcision, but a new creation" (Gal 6:15).

Thanks to a reference which Paul makes (in Gal 4:13) when he reminds those he is addressing of the time he preached to them "at first" (which implies that he spent time in Galatia on at least two separate occasions), there is good reason to believe that the epistle was written during his third apostolic journey, when, after strengthening the faith of the churches in Galatia and Phrygia (cf. Acts 18:23) he sojourned for a period – two or three years – in Ephesus (cf. Acts 19:10; 20:31). And in view of the fact that Paul refers to having been recently in Galatia (cf. Gal 1:6), there is good reason for thinking that he wrote this letter around the year 54.

2. *Romans* The Epistle to the Romans was written in very different circumstances, which explains the particular tone of this letter. The Judaizers had not reached as far as Rome, which meant that there was no threat to the internal unity of the Christian community living in the capital of the Empire. The only serious problem in the Roman church had to do with a moral and disciplinary matter connected with clean and unclean food, and fasting (subjects dealt with in the second half of the letter). Paul's aim may have been to cement the bonds of unity between Christians of both backgrounds, Jewish and Gentile: he reminds them of the common vocation they have received from God and of how, previously, both of them had been in a state of sin: recognition of this fact should make them humble and charitable towards one another. As we have said, there were no pressing problems for Paul to solve at this time; however, in writing to the Romans Paul is extending his own apostolic horizons and God inspires him to develop the subject already covered in Galatians – the connexion between justification and the Law; faith and good works; freedom and sin.

At the time of writing, the Apostle is conscious that his activity in the eastern regions of the Empire has produced lasting fruit. The Gospel of Christ has been preached from Jerusalem right to the eastern coast of the Adriatic (cf. Rom 15:19). Paul has been the principal sower, the layer of foundations; his disciples and companions will develop his work and make the offering of the Gentiles an acceptable one, sanctified by the Holy Spirit (cf. Rom 15:16). Paul feels that there is no further scope for him in those regions (cf. Rom 15:23), and he is beginning to think about going further afield. First of all he is thinking of the potential of Rome itself, but there were already small Christian communities in Mediterranean coastal cities and provinces, and still further away lay the rest

4 Cf. 2 Cor 11:21-23; Phil 3:18-19; Col 2:8, 16; 1 Tim 1:3, 7; Tit 1:14.

of Italy, and Iberia and Gaul (modern France, Belgium, Switzerland and Northern Italy).

The Apostle's heart thrilled at the prospect Rome itself presented for the spread of the Gospel. Its cosmopolitan population and its position as a political, commercial and cultural centre meant that its influence extended across the known world. Only a few miles from Rome lay Ostia, the most important port of the Mediterranean, with a population of two hundred thousand; Rome itself had a million: both cities were very large by the standards of the time. Paul had also heard about there being Christians in the Roman provinces of the Iberian peninsula, places he was already aware of through the Bible where they were known by the name of Tarshish.[5] Here also he would have to bring the light and love of Christ, to dispel the darkness of idolatry, magical cults and primitive superstitions.

St Paul writes with a certain boldness (cf. Rom 15:15) to those people who have already been preached to by others (cf. Rom 15:20) – undoubtedly St Peter and some of the earliest converts. He wants to plan his journey to the West and would like the Christians of Rome to help him (cf. Rom 15:24), perhaps by giving him some money and letters of introduction. But what he especially wants to do is to strengthen their faith (cf. Rom 1:11-12; 15:32), to be consoled by their fidelity and also to "reap some harvest" among them (cf. Rom 1:13). He feels under an obligation to all – Greeks and barbarians, wise and foolish: that is why he is so keen to go to Rome (cf. Rom 1:11-15; 15:22-23).

Paul is writing, in all probability, from Corinth. This would explain his reference to Phoebe and the church at Cenchreae,[6] and why we find among his fellow workers Erastus (cf. 2 Tim 4:20), and Gaius or Caius, one of the few Corinthians whom Paul himself baptized (cf. 1 Cor 1:14). At the end of the letter we read that the Teacher of the Gentiles is planning to bring up to Jerusalem the monies collected in Macedonia and Achaia (cf. Rom 15:25-26; Acts 19:21; 1 Cor 16:1). This suggests that the letter was written near the end of his third apostolic journey, probably during the three months he spent in Greece after the riot in Ephesus and before his dramatic journey to Jerusalem (cf. Acts 20:3): that would make it the winter of 57-58, very probably 58, just before he took ship.

---

5   St Paul refers on two occasions to a future visit to Spain – in Rom 15:24 and 28. Various Jewish communities are known to have existed in Spain in the first century A.D. We also know that there were close commercial links between Spain and Carthage, a city to which Christianity arrived quite early on: Acts 2:10 refers to some of those who heard the Apostles preaching on Pentecost as coming from Cyrene, that is the province contiguous to Carthage. According to early geographers, the sea journey from Ostia to Tarragona took three or four days, and that from Puzzuoli to Cadiz seven days. All this suggests that before St Paul's visit there could well have been some pockets of Christianity in existence. Regarding the name Tarshish (cf. Is 2:16; 23:1; Ezek 27:12; 38:13; Ps 48:4; 72:10; etc.) it is well known that this was used to refer to the western limits, from whence came big ships laden with precious and base minerals.

6   Cenchreae was the maritime port of Corinth on the Aegean Sea (cf. Act 18:18). Corinth had another port, Lecheos, on the Ionian Sea.

1. *The Christians of Galatia*   Galatia was an inland region of Asia Minor, occupying the central part of the plateau of Turkey. In the centre of the region lay Ancyra, present-day Ankara. In St Paul's time the Roman province of Galatia also included, to the south, the territory of the ancient country of Lycaonia, where were located many cities we are familiar with through Acts – Derbe, Lystra, Iconium and Pisidian Antioch. Galatia was bordered, then, on the east by Cappodocia, on the north by Bythinia and Paphlagonia (both on the Black Sea), on the west by Phrygia (where Colossae and Laodicea were located) and to the south, as we have said, by Lycaonia and Pisidia. The Galatians were of Celtic stock and were descended from people who had migrated there in the third century B.C.; many of them were shepherds, honest, upright people, warm and affectionate. St Paul had made contact with them on his very first missionary journey, when he evangelized the south of the province. But his most intensive ministry to them took place during his second journey, between 49 and 52, possibly because illness forced him to stay there for a period (cf. Gal 4:13; Acts 16:1-8). The Galatians welcomed him with open arms – received him "as an angel of God", as if he were our Lord himself (cf. Gal 4:14); they rejoiced at their good fortune in having Paul with them and showed him affection in all kinds of ways: as he reminds them, "if possible, you would have plucked out your eyes and given them to me" (Gal 4:15).

Even though the Apostle has not been in Galatia for some time he still addresses them with great tenderness: "My little children, with whom I am once again in travail until Christ be formed in you" (Gal 4:19). He calls them "foolish Galatians": they are easily swayed, too ready to listen to new preachers, too inclined to look for excitement or consolation in religion (cf. Gal 3:1- 4); but he finds it difficult to reprove them and soon changes his tone, for his spiritual children make him feel affectionate and understanding (cf. Gal 4:20). The Apostle had actually been back to Galatia twice in the year 53 or 54 (cf. Acts 18:23), and then, on learning about the threat from the Judaizers, he wrote them this letter so full of anguish and love.

2. *The Christian community in Rome*   It is estimated that in Nero's time Rome had a population of about one million. Obviously, it would have been made up of all kinds of people; as Seneca put it, "Every sort of person flocks to the City which offers, at a high price, virtues and vices."[7] There is every reason to suppose that Christian converts were to be found there from very early on. In fact, at Pentecost, the Acts of the Apostles tell us, there were visitors from Rome in Jerusalem (Acts 2:10), some of whom may well have been baptized on that day (cf. Acts 2:41). Besides, it is known that the Jewish community in the Eternal City was perhaps as large as 50,000, with thirteen synagogues. Suetonius, in his *Life of Claudius*, tells us that during that emperor's reign there was such unrest among the Jews "provoked by one Chrestus" that the emperor

7   *Consolatio ad Helviam*, 6, 2-3.

had to decree their expulsion:[8] this was what led Aquila and Priscilla to leave Rome and go to Corinth (cf. Acts 18:2), where they met St Paul (they were already Christians). Also among the people whom the Apostle greets at the end of his epistle we find Andronicus and Junias, who "were in Christ before me" (cf. Rom 16:7) that is, before the year 38.

Although it is more than likely that some members of the Jewish community in Rome were Christians from very early on, the actual foundation of the local church at Rome must be attributed to St Peter, who went there shortly after he escaped miraculously from Herod Agrippa's prison (cf. Acts 12:17). The unanimous tradition about St Peter's stay in Rome is recorded in two main sources: Eusebius, in his *Ecclesiastical History*, tells us that Simon Peter arrived in Rome during the reign of Claudius (41-54); and the *Catalogus libri pontificalis* speaks of his preaching there for twenty-five years. From Paul's letters we can see that he recognizes the Christians of the City as constituting a flourishing community whose "faith is proclaimed in all the world" (Rom 1:8), a community which merits being greeted by "all the churches of Christ" (Rom 16:16) and which has been in existence for some considerable time (cf. Rom 15:22) – all of which confirms what tradition tells us. This explains how, when Paul, after so many vicissitudes, was eventually able to fulfil his long-felt desire to visit Rome,[9] the brethren went "as far as the Forum of Appius and Three Taverns" to meet him (Acts 28:15).

Who were responsible for the establishment of this very important local church? Was it Jewish Christians or Gentile converts? Probably both. Certainly there must have been many Jews in the Roman church; otherwise, there would be no reason for Paul to have so many Jewish references in his letter – quotations from books of the Old Testament (cf. e.g. Rom 3:10-18), the long point he makes about the calling of Abraham (cf. chap. 4), his outline of the history of Israel (cf. chaps. 9-11), the various possible objections he deals with,[10] and, perhaps, his reference to those who are "weak in faith", who continue to follow superseded practices (cf. Rom 14:1-6). However, the Gentiles must have been in the majority, because essentially the letter is addressed to them. To them specifically the Apostle has been sent (cf. Rom 1:5, 13-14; 15:15-16); Paul considers himself "under obligation" to them for the sake of the Gospel; the letter is written to people who have been slaves of sin (cf. Rom 6:17); they do not belong to Israel according to the flesh;[11] the Apostle is speaking to them directly (Rom 11:13); they must not feel superior to the Jews (cf. Rom 11:20, 24), but rather revere and adore God's mercy and justice (cf. Rom 11:22, 28-32).

And, lastly, they are the "strong": they know that for God there is no such thing as "unclean" food; all food is good; but they should not "let what is good

8 *Life of Claudius*, 25.
9 Cf. Rom 1:10, 15; 15:23; Acts 19:21.
10 Cf. Rom 2:17-22; 3:1-5; 6:1-3; 7:1; etc.
11 Cf. Rom 4:11-12, 9:3ff; 10:1; etc.

[. . .] be spoken of as evil" (Rom 14:16), that is, they should be careful not to give scandal.

In that early Christian community in Rome we see at work the universal ideal of Christianity: "Christ became a servant to the circumcised [. . .] in order to confirm the promises given to the patriarchs, and in order that the Gentiles might glorify God for his mercy" (Rom 15:8-9).

CONTENT AND STRUCTURE OF THE TWO EPISTLES

1. *St Paul's literary style*   Various collections of letters by important people or writers have come down to us from classical times: for example, there are those of Cicero, which give clear insights into the mind of the man and the turbulent times he lived in; or Pliny the Younger's letters, a most valuable source of information on men and affairs in the first and second century A.D. We also have some letters of Fathers of the Church – Athanasius, Basil, Gregory Nazianzen, Paulinus of Nola, Ambrose, Jerome, Augustine . . . ; and indeed some of the oldest documents preserved by immediate post-biblical Christian traditions are letters – St Clement of Rome's *Epistle to the Corinthians* and the series of *Letters* written by St Ignatius, bishop of Antioch, during his long journey to Rome to be put to death for the faith.

All this helps us to understand the kind of letters we meet in the New Testament – the Pauline epistles and the other seven "catholic" epistles. Even from a literary point of view the Pauline letters are quite outstanding. The other inspired letters are short doctrinal essays, sometimes very profound, but they do not have the vigour and energy of St Paul's writings. No writer of ancient times can be compared to him. Leaving other New Testament authors aside, perhaps only the very earliest Christian writers, such as St Clement and St Ignatius, can approach the depth, strength, passion and vision of the Apostle of the Gentiles. But those early writers were in fact disciples of St Paul, dedicated apprentices of his. Moreover, in addition to the characteristic features of Paul's letters, it must also be said that they have all the features of real correspondence; one realizes immediately that these are not letters written with a literary purpose, nor are they intellectual reflections cast in letter form (quite a common practice in all languages), nor elaborations of some earlier text. They have all the immediacy of things said or dictated on the spot. St Paul links ideas by association, he goes back a number of times over things he has already spoken about and keeps repeating ideas which he sees as very important; he develops his arguments slowly, moving in concentric circles; sometimes he rises suddenly to dizzy heights, pursuing an insight; on other occasions he writes straight from the heart and the tone is warm and passionate; he some-times uses irony, reproach and even cutting words if he feels that is what his readers need.

Paul's style does not follow any fixed method; but there is a basic order to it. In each letter there are one or more core themes, to which the Apostle keeps returning, and these lead him on to other ideas which seem to be incidental.

This explains why we sometimes find unfinished sentences: the writer's thought has gone off on a tangent and does not come back, but it is easy to see what he is saying: in fact, these unfinished sentences have a poetry and strength and vitality of their own.

Still, these epistles largely do keep to the general structure of a traditional letter. Paul begins with a greeting, which is not a stereotyped form of words but a vibrant, supernatural recollection. He gives a little news about himself and sends his best wishes – for peace, grace and divine assistance. He then moves on to deal with the matter(s) he wants to expound. He reminds his readers of their duty, in all situations, to be charitable, and, always using new imagery, he paints an attractive picture of what the Christian life involves – how magnificent it is, and how demanding it is also. He ends the letter renewing his good wishes and greetings, and praising God.

2. *Galatians* The Apostle uses this structure as a framework into which he builds the particular things he wants to deal with in each letter. In the case of the Epistle to the Galatians, which was written before that to the Romans, he starts off with his usual greetings (1:1-5), recalling that he has been chosen not by men but by God, and immediately making complaint at the inconstancy of his spiritual children (1:6-10). He is very outspoken and goes as far as to put a curse on anyone who preaches a gospel other than his. This ends the introductory part of the letter. It is followed by one of the most historically interesting texts: in order to defend his right to preach the Gospel, and to argue the supernatural character of his mission, Paul recalls the main stages in his life – his vocation (1:11-24), his visit to Jerusalem with Barnabas and Titus, probably in connexion with the Apostles' council (2:1-10), and the Antioch incident (2:11-21).

The *doctrinal part* of this letter is the first time Paul deals with the key question in his controversy with the Judaizers – justification through faith in Jesus Christ and not through adherence to the Law of Moses. In dealing with this truth he goes right back to God's promises to Abraham, recalling that the Patriarch was justified by his faith, recalling too the curse the Law imposed on transgressors. Justification finds its basis in the promises made to Abraham, not in the Law promulgated 430 years later: the Law's function was one of education, preparing the way for the new Law of freedom preached by Christ (3:15-29).

To explain what being a Christian means, the Apostle makes two comparisons – one taken from ordinary life and one from Sacred Scripture. Christians are sons and daughters of God: before Christ they were like small children, in need of guardians; now they are mature sons and daughters, heirs, who can relate to God as to their Father (4:1-11). Or, to put it in biblical terms: the contrast between slavery and freedom recalls the two sons of Abraham – Ishmael, the son of Hagar, a slave, and Isaac, the son of Sarah, a free woman. Ishmael stands for the Old Testament, Isaac for the New (4:21-31). In between making these comparisons, St Paul opens his heart to the Galatians, showing how fatherly are his feelings for them (4:12-20).

After expounding this teaching, the Apostle shows how it applies in everyday life. This is the moral section of the letter (5:1 - 6:10). He begins by recalling that the Law of Christ is a law of freedom, whereas the Law of circumcision involves a whole series of obligations (5:1-12); then he goes on to develop a very important idea – the opposition between the works of the Spirit, and the works of the flesh and of sin (5:13-26). He finishes by pointing out that the key precept in the Law of Christ is charity, and he describes charity by showing how it expresses itself in the area of brotherhood (6:1-10).

The epistle ends with lines written by St Paul in his own hand, a brief summary of what he has been saying, and warm words of farewell (6:11-18).

3. *Romans* The Epistle to the Romans deals with the same subject, but more extensively and in more depth. It begins with a very long and elaborate *prologue*, one of the most moving passages in all the Apostle's letters. In it he declares himself to be a servant of Jesus Christ, and, in referring to his mission, he gives a vivid summary of the process of Redemption (1:1-15). He is writing this letter to speak about the justification which comes through faith, for "he who through faith is righteous shall live" (1:16-17).

The *dogmatic section* of the letter, which takes up over half of the text, centres on the meaning, content and implications of the justification opened up to us through Jesus Christ (1:18 - 11:36). He begins by showing the need for justification (1:18 - 4:25), describing the sinful situation in which all men, without exception, find themselves – pagans, through their idolatry and perversion (1:18-32), Jews through their sins and transgressions (2:1-24). Physical circumcision cannot save anyone: a person must be inwardly circumcised, that is, be inwardly clean (2:25 - 3:8). In God's sight all are sinners, whether they be Jews or Gentiles (3:9-20), and all are in need of the justification which comes through faith in Christ and which cannot be merited; it is a free gift of God (3:21-31). This first part of the doctrinal section of the letter ends with Paul giving an example he has already used in Galatians – that of Abraham, to whom God made promises not because Abraham had adhered to the Law (it had not yet been promulgated) but because of his faith (4:1-25).

But faith, like justification, is itself a gift from God. No merits of ours can win it: God gratuitously saves us through Christ. In this second part of his doctrinal exposition, St Paul explains what the effects of justification are – liberation from sin, from death (temporal and, above all, eternal death) and from the Mosaic Law. He shows us how salvation comes through Christ's self-sacrifice and how this salvation is applied to us (5:1 - 8:39). By his death Christ reconciles us with the Father; his death, therefore, is the ground of our hope (5:1-11). Oppressed by the sin of Adam, we find in Christ the new Adam, the new head of the human race; Christ liberates us and gives us back the life which the first man's sin took away from us. Where sin increased, grace abounded all the more (5:12-21). This liberation and this new life are communicated to us through Baptism, which makes us sharers in the Death and Resurrection of Jesus Christ (6:1-11).

The opposition between sin and redemption, between death and life, is compared with the opposition between enslavement and freedom: Christ has freed us from original sin and given us the opportunity to set ourselves free from personal sins so as to freely serve righteousness (16:12-23). What enslaves man is sin – original sin, in the first place; personal sins, made worse by knowledge of the Law; and concupiscence, which, though it is not sin, derives from sin and inclines us to sin. The freedom which Christ gives us is, therefore, freedom from the Law (7:1- 6)[12] and freedom from concupiscence (7:7-13). There is a third enemy – the flesh (the soil on which concupiscence grows), which works against the spirit. There is a law of the flesh (concupiscence, which inclines one to sin) which goes against grace; this law needs to be striven against. This interior striving is a normal and necessary part of the Christian life, because sin constitutes a threat even after we are justified: we can see what it did to the first man; it conquered him and held him in thrall until the coming of Christ (7:14-25).[13]

But a Christian's life is not all one long struggle, nor is justification only a matter of forgiveness of sins. The most important thing about justification is its positive aspect – the new life which the Spirit gives us (8:1-13). Through the action of the Holy Spirit we become true sons and daughters of God (8:14-30) and are filled with confidence despite any difficulties that may arise. Our hope has a supernatural basis; our morale is based on awareness that God is our Father (8:31-39).

With the example of Abraham's calling and his faith, we come to the end of the letter's first series of doctrinal observations about sin, faith, redemption, and justification through Christ. Paul uses a similar comparison at the end of his next discussion on the same subject (9:1 - 11:36) – God's free choice of the people of Israel. Here Paul is not so much copper-fastening what he has already said in chapters 5-8, as answering a question which follows on from that earlier discussion: what do the promises made to the chosen people mean? The example he uses is God's free choice of Jacob as heir of the promise, and the passing over of Esau when he rejects his birthright (9:1-13).

This example reveals the mystery of predestination, which is not in con-

---

12 Freedom from the Law here means the Christian's freedom from the ritual precepts of the Mosaic Law and from the condemnation of sin which the Law brought with it. Prior to the Redemption, because he found it more difficult to keep the commandments, man incurred greater condemnation. This freedom from the Law of Moses does not of course mean that the Christian is not subject to any law: he has his own law, the Law of Christ (which is based on the double precept of love), the commandments of the Church, and the precepts of the natural law. Cf. "Introduction to the 'Theology' of St Paul", p. 31 above.

13 The notions of sin, flesh, death and Law, referred to here, are explored in more detail in the section called "Introduction to the 'Theology' of St Paul" (cf. pp. 29-32 above). The notion of Redemption is examined later in that section (cf. "Note", p. 36) and that of concupiscence is dealt with in the context of "flesh" (p. 30).

tradiction with human freedom (9:14-33). Paul also points out that the previous chosen people have been unfaithful to their calling and that this opened the way for God to pour his mercy upon the Gentiles (10:1-21). But not all Israel will be rejected: a remnant will be saved (11:1-12). The doctrinal part of Romans ends in fact with reflections on the difference between the new chosen people and the old (11:13-24); and Paul proclaims that divine Wisdom has arranged for the conversion of Israel and the bringing together of all the faithful during the last times (11:25-36).

This revelation about all men becoming one in Christ leads the way to the *morality section* of the letter (12:1 - 15:13). As in Galatians, this section deals with life based on love, but here the scale is worldwide. Love, charity, is, in the first place, the bond uniting the members of Christ's Body, the Church (12:1-8). In Christ we all form a single body, are all members of one body – hence the need for fraternal charity (12:9-21). This same love guarantees the good order of society, because social order depends on recognition that all authority comes from God and must obey him (13:1-7). Therefore, charity is the fulfilling of the Law (13:8-14).

After giving the general principles governing the Christian life (12:1 - 13:14), St Paul examines one particular area; this leads on to his final observations (14:1 - 15:13). The particular matter is the distinction between people who are "strong" and those who are "weak" in faith – those who do not make distinctions between different kinds of food or days, and others who feel obliged not to eat the flesh of unclean animals, and to observe Jewish fasts on certain days of the year. The principle to apply here is that of love and respect for others: one has to put oneself in one's neighbour's shoes (14:1-12), avoid causing others to stumble (14:13-23) and follow Christ's example in all things (15:1-13).

The Letter to the Romans ends with an *epilogue*, which is longer than usual (15:14 - 16:27), perhaps because of the importance of the Christian community living in the capital city of the Empire and also because Paul describes his future plans in some detail. He explains why he has written to the Christians of Rome (15:14-21) and what his own plans are (15:22- 33), and ends his letter with a long series of warm greetings and introductions (16:1-24). His closing words are a splendid paean in praise of God, through Jesus Christ (16:25-27): he concludes his letter as if it were a prayer, just as he began it in the name of God and of Jesus Christ.

THE PRESENT TEXT OF ROMANS

In general, the text of these two letters has been very well preserved – which indicates the great reverence and respect the churches showed towards inspired writings attributed to the Apostle of the Gentiles. However, certain small variations should be remarked upon. They concern mainly the position of the final doxology (Rom 16:25-27). The letter seems to end as early as 15:33, with the customary words of farewell: this would explain why a very ancient papyrus puts the doxology at that point; other manuscripts, however, put it at the end of chapter 14, and most of these then repeat it at the very end of the epistle. It is not difficult to suggest an explanation for this. The liturgical reading of Romans usually omitted chapters 15 and 16 because they contained mainly "news items". However, the liturgy did not want to lose the beautiful doxology at the very end, and so it tagged it on to the text proper, as it were, as an extension of chapter 14 or chapter 15. Liturgical reading would have influenced the copying of the manuscripts and thereby given rise to the variations. Therefore, there seems to be no doubt about the final doxology being by St Paul and having always occupied the position it now holds at 16:25-27.

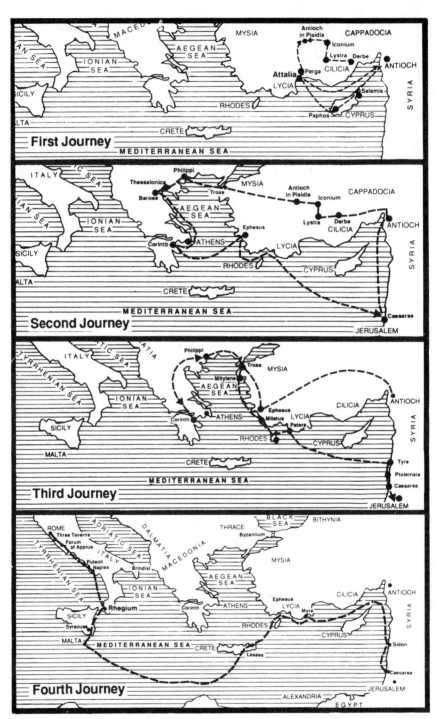

First Journey

MACEDO...
IONIAN SEA
AEGEAN SEA
MYSIA
Antioch in Pisidia
CAPPADOCIA
Iconium
Lystra
Derbe
ANTIOCH
Attalia
Perga
CILICIA
LYCIA
SYRIA
RHODES
Salamis
...AN SEA
SICILY
Paphos
CYPRUS
...LTA
CRETE
MEDITERRANEAN SEA

Second Journey

ITALY
...C SEA
Philippi
Thessalonica
Beroea
Troas
MYSIA
Antioch in Pisidia
CAPPADOCIA
Iconium
...AN SEA
IONIAN SEA
AEGEAN SEA
Ephesus
Lystra
Derbe
CILICIA
ANTIOCH
SICILY
Corinth
ATHENS
LYCIA
SYRIA
...LTA
RHODES
CYPRUS
CRETE
MEDITERRANEAN SEA
Caesarea
JERUSALEM

Third Journey

TYRRHENIAN SEA
ITALY
...TIA
...C SEA
...MATIA
Philippi
Troas
MYSIA
Mitylene
AEGEAN SEA
IONIAN SEA
Corinth
ATHENS
Ephesus
Miletus
CILICIA
ANTIOCH
LYCIA
Patara
SICILY
SYRIA
MALTA
RHODES
CYPRUS
CRETE
Tyre
MEDITERRANEAN SEA
Ptolemais
Caesarea
JERUSALEM

Fourth Journey

ROME
Three Taverns
Forum of Applus
ADRIATIC SEA
DALMATIA
BLACK SEA
THRACE
BITHYNIA
Byzantium
TYRRHENIAN SEA
Puteoli
Naples
ITALY
Brindisi
MACEDONIA
MYSIA
IONIAN SEA
AEGEAN SEA
Rhegium
Corinth
ATHENS
Ephesus
LYCIA
CILICIA
ANTIOCH
SICILY
Myra
Syracuse
RHODES
SYRIA
MALTA
CYPRUS
MEDITERRANEAN SEA
CRETE
Sidon
Lasaea
Caesarea
JERUSALEM
ALEXANDRIA
EGYPT

MISSIONARY JOURNEYS OF SAINT PAUL

The Epistle of St Paul
to the Romans

ENGLISH AND LATIN VERSIONS, WITH NOTES

1

PROLOGUE *by Christ himself*

Phil 1:1
Tit 1:1
Gal 1:10
Jas 1:6
Gal 1:15

Greeting

¹Paul, a servant[a] of Jesus Christ, called to be an apostle, set apart for the gospel of God ²which he promised beforehand

---

¹Paulus servus Christi Iesu, vocatus apostolus, segregatus in evangelium Dei, ²quod ante promiserat per prophetas suos in Scripturis sanctis ³de Filio suo, qui

---

1-15. These opening verses of the letter are a combination of greeting, introduction of the writer and the prologue to the entire text. The passage deals with themes in no particular order – in line with the style of some other Pauline letters, especially Romans itself.

Three matters are being covered here – Paul's introduction of himself, and his plans to visit Rome (vv. 1, 5, 9-15); who the immediate recipients are and their particular situation (vv. 6-8, 11, 15); and, finally, Paul's purpose in writing to the faithful at Rome (outlined in his greeting — vv. 2-4, 15 and, to a lesser degree, v. 9).

1-2. The word "gospel", which St Paul uses very often, here refers to the purpose of his vocation: he has been designated to preach the Gospel of God. This is obviously not a reference to the written Gospels; he is speaking of something complex and profound, already articulated by Christ in his preaching. Jesus said of himself that he had come to bring Good News (cf. Mt 11:15; Mk 1:14-15; Lk 4:18; etc.), as the prophets had foretold (especially Is 61:1, which Jesus quoted). "As an evangelizer, Christ first of all proclaims a kingdom, the Kingdom of God; and this is so important that, by comparison, everything else becomes 'the rest', which is 'given in addition' (cf. Mt 6:33).

"As the kernel and centre of this Good News, Christ proclaims salvation, this great gift of God which is liberation from everything that oppresses man but which is above all liberation from sin and the Evil One" (Paul VI, *Evangelii nuntiandi*, 8 and 9).

When he was about to ascend into heaven, Jesus charged his Apostles to proclaim the Good News (Mk 16:15; cf. Mt 28:19-20) which was to be "the source of all saving truth and moral discipline" (Vatican II, *Dei Verbum*, 7). For the Apostles this Good News was nothing more or less than Jesus Christ and his work of salvation. That is why the Gospel (which the Church is given to hand on to all generations) is centred on the life and teachings of Jesus Christ, as passed on to us by the Apostles. "The promises of the New Alliance in Jesus Christ, the teaching of the Lord and the Apostles, the Word of life, the sources of grace and of God's loving kindness, the path of salvation – all these things

[a]Or *slave*.

have been entrusted to her. It is the content of the Gospel, and therefore of evangelization" (*Evangelii nuntiandi*, 15). Thus we can say with St Thomas Aquinas (cf. *Summa theologiae*, I-II, q. 108, a.1; *Commentary on Rom.* 1, 1) that the core of the Gospel has to do with uniting men and God, a union which takes a perfect form in Christ but an imperfect one in us. The superiority of the Gospel over the Old Law consists in the grace of the Holy Spirit, which Christ confers on us. Therefore, the Gospel, to which the Apostles dedicated themselves, is, at one and the same time, a series of truths revealed by our Lord, the saving power of grace and the Church-in-action.

1. In addressing the Christians at Rome the Apostle uses, of his two names – Saul and Paul – the one he has used since his first missionary journey (cf. Acts 13:9), a Roman name indicating his Roman citizenship (cf. Acts 16:37; 22:25-28). It was in fact quite common for Jews to use two names – a national name, Hebrew or Aramaic, and another name, Greek or Latin, for dealings with people from other countries in the Empire. We find a number of examples of this in the New Testament – John-Mark, Symeon-Niger (Acts 13:1), Tabitha-Dorcas (Acts 9:36), etc.

Paul, who had been born a Roman citizen, was deeply conscious of his Jewish roots. He was of the tribe of Benjamin (Rom 11:1; Phil 3:5) and bore the name of one of the most famous members of that tribe – King Saul, son of Kish (Acts 13:21). He was well able to show his pride in his Jewish descent (cf. 2 Cor 11:22; Gal 1:13-14) yet was ready to become all things to all men in order to save even some (cf. 1 Cor 9:22).

St Paul wants to speak about Christ and his saving Gospel, but he cannot avoid making reference to himself and the mission entrusted to him; this he does by using three words which are full of meaning: he is a "servant" of Jesus Christ, called by God to be his "apostle" (envoy), "set apart" or designated by God to preach the Gospel. These three words tell the whole story of his vocation, and each of them encapsulates something of the mystery which Paul will expound in his epistle – the mercy of God, who saves men, justifies them, sanctifies them and sends them out.

"Servant": this title, also used by St James (Jas 1:1), St Peter (2 Pet 1:1) and St Jude (Jud 1), comes from the Old Testament. There the great prophets and guides of the chosen people described themselves as "servants" of Yahweh (cf., for example, Samuel: 1 Sam 3:9f; Abraham: Ps 104:6; David: 2 Sam 24:10; Moses, Aaron, Solomon, etc.), and the entire people of Israel is called the "servant" of God (Is 49:3); but most prominently there is the Messiah, the "Servant" of God to the extent of actually giving his life (Is 41:9; 42:1; 49:6; 53:11). In the world of the Hebrew religion "servant of God" is the equivalent of "worshipper of God", one who offers religious worship: this notion of servant did not carry the overtones of inhuman debasement that it had in Greco-Roman culture. When St Paul says that he is a "servant" (or "slave") of Jesus Christ he is implicitly saying that he renders him religious adoration.

"Apostle": this word designates preachers of the Gospel, particularly the

64

through his prophets in the holy scriptures, [3]the gospel
concerning his Son, who was descended from David
according to the flesh [4]and designated[a2] Son of God in
power according to the Spirit of holiness by his resurrection

---

factus est ex semine David secundum carnem, [4]qui constitutus est Filius Dei in
virtute secundum Spiritum sanctificationis ex resurrectione mortuorum, Iesu

---

twelve chosen disciples of Jesus (cf. Mt 10:2-4 and Mk 3:16-19). It was quite
logically applied to Matthias when he became one of the Twelve (Acts 1:25).
Christ himself designated Paul an apostle when he appeared to him on the road
to Damascus (Acts 26:16-18; Gal 1:15-16), called him to the faith and charged
him with his mission to preach. By describing himself as "called to be an
apostle", St Paul is saying that he is on an equal footing with the Twelve – for
example, Peter, James and John, whom he calls "pillars" of the Church (Gal
2:9) – since he received his calling from Christ himself, as had been the case
with the other Apostles (cf. Acts 9:3-18), and not from the leaders of the
community of Antioch (Acts 13:2-3).

"Set apart": this refers to the mission entrusted to St Paul of preaching the
Gospel to the Gentiles. Possibly it also refers to Paul's place in God's eternal
plan; in this sense he can say that he was "set apart" ever since he was in his
mother's womb (Gal 1:15; cf. Jer 1:5; Is 49:1).

St John Chrysostom comments on this verse as follows: "If Paul constantly
recalls his vocation it is in order to show his gratitude. This gift, which he did
not solicit, took him by surprise; he simply obeyed and followed the divine
inspiration. As regards the faithful, they too, as he himself says, have been
called to holiness" (*Hom. on Rom*, 1).

3-4. Scholars are now confident that in Rom 1:3-4 St Paul is quoting from a
Christological formula or hymn (like that in 1 Tim 3:16 or Phil 2:6-11) –
probably used in the very earliest Christian liturgy. In these two verses St Paul
offers, as it were, a summary of Christology: Jesus Christ, true God and true
Man, is the Son sent by his Father God (v. 3). From all eternity he is God, equal
to the Father, and in the fullness of time he has taken up a human nature which
was initially capable of experiencing pain (v. 3) and was later glorified (v. 4).

The Incarnation did not involve any change, as far as the Word was
concerned, either in his divine nature (which he did not shed and which did not
alter) or in his being a Person distinct from the Father and the Holy Spirit.
However, by the Incarnation he assumed a human nature, being born of a Virgin
(cf. Lk 1:27, 35): and so the Son of God became the Son of David, of the lineage
of David. The phrase "according to the flesh" actually emphasises the
lowliness which the Incarnation implied – fragility, suffering, self-emptying,
humiliation (cf. Jn 1:14 and note; Phil 2:7).

[a2]Or *constituted.*

from the dead, Jesus Christ our Lord, ⁵through whom we have received grace and apostleship to bring about the obedience of faith for the sake of his name among all the nations, ⁶including yourselves who are called to belong to Jesus Christ:

Christo Domino nostro, ⁵per quem accepimus gratiam et apostolatum ad oboeditionem fidei in omnibus gentibus pro nomine eius, ⁶in quibus estis et vos

---

During Christ's life on earth prior to his Resurrection, although it was united to the Word, his human nature, especially his body, was not fully glorified. Moreover, although it is true that during that period of his life he showed his divinity by his miracles (cf. Jn 2:11) and by words confirmed by those miracles (cf. Jn 10:37ff), it is also true that his human nature was to the forefront most of the time. After the Resurrection, his human body and soul were fully glorified and therefore from then on his divine nature was the more apparent. This real change which took place in Christ's human nature when he rose from the dead, and the fact that his divinity became more manifest and he was more easily recognized to be God, are captured in what St Paul says here in v. 4.

The words "according to the Spirit of holiness" can refer both to Christ's divine nature (in the same way as "according to the flesh" refers to his human nature) and to the action of the Holy Spirit, whose effects were more easily seen after the Resurrection, especially from Pentecost onwards (cf. Jn 7:39 and note on same).

5. Here St Paul refers to the mission given him by God the Father through Jesus Christ at the time of his conversion (cf. Acts 9:15) and which he mentions explicitly in his letter to the Galatians (cf. Gal 2:7). Within the world-wide mission implied in being an apostle called by Christ himself, St Paul was given a special mission of his own – to be the Apostle of the Gentiles; he mentions this mission at the beginning of this letter to show why he should be addressing the Christians at Rome, a church which he had not founded.

The purpose and effect of the apostolic ministry is to bring about the "obedience of faith": when a person believes, he submits his mind and will to God's authority, freely accepting the truths which God proposes. Apropos of this obedience proper to faith the Second Vatican Council says: "'The obedience of faith' (Rom 16:26; cf. Rom 1:5; 2 Cor 10:5-6) must be given to God as he reveals himself. By faith man freely commits his entire self to God, making 'the full submission of his intellect and will to God who reveals' (Vatican I, *Dei Filius*, chap.3) and willingly assenting to the Revelation given by him. Before this faith can be exercised, man must have the grace of God to move and assist him; he must have the interior help of the Holy Spirit, who moves the heart and converts it to God, who opens the eyes of the mind and 'makes it easy for all to accept and believe the truth' (Second Council of Orange III, *De gratia*, can. 7; *Dei Filius, ibid.*)" (Vatican II, *Dei Verbum*, 5).

segregatus in evangelium Dei (i)

7To all God's beloved in Rome, who are called to be saints:
Grace to you and peace from God our Father and the Lord Jesus Christ.

---

vocati Iesu Christi, **7**omnibus, qui sunt Romae dilectis Dei, vocatis sanctis:

---

7. "Called to be saints": literally "called saints". This is not just a way of speaking: St Paul really is saying that Christians are "called" in the same kind of way as the Israelites were so often called through Moses (Num 10:1-4). In the Christians' case, the calling is to form the new people of God, one of whose characteristic features is holiness. Basing itself on this and other Pauline texts, the Second Vatican Council has this to say: "As Israel according to the flesh which wandered in the desert was already called the Church of God (cf. 2 Ezra 13:1; cf. Num 20:4; Deut 23:1ff), so too, the new Israel, which advances in this present era in search of a future and permanent city (cf. Heb 13:14), is called also the Church of Christ (cf. Mt. 16:18) [. . .]. The followers of Christ, called by God not in virtue of their works but by his design and grace, and justified in the Lord Jesus, have been made sons of God in the baptism of faith and partakers of the divine nature, and so are truly sanctified" (*Lumen gentium*, 9 and 40).

This is in fact the basis of the "universal call to holiness". All Christians, by virtue of their Baptism, should live in line with what that means: they are called to be saints and their whole life should be a pursuit of holiness: "In baptism, our Father God has taken possession of our lives, has made us share in the life of Christ, and has given us the Holy Spirit" (J. Escrivá, *Christ is passing by*, 128). "We are deeply moved, and our hearts profoundly shaken, when we listen attentively to that cry of St Paul: 'This is the will of God, your sanctification' (1 Thess 4:3). Today, once again, I set myself this goal and I also remind you and all mankind: this is God's Will for us, that we be saints" (J. Escrivá, *Friends of God*, 294).

The formula "grace and peace" seems to be St Paul's own: it is a combination of the usual Greek greeting at the start of letters and the Hebrew *shalom* (peace). The Apostle uses this double greeting very often (cf., for example, 1 Cor 1:3; 2 Cor 1:2; Gal 1:3; Eph 1:2; etc). It is a Christian greeting, referring to the gifts the Holy Spirit brings us. Jewish and pagan greetings wished people material prosperity or good fortune; the Apostle's are wishes for something higher – divine benevolence, which comes in the form of the gift of sanctifying grace, and the virtues and gifts of the Holy Spirit, and interior peace, which derives from reconciliation with God brought about by Christ. These gifts, according to the Apostle, come to us from God our Father, and from Jesus Christ, the Lord, who is equal to the Father. Thus we see Christian life as being inserted in the intimate life of the Blessed Trinity, for "grace and peace" came from the goodness and mercy of God, by way of the Incarnation of the Word and the Redemption wrought by him.

Rom 16:19
1 Thess 1:8
Rom 1:1, 16;
15:16
Phil 1:8
Eph 1:16
Rom 15:23-32
Acts 19:21

⁸First, I thank my God through Jesus Christ for all of you, because your faith is proclaimed in all the world. ⁹For God is my witness, whom I serve with my spirit in the gospel of his Son, that without ceasing I mention you always in my prayers, ¹⁰asking that somehow by God's will I may now

---

gratia vobis et pax a Deo Patre nostro et Domino Iesu Christo. ⁸Primum quidem gratias ago Deo meo per Iesum Christum pro omnibus vobis, quia fides vestra annuntiatur in universo mundo; ⁹testis enim mihi est Deus, cui servio in spiritu

---

8. After greeting the people he is writing to, St Paul pours out his soul in an act of thanksgiving to God, as he recalls the fidelity and perseverance of the Christians at Rome: this is very typical of the Apostle; we find him doing it in almost all his letters (cf. for example, 1 Cor 1:4-5; Eph 1:15-16; Phil 1:3-4; Col 1:3-4; 1 Thess 1:2; etc.).

Here he gives thanks for the faith of the Roman Christians, that is, for their loyalty to the faith and for their many converts despite their difficult circumstances and the immorality that was a feature of Roman society. The Christians at Rome must have been an example and encouragement to all the Christian communities in the Empire: the Apostle says that their faith is "proclaimed", praised, the world over.

9. St Paul calls on God as his witness to prove his affection for the faithful at Rome, and his constant prayer for them. This invocation of God, which is like taking an oath and is full of religious feeling, is a spontaneous expression of his love of God. For St Paul God is the One whom he serves as a worshipper (the Greek word *latreúo*, translated as 'serve', has tones of the adoration that is due to God) with every fibre of his being. It is as if the Apostle were saying: I give him my entire life, all my energy, my sweat and blood; I shall serve him to my last breath, working and striving on his behalf. The sincerity of this total dedication is expressed in the word "spirit", as opposed to the "letter" of external forms or mere ceremonial behaviour (cf. Rom 2:9; 7:6; 2 Cor 3:6) so prevalent in the Judaism of his time. Some Fathers of the Church see in these words an allusion to the "new life" of the Christians, who worship God "in spirit and truth", as Christ explained to the Samaritan woman (Jn 4:23), and even as implying the presence of the Holy Spirit. For example, St John Chrysostom comments: "When Paul says, 'whom I serve with my spirit in the gospel of the Son', while pointing to the grace of God he also reveals his humility; the grace of God, because the Lord entrusted him with an important mission, that of preaching; his humility, because he attributes all the glory of his success, not to his own efforts, but to the presence of God" (*Hom. on Rom*, 2). This connexion between apostolate and intimacy with God reminds us of a basic aspect of every Christian's life: "You have got to be a 'man of God', a man of interior life, a man of prayer and sacrifice. Your apostolate must be the overflow of your life 'within'" (J. Escrivá, *The Way*, 961).

at last succeed in coming to you. [11]For I long to see you, that I may impart to you some spiritual gift to strengthen you, [12]that is, that we may be mutually encouraged by each other's faith, both yours and mine. [13]I want you to know, brethren, that I have often intended to come to you (but thus far have been prevented) in order that I may reap some harvest among you as well as among the rest of the Gentiles. [14]I am under obligation both to Greeks and to barbarians, both to the wise and to the foolish: [15]so I am eager to preach the gospel to you also who are in Rome.

Rom 1:7;
15:22

Mt 10:33
Mk 8:38
1 Cor 1:18,
24; 2:4-5
Acts 13:46

The theme of the epistle

[16]For I am not ashamed of the gospel: it is the power of

---

meo in evangelio Filii eius, quomodo sine intermissione memoriam vestri faciam [10]semper in orationibus meis obsecrans si quo modo tandem aliquando prosperum iter habeam in voluntate Dei veniendi ad vos. [11]Desidero enim videre vos, ut aliquid impertiar gratiae vobis spiritalis ad confirmandos vos [12]id est una vobiscum consolari per eam, quae invicem est, fidem vestram atque meam. [13]Nolo autem vos ignorare, fratres, quia saepe proposui venire ad vos et prohibitus sum usque adhuc, ut aliquem fructum habeam et in vobis, sicut et in ceteris gentibus. [14]Graecis ac barbaris, sapientibus et insipientibus debitor sum. [15]Itaque, quod in me est, promptus sum et vobis, qui Romae estis, evangelizare. [16]Non enim erubesco evangelium: virtus enim Dei est in salutem

---

13. On St Paul's desire to extend his apostolate to the western part of the Roman empire, cf. "Introduction to the Epistles of St Paul", pp. 17-18 above.

14-15. "To Greeks and to barbarians": in other words, the entire Gentile world. "Greek" as opposed to "barbarian" referred to someone who was educated and who spoke Greek. The Greeks regarded as barbarians everyone who spoke a language other than Greek (cf. Act 28:2; 1 Cor 14:11): even Romans were barbarians if they spoke only Latin. The Christian community at Rome would have had both kinds of Gentiles in it. However, elsewhere in the letters the term "Greek" includes all Gentiles as distinct from Jews (cf. Rom 1:16; 2:9-10; 10:12; Acts 11:20). The Gospel is addressed to everyone, irrespective of race, nation or culture. However, often it is simple, humble people who prove to be most ready to receive Christ's message.

16. St Paul continues to speak about the "Gospel". The proclamation of the saving power of Christ's death on the Cross is a stumbling block to the Jews and foolishness to the Gentiles, whereas a Christian is proud of the Cross and draws strength from it. When writing to the Romans, the Apostle, who was quite familiar with the noise of triumphal marches and the divinization of

God for salvation to every one who has faith, to the Jew first and also to the Greek. [17]For in it the righteousness of God is revealed through faith for faith; as it is written, "He who through faith is righteous shall live."[b]

omni credenti, Iudaeo primum et Graeco. [17]Iustitia enim Dei in eo revelatur ex

emperors, simply says that "he is not ashamed; he does so to encourage them also not to be ashamed but, rather, to boast as he did. If today someone approaches you and asks you, 'But . . . do you adore a crucified man?', far from hanging your head and blushing with confusion, use this reproach as an opportunity to boast and let your eyes and your face show that you are not ashamed. If they come back and ask you aloud, 'What, adore the crucified?', reply: 'Yes, I adore him [. . .]. I adore and boast of a crucified God who, by his Cross, reduced the demons to silence and did away with all superstition: for me his Cross is the ineffable trophy of his benevolence and of his love'" (St John Chrysostom, *Hom. on Rom*, 2).

17. The expression "righteousness of God" refers to the state of righteousness or justice (= justness) in which a person is placed when God gives him grace. It is called the righteousness of God because man cannot attain it through his own efforts: it is a free (gratuitous, hence "grace") gift of God. The fact that "righteousness" comes from God does not mean that it is something external to man, for righteousness does not mean merely that we are called "righteous" but that we really are righteous in God's eyes. The Magisterium of the Church has given solemn teaching on this matter in the context of explaining the various factors which cause man's justification: "Finally", says the Council of Trent, "the only formal cause is 'justice of God, not the justice by which he is himself just, but the justice by which he makes us just' (St Augustine, *De Trinitate*, XIV, 12, 15), namely, the justice which we have as a gift from him and by which we are renewed in the spirit of our mind. And not only are we considered just, but we are truly said to be just, and we are just" (*De iustificatione*, chap. 7).

"Through faith for faith": Sacred Scripture tends to use this kind of phrase to indicate on-going growth in something that is living (cf. Ps 84:8; 2 Cor 2:16; 3:18; Rom 6:19). What is being spoken about here is a steady progression from the imperfect understanding of divine truths possible in this life to the perfect understanding that is experienced in heaven. The full meaning of the phrase can be seen from St Paul's statement that in the Gospel justice is made manifest: it begins and is nourished and grows through faith, until the believer at last attains eternal salvation.

The statement that "he who through faith is righteous shall live" comes from Hab 2:4; St Paul here applies it to the position of the Christian. What the prophet meant was that those Jews who kept the Law and trusted in its promises would

[b]Or *The righteous shall live by faith.*

JUSTIFICATION THROUGH JESUS CHRIST

JUSTIFICATION THROUGH FAITH

The fault and punishment of the Gentiles

Zeph 1:15
1 Thess 2:16

¹⁸For the wrath of God is revealed from heaven against all ungodliness and wickedness of men who by their

---

fide in fidem, sicut scriptum est: *"Iustus autem ex fide vivet."* ¹⁸Revelatur enim ira Dei de caelo super omnem impietatem et iniustitiam hominum, qui veritatem

---

not succumb when the Babylonians invaded. St Paul applies the test to the righteous of the New Testament: if they stay firm in their faith in the Gospel, they will continue in the life of grace and will attain everlasting beatitude. The faith of good Israelites was a prefiguring of the faith of good Christians. The just man will live by faith, which "faith is the beginning of man's salvation, the foundation and source of all justification, 'without which it is impossible to please God' (cf. Heb 11:6) and to be counted as his sons" (Council of Trent, *De iustificatione*, chap. 8).

St Paul's statement can also be understood as meaning that he who through faith is just will live. This puts the emphasis on the fact that faith is the beginning of the process of justification, and that a person who is justified will attain salvation.

18-32. The Apostle is saying that the righteousness of God (= justness) can only come about through faith in Jesus Christ – and that neither Jews nor Gentiles possess this righteousness. He develops this point up as far as 3:20.

In the present passage he describes two stages in the position of the Gentiles. In the first (vv. 18-23) he points out their blameworthiness, and then in the second he goes on (vv. 24-32) to speak about the punishment of their sins. Justice as the righteousness of God refers to God's action of saving sinful man by pouring his grace into him; God's "wrath" is the punishment which the Almighty inflicts on him who persists in sin. For, as St Thomas says, "Anger and the like are ascribed to God by an analogy drawn from their effects. Because it is characteristic of anger that it stimulates men to requite wrong, divine retribution is analogically termed anger" (*Summa theologiae*, I, q. 3, a. 2 ad 2).

There is a connexion between faith and righteousness, on the one hand, and sin and God's wrath, on the other. This Pauline teaching ties in with the last thing St John the Baptist is recorded as saying in bearing witness to Christ: "He who believes in the Son has eternal life; he who does not obey the Son shall not see life, but the wrath of God rests upon him" (Jn 3:36).

Wis 13:1-9
Acts 14:15-17;
17:24-29
Eccles 17:7-8

wickedness suppress the truth. [19]For what can be known about God is plain to them, because God has shown it to them. [20]Ever since the creation of the world his invisible

---

in iniustitia detinent, [19]quia, quod noscibile est Dei, manifestum est in illis; Deus enim illis manifestavit. [20]Invisibilia enim ipsius a creatura mundi per ea, quae

---

Christian teaching often points out how God's desire that all sinners be saved (the "righteousness of God" as instrument of salvation) combines with his punishment of sin (the "wrath of God"). How perfect justice interfaces with perfect mercy is ultimately a mystery.

18. "Who by their wickedness suppress the truth": commenting on these words St Thomas writes: "Genuine knowledge of God has the effect of inclining a person to goodness. However, this knowledge of God can be frustrated, as if enchained, by a person's attachment to vice" (*Commentary on Rom, ad loc.*)

Clearly St Paul is speaking here of those Gentiles who do know about God but who fail to appreciate their good fortune; their knowledge of God does not produce the result which should naturally flow from it – an upright life. We can see from what Paul says that man is naturally religious. He has a knowledge of God which is not just theoretical: it has implications for his whole life because it implies that he is intimately united to God. When a person does not follow the impulse of his very nature he is guilty of unrighteousness, for he should render God homage for being his Creator.

"All men, because they are persons, that is, beings endowed with reason and free will and therefore bearing personal responsibility, are both impelled by their nature and bound by a moral obligation to seek the truth, especially religious truth. They are also bound to adhere to the truth once they come to know it and direct their whole lives in accordance with the demands of truth" (Vatican II, *Dignitatis humanae*, 2).

Our dependence on God does not mean that we are less than free; on the contrary, it is rejection of all religious duties that leads to the shameful slaveries which Paul now goes on to list, for "religion is the greatest rebellion of a person who does not want to live like an animal, who is not satisfied and will not rest until he reaches and comes to know his Creator" (J. Escrivá, *Conversations*, 73).

19-20. It is possible to know about God without his having to reveal himself in a supernatural way; we know this from the book of Wisdom (Wis 13:1-9), which says that pagans, who, led astray by the beauty and power and greatness of created things, took these things for gods, should have known that all this perfection etc. came from their Author, for "from the greatness and beauty of created things comes a corresponding perception of their Creator" (Wis 13:5). This knowledge of God, which we term "natural", is not something easy to attain; but it can be attained and it is the best form of preparation for accepting supernaturally revealed truths, and for disposing us to honour and worship our Creator. Moreover, Revelation confirms the certainty which natural knowledge gives: "The heavens are telling the glory of God", the Psalmist exclaims, "and the firmament proclaims his handiwork" (Ps 19:2). St Augustine reminds us that traces of the Creator are to be found in man, and, as we all know from experience, we have been made to know and love God and therefore our heart is restless until it rests in him (cf. *Confessions*, I, 1, 1).

To sum up, we can say with St Thomas Aquinas that, in the natural order, man has two ways of discovering the existence of God – one, through reason, that inner light by means of which a person acquires knowledge; the other, through certain external pointers to the wisdom of God, that is, created things perceivable through the senses: these things are like a book on which are imprinted traces of God (cf. *Commentary on Rom*, 1:6).

Whichever of these routes is taken, "God, the origin and end of all things, can be known with certainty by the natural light of human reason from the things that he created" (Vatican I, *Dei Filius*, chap. 2).

Recalling the core of Christian teaching about the nature of man, the Second Vatican Council states that "sacred Scripture teaches that man was created 'in the image of God' as able to know and love his Creator", and that "the dignity of man rests above all on the fact that he is called to communion with God. The invitation to converse with God is addressed to man as soon as he comes into being. For if man exists it is because God has created him through love, and through love continues to hold him in existence" (*Gaudium et spes*, 12 and 19). The human mind, therefore, even when relying on its own resources can grasp various truths concerning God – first of all, his existence, and secondly, certain of his attributes, which St Paul sums up here as his "invisible nature", "eternal power" and "deity". By reflecting on the created world, we can learn about some of God's perfections; but, St Thomas Aquinas comments, only in heaven will we be able to see that these various perfections are all one with the divine essence. This is why St Paul talks about God's "invisible nature". Contemplation of the works of creation leads us to posit the presence of an ever-existing Creator, and brings us to discover his "eternal power". Finally, the word "deity" implies that God is transcendent: he is the Cause, superior to all other causes, and in him everything finds its explanation and ultimate purpose.

The fact that it is possible to know God by the use of natural reason means that pagans who chose not to worship him were blameworthy. Their position is comparable to that of contemporary atheists and unbelievers who deny or doubt the existence of God despite the fact that as human beings they do know him in some way in the depths of their conscience. The culpability of pagans as of modern unbelievers ("they are without excuse") derives from the fact that they fail to accept that God is knowable through the use of human reason; they both commit the same fault – that of refusing to render worship to God.

Of course, to some degree the attitude of atheists can be explained by

nature, namely, his eternal power and deity, has been clearly perceived in the things that have been made. So they
Is 40:26
Eph 4:17-18
are without excuse; [21]for although they knew God they did not honour him as God or give thanks to him, but they became futile in their thinking and their senseless minds
1 Cor 1:18-21
were darkened. [22]Claiming to be wise, they became fools,
Ps 106:20
Ex 32
Ps 115:1-8
Wis 15:14-19
[23]and exchanged the glory of the immortal God for images resembling mortal man or birds or animals or reptiles.
      [24]Therefore God gave them up in the lusts of their hearts

---

facta sunt, intellecta conspiciuntur, sempiterna eius et virtus et divinitas, ut sint inexcusabiles; [21]quia, cum cognovissent Deum, non sicut Deum glorificaverunt aut gratias egerunt, sed evanuerunt in cogitationibus suis, et obscuratum est insipiens cor eorum. [22]Dicentes se esse sapientes, stulti facti sunt, [23]et

---

historical, environmental, personal and other factors. However, it should not be forgotten that these do not justify atheism. However, "those who wilfully try to drive God from their heart and to avoid all questions about religion, not following the biddings of their conscience, are not free from blame" (Vatican II, *Gaudium et spes*, 19).

21-23. The Gentiles knew God but they failed to give him his due – to worship him in a spirit of adoration and thanksgiving. As a result they fell into polytheism (belief in a multiplicity of gods) and idolatry, as St Paul vividly describes: they worshipped images depicting men and women (the Greeks gave their gods human form) or animals (as was the case in Egyptian and other eastern religions).

In our own time idolatry does not take that form, but there are practices which can properly be called idolatrous. Man is naturally religious and if he does not worship the true God he necessarily has to find other things to take God's place. Sometimes it is himself that man makes the object of worship: the Second Vatican Council points out that "with some people it is their exaggerated idea of man that causes their faith to languish; they are more prone, it would seem, to affirm man than to deny God [. . .]. Those who profess this kind of atheism maintain that freedom consists in this, that man is an end to himself and the sole maker, with supreme control, of his own history" (*Gaudium et spes*, 19 and 20). It also happens that people, by becoming enslaved to them, make gods out of the good things created by God for man's benefit – money, power, sensuality.

24-32. The sin of idolatry leads to the kind of moral disorder described by St Paul: every time man knowingly and willingly tries to marginalize God, that religious aberration leads to moral disorder not only in the individual but also in society.

to impurity, to the dishonouring of their bodies among themselves, [25]because they exchanged the truth about God for a lie and worshipped and served the creature rather than the Creator, who is blessed for ever! Amen.

Rom 9:5

[26]For this reason God gave them up to dishonourable passions. Their women exchanged natural relations for unnatural, [27]and the men likewise gave up natural relations with women and were consumed with passion for one another, men committing shameless acts with men and receiving in their own persons the due penalty for their error.

---

mutaverunt gloriam incorruptibilis Dei in similitudinem imaginis corruptibilis hominis et volucrum et quadrupedum et serpentium. [24]Propter quod tradidit illos Deus in concupscentiis cordis eorum in immunditiam, ut ignominia afficiant corpora sua in semetipsis, [25]qui commutaverunt veritatem Dei in mendacio et coluerunt et servierunt creaturae potius quam Creatori, qui est benedictus in saecula. Amen. [26]Propterea tradidit illos Deus in passiones ignominiae. Nam et feminae eorum immutaverunt naturalem usum in eum, qui est contra naturam; [27]similiter et masculi, relicto naturali usu feminae,

---

God punishes the sin of idolatry and impiety by withdrawing his graces: that is what the Apostle means when he says that he "gave them up to the lusts of their hearts" (v. 24), "gave them up to dishonourable passions" (v. 26). St John Chrysostom, explaining these words, says: "The Apostle shows here that ungodliness brings with it violation and forgetfulness of every law. When Paul says that God gives them up, this must be understood as meaning that God leaves them to their own devices. God abandons the evildoer but he does not impel him towards evil. When the general withdraws in the thick of the battle, he gives his soldiers up to the enemy, not in the sense of physically shackling them but because he deprives them of the help of his presence. God acts in the same way. Rebels against his law, men have turned their back on him; God, his goodness exhausted, abandons them [. . .]. What else could he do? Use force, compel them? Those means do not make men virtuous. The only thing he could do was let them be" (*Hom. on Rom*, 3).

It may be that God counts on the experience of sin to move people to repentance. In any event, we should not read into this passage unconcern, much less injustice, on God's part: he never abandons people unless they first abandon him (cf. Council of Trent, *De iustificatione*, chap. 11).

25. When describing the blasphemous behaviour of Gentiles who worship created things rather than the Creator, St Paul cannot but utter an ejaculation, in a spirit of atonement. This should teach us to do the same whenever we witness offence being offered to God.

²⁸And since they did not see fit to acknowledge God, God gave them up to a base mind and to improper conduct. ²⁹They were filled with all manner of wickedness, evil, covetousness, malice. Full of envy, murder, strife, deceit, malignity, they are gossips, ³⁰slanderers, haters of God, insolent, haughty, boastful, inventors of evil, disobedient to parents, ³¹foolish, faithless, heartless, ruthless. ³²Though

1 Cor 6:9-10
Gal 5:19-21

---

exarserunt in desideriis suis in invicem, masculi in masculos turpitudinem operantes et mercedem, quam oportuit, erroris sui in semetipsis recipientes. ²⁸Et sicut non probaverunt Deum habere in notitia, tradidit eos Deus in reprobum sensum, ut faciant, quae non conveniunt, ²⁹repletos omni iniquitate, malitia, avaritia, nequitia, plenos invidia, homicidio, contentione, dolo, malignitate, susurrones, ³⁰detractores, Deo odibiles, contumeliosos, superbos, elatos, inventores malorum, parentibus non oboedientes, ³¹insipientes, incompositos, sine affectione, sine misericordia. ³²Qui cum iudicium Dei cognovissent,

---

29-31. After describing how men have sinned against the commandments to love and honour God (vv. 21-23, 25), he now goes on to list the sins that go against love of neighbour. Love of neighbour derives from love of God, therefore, if one fails to give God the love that is his due, who is the object of the first commandment, one ends up offending others, in violation of the second precept of the Law (cf. Mt 22:34-39; Mk 12:28-31; Lk 10:25-28).

St Paul includes in his list both internal sins or sins of desire (wickedness, malice, greed, envy) and external sins (murder, strife); and sins of omission (disloyalty, heartlessness) as well as sins of commission or actually breaking a commandment (tale-bearing, slander).

St Paul's mention of sins here and in other epistles (cf. 1 Cor 5:11-13 and note; 1 Cor 6:9-10; Gal 5:19.21; Eph 4:31; Col 3:8; 1 Tim 1:9-10 and 2 Tim 3:2-5) should lead us to examine our conscience to see how far we are living up to the demands of the Christian life. However, what he says affects not only Christians: everyone, Christian or not, comes under the natural law, whose principles are unchanging, for "the moral obligations of the natural law are based on the very nature of man and of his essential relationships – those between man and God, between man and man, between husband and wife, between parents and children; from violation of essential relationships in the community – in the family, in the Church, in the State – it follows, among other things, that hatred of God, blasphemy, idolatry, abandonment of the true faith, denial of the faith, perjury, false witness, murder, calumny, adultery and fornication, abuse of marriage, solitary sin, robbery [. . .] – are all severely forbidden by the divine Lawgiver" (Pius XII, *Address*, 18 April 1952).

32. Particularly serious is the position of those who sin and know that they sin and yet do not repent but actually keep others from repentance also. "It is

they know God's decree that those who do such things deserve to die, they not only do them but approve those who practise them.

2

The Jews also are guilty

¹Therefore you have no excuse, O man, whoever you are, when you judge another; for in passing judgment upon him you condemn yourself, because you, the judge, are doing the very same things. ²We know that the judgment of God

Mt 7:2

---

quoniam qui talia agunt, digni sunt morte, non solum ea faciunt, sed et consentiunt facientibus.

¹Propter quod inexcusabilis es, o homo omnis, qui iudicas. In quo enim iudicas alterum, teipsum condemnas; eadem enim agis, qui iudicas. ²Scimus

---

certainly a crime", St John Chrysostom comments, "to sin against one's conscience, but it is an even greater crime to praise the guilty" (*Hom. on Rom*, 5). This not only clearly goes against the constant teaching of Scripture, that one should correct an erring person (cf. 2 Sam 12:1ff; Mt 18:12-17; Gal 6:1ff) but it implies flagrant cooperation in evil (a sin of false prophets, cf. Jer 23:11-16; Mt 7:15). This form of cooperation in evil – approval of sin – is sometimes described as "adulation". People who are guilty of it, "although they do not speak evil of their neighbour, nevertheless do him much harm, because, by praising his sins, they encourage him, for one thing, to persist in his vice" (*St Pius V Catechism*, III, 9, 11).

1. The Apostle now addresses the Jews to make them see that, despite their privileged position, they too are unrighteous. He does this by setting up an imaginary conversation with a person representing the Jewish people, whose attitude is like that of those who "trusted in themselves that they were righteous and despised others" (Lk 18:9). If the pagans, who could only know God through the use of natural reason, cannot be excused for not worshipping him and for committing sin, how much more inexcusable is the behaviour of Jews who, despite receiving supernatural Revelation, commit the very same sins as those for which they reproach the Gentiles. St Paul's invective against the Jews (vv. 17-24) is reminiscent of our Lord's criticism of the scribes and Pharisees (cf. Mt 23:13-33).

2-11. These verses contain the following truths : 1) God rewards and punishes, and therefore there is a close connexion between a person's behaviour in this life (meritorious or blameworthy) and what happens to him or her in the

77

rightly falls upon those who do such things. ³Do you suppose, O man, that when you judge those who do such things and yet do them yourself, you will escape the judgment of God? ⁴Or do you presume upon the riches of his kindness and forbearance and patience? Do you not know that God's kindness is meant to lead you to repentance? ⁵But by your hard and impenitent heart you are storing up wrath for yourself on the day of wrath when God's righteous judgment will be revealed. ⁶For he will render to every man according to his works: ⁷to those who by patience in well-doing seek for glory and honour and immortality, he will give eternal life; ⁸but for those who are factious and do not obey the truth, but obey wickedness, there will be wrath and fury. ⁹There will be tribulation and

2 Pet 3:15

Rom 1:18
Zeph 1:14-18
2 Thess 1:5-10

Ps 62:13
Prov 24:12
2 Cor 5:10
Mt 16:27
Jn 5:29

---

enim quoniam iudicium Dei est secundum veritatem in eos, qui talia agunt. ³Existimas autem hoc, o homo, qui iudicas eos, qui talia agunt, et facis ea, quia tu effugies iudicium Dei? ⁴An divitias benignitatis eius et patientiae et longanimitatis contemnis, ignorans quoniam benignitas Dei ad paenitentiam te adducit? ⁵Secundum duritiam autem tuam et impaenitens cor thesaurizas tibi iram in die irae et revelationis iusti iudicii Dei, ⁶qui reddet unicuique secundum opera eius: ⁷his quidem, qui secundum patientiam boni operis gloriam et honorem et incorruptionem quaerunt, vitam aeternam; ⁸his autem, qui ex contentione et non oboediunt veritati, oboediunt autem iniquitati, ira et indignatio.⁹Tribulatio et angustia in omnem animam hominis operantis malum,

---

next life (cf. especially vv. 2, 5, 7-10).   2) God is a just and impartial Judge; he does not look to whether a person is Jew or Gentile but simply to how he lives. 3) The passage also tells us when this judgment will take place (v. 5, elaborated on by v. 16).

In the course of speaking about God as rewarding the good, St Paul describes the glorious state of the blessed in heaven ("eternal life", "glory", "honour", "peace": vv. 7, 10) and the fact that it will last for ever ("immortality": v. 7). He also teaches that in order to attain this state one must persevere in good works ("patience in well-doing": v. 7); this echoes what our Lord said: "he who endures to the end will be saved" (Mt 10:22; cf. 24:13).

Parallel with this, St Paul speaks of how God will punish sinners ("wrath and fury": v. 8) and of the unhappy fate of those condemned to hell ("tribulation and distress": v. 9).

The meaning of this passage becomes clearer in the light of many other passages of Sacred Scripture and, also, of the Church's teaching about the Judgment and when it will take place. There are two different occasions "when everyone must appear in the presence of the Lord to render an account of all

distress for every human being who does evil, the Jew first
and also the Greek, [10]but glory and honour and peace for
every one who does good, the Jew first and also the Greek.
[11]For God shows no partiality.

[12]All who have sinned without the law will also perish
without the law, and all who have sinned under the law will
be judged by the law. [13]For it is not the hearers of the law
who are righteous before God, but the doers of the law who
will be justified. [14]When Gentiles who have not the law do

Deut 10:17
Acts 10:34
Gal 2:6
1 Pet 1:17

Mt 7:21
Jas 1:22, 25
Lk 8:21

Iudaei primum et Graeci; [10]gloria autem et honor et pax omni operanti bonum,
Iudaeo primum et Graeco. [11]Non est enim personarum acceptio apud Deum.
[12]Quicumque enim sine lege peccaverunt, sine lege et peribunt; et quicumque
in lege peccaverunt, per legem iudicabuntur. [13]Non enim auditores legis iusti
sunt apud Deum, sed factores legis iustificabuntur. [14]Cum enim gentes, quae

---

his thoughts, words and actions [. . .]. The first takes place when each of us
departs this life; for then he is instantly placed before the judgment seat of God,
where all that he has ever done shall be subjected to the most rigid scrutiny.
This is called the particular judgment. The second occurs when on the same
day and in the same place all men shall stand together before the tribunal of
their judge, that in the presence and hearing of all human beings of all times
each may know his final doom and sentence" (*St Pius V Catechism*, I, 8, 3).

12-14. The Jews received the Law from God through Moses; the pagans or
Gentiles, however, only received, through the exercise of reason, the principles
of the natural moral law. By acting in accordance with nature they adhered to
the same moral precepts as God specified more exactly in the ten
Commandments. For pagans, therefore, the natural moral law was "a law to
themselves", a law applying to them. What God requires of everyone is that he
or she keep the natural moral law, that is, the law that is "written and engraved
in the mind of every man; and this is nothing but our reason, commanding us
to do right and forbidding sin" (Leo XIII, *Libertas praestantissimum*, 8).

The Church teaches that even though human reason in theory is capable of
grasping the natural law written on our souls by our Creator, many factors
prevent us from obeying that law: our senses, our imagination, and our evil
desires deriving from original sin give rise to difficulties. As a result, people
can easily convince themselves that what they do not want to accept as the right
thing to do is in fact the wrong thing, or at least that the matter is in doubt (cf.
Pius XII, *Humani generis*, 2).

In order to help man overcome difficulties of this sort and attain a grasp of
the natural law easily, God chose to reveal himself in another, supernatural,
way; this shows that divine revelation of the content of the natural law is *morally*
necessary (cf. *ibid.*, and Vatican I, *Dei Filius*, chap. 2). This is why Christians,

by nature what the law requires, they are a law to themselves, even though they do not have the law. [15]They show that what the law requires is written on their hearts, while their conscience also bears witness and their conflicting

legem non habent, naturaliter, quae legis sunt, faciunt, eiusmodi legem non habentes ipsi sibi sunt lex; [15]qui ostendunt opus legis scriptum in cordibus suis, testimonium simul reddente illis conscientia ipsorum, et inter se invicem cogitationibus accusantibus aut etiam defendentibus, [16]in die cum iudicabit

who, thanks to the faith and teaching of the Church, have a good grasp of the natural law, are also best equipped to ensure that "the divine law be impressed on the affairs of the earthly city" (Vatican II, *Gaudium et spes*, 43) and to teach others the way to live in harmony with human nature and thereby attain salvation.

When he says that the Gentiles keep the law if they follow the dictates of nature, the Apostle does not mean that supernatural grace is not necessary for salvation. Human nature has certainly been wounded by original sin, but it is not completely vitiated, for "the likeness of God impressed upon the human soul cannot be destroyed by a person's attachment to earthly things to the point that it does not retain even the faintest traces of that likeness; and so, it is correct to say that a sinner, despite the irregularity of his life, is aware of and does keep some part of the Law" (St Augustine, *De spiritu et littera*, XXVII, 48).

However, without the help of grace it is impossible to keep all the precepts of the natural law all the time.

15. This verse says something which is extremely important. Earlier the Apostle speaks of the existence of a law, of divine origin; here he adds that it is written on men's hearts. The voice of this law, "ever calling him to love and to do what is good and to avoid evil, tells him inwardly at the right moment: do this, shun that" (Vatican II, *Gaudium et spes*, 16). Conscience and law reinforce each other.

Because of the divine source of this law, a law which conscience applies in each particular situation, it has been called "the voice of God"; it is at the secret, intimate core of a person, where he is alone with himself and God. All through life this voice will be with him; and it will be present when he appears before God's judgment seat (cf. *Gaudium et spes*, 16; Pius XII, *Address*, 23 March 1952).

As well as listening to the interior voice of divine law, moral conscience also needs to be instructed by someone endowed with authority, to enable it to determine how the law must be applied in each case. St Paul provided this teaching for the first Christians in Rome (Rom 14:17) and Corinth (1 Cor 8) on moral questions about the use of meat of sacrificed animals. We too need someone to give us guidelines, for "in order to walk in the right direction when it is dark, that is, when the Christian is entering the mystery of the Christian

thoughts accuse or perhaps excuse them [16]on that day when, according to my gospel, God judges the secrets of men by Christ Jesus.

Rom 2:6-8
1 Cor 4:5

[17]But if you call yourself a Jew and rely upon the law and boast of your relation to God [18]and know his will and approve what is excellent, because you are instructed in the law, [19]and if you are sure that you are a guide to the blind, a light to those who are in darkness, [20]a corrector of the foolish, a teacher of children, having in the law the embodiment of knowledge and truth – [21]you then who teach others, will you not teach yourself? While you preach against stealing, do you steal? [22]You who say that one must not commit adultery, do you commit adultery? You who abhor idols, do you rob temples? [23]You who boast in the law, do you dishonour God by breaking the law? [24]For, as it is written, "The name of God is blasphemed among the Gentiles because of you."

Mt 3:7-9
Jn 8:33-40

Jn 9:40-41
Mt 15:14
Lk 6:39

Ps 50:16-21

Is 52:5 (LXX)
Ezek 36:20-22
Jas 2:7
2 Pet 2:2

Real circumcision, a matter of the heart

1 Cor 7:19
Gal 5:3, 6
Jer 9:24-25

[25]Circumcision indeed is of value if you obey the law; but

Deus occulta hominum secundum evangelium meum per Christum Iesum. [17]Si autem tu Iudaeus cognominaris et requiescis in lege et gloriaris in Deo, [18]et nosti Voluntatem et discernis potiora instructus per legem, [19]et confidis teipsum ducem esse caecorum, lumen eorum, qui in tenebris sunt, [20]eruditorem insipientium, magistrum infantium, habentem formam scientiae et veritatis in lege. [21]Qui ergo alium doces, teipsum non doces? Qui praedicas non furandum, furaris? [22]Qui dicis non moechandum, moecharis? Qui abominaris idola, templa spolias? [23]Qui in lege gloriaris, per praevaricationem legis Deum inhonoras? [24]"*Nomen* enim *Dei propter vos blasphematur inter gentes*", sicut scriptum est. [25]Circumcisio quidem prodest, si legem observes; si autem praevaricator legis

---

life, he cannot rely on his eyes, he needs a lamp, a light. And this *light of Christ* does not distort, does not inhibit or contradict our conscience; on the contrary, it illuminates it and enables it to follow Christ along the straight road of our pilgrimage towards that vision which is eternal" (Paul VI, Address, 12 February 1969).

25-29. Through circumcision man became party to the Covenant God made with Abraham (Gen 17:10-11), and heir to the promises. In accordance with that Alliance, circumcision obliged the Israelite to keep the Mosaic Law, especially its moral precepts: according to God's design all the rites and other requirements of the Old Law were directed to that end. Therefore, the letter of

81

if you break the law, your circumcision becomes uncircumcision. ²⁶So, if a man who is uncircumcised keeps the precepts of the law, will not his uncircumcision be regarded as circumcision? ²⁷Then those who are physically uncircumcised but keep the law will condemn you who have the written code and circumcision but break the law. ²⁸For he

Deut 30:6
Jew 4:4
Rom 7:6; 8:2-4
2 Cor 3:6
Phil 3:2-3

is not a real Jew who is one outwardly, nor is true circumcision something external and physical. ²⁹He is a Jew who is one inwardly, and real circumcision is a matter of the heart, spiritual and not literal. His praise is not from men but from God.

3

Rom 9:4-7
Deut 4:7-8

¹Then what advantage has the Jew? Or what is the value of circumcision? ²Much in every way. To begin with, the Jews

---

sis, circumcisio tua praeputium facta est. ²⁶Si igitur praeputium iustitias legis custodiat, nonne praeputium illius in circumcisionem reputabitur? ²⁷Et iudicabit, quod ex natura est praeputium legem consummans, te, qui per litteram et circumcisionem praevaricator legis es. ²⁸Non enim, qui manifesto Iudaeus est, neque quae manifesto in carne circumcisio, ²⁹sed qui in abscondito Iudaeus est, et circumcisio cordis in spiritu non littera, cuius laus non ex hominibus sed ex Deo est.

¹Quid ergo amplius est Iudaeo, aut quae utilitas circumcisionis? ²Multum per

---

the Law, and physical circumcision, were important only to the degree that they helped promote these plans of God. This is why St Paul asserts that the true circumcision is not a physical thing but what he calls "circumcision of the heart", which he also describes as being spiritual rather than literal: the content of the Law can be practised without one's having a written law (vv. 14-16), as can happen in the case of Gentiles, who are physically uncircumcised.

1-8. In this passage St Paul is still replying to objections raised by an imaginary Jewish questioner. What makes it difficult to follow is the fact that the reply to each question gives rise to the next objection.

First (v. 1), the questioner asks, if Jews as well as Gentiles are going to be rewarded or punished in the light of their deeds, then in what way is the Jew better off? The Apostle replies that the Jewish people – and they alone – were given Revelation by God for them to pass it on to other nations. The fact that some Jews were not faithful to this mission did not mean that God changed his plans, for it was to the Jewish people as such – and not to each individual Jew

are entrusted with the oracles of God. ³What if some were
unfaithful? Does their faithlessness nullify the faithfulness
of God? ⁴By no means! Let God be true though every man
be false, as it is written,

Ps 89:31-38
2 Tim 2:13

Ps 116:11; 51:6
(LXX)

"That thou mayest be justified in thy words,
and prevail when thou art judged."

⁵But if our wickedness serves to show the justice of God,
what shall we say? That God is unjust to inflict wrath on
us? (I speak in a human way.) ⁶By no means! For then how
could God judge the world? ⁷But if through my falsehood
God's truthfulness abounds to his glory, why am I still
being condemned as a sinner? ⁸And why not do evil that
good may come? – as some people slanderously charge us
with saying. Their condemnation is just.

---

omnem modum. Primum quidem, quia credita sunt illis eloquia Dei. ³Quid
enim, si quidam non crediderunt? Numquid incredulitas illorum fidem Dei
evacuabit? ⁴Absit! Exstet autem Deus verax, omnis autem homo mendax, sicut
scriptum est: *"Ut iustificeris in sermonibus tuis et vincas cum iudicaris."* ⁵Si
autem iniustitia nostra iustitiam Dei commendat, quid dicemus? Numquid
iniustus Deus, qui infert iram? Secundum hominem dico. ⁶Absit! Alioquin
quomodo iudicabit Deus mundum? ⁷Si enim veritas Dei in meo mendacio
abundavit in gloriam ipsius, quid adhuc et ego tamquam peccator iudicor? ⁸Et

---

– that he gave this mission. God's fidelity to his promises is not affected by the
way man responds; in fact human infidelity only serves to highlight God's
fidelity (vv. 2-4).

The imaginary questioner now goes on to raise a new objection, but he is
oversimplifying things and has a narrow, human outlook; he argues that if
human wickedness does God no harm, but actually highlights his justice, then
God is unjust to punish it (vv. 5 and 7). St Paul counters this with another
question, which he uses to show that his opponent has no case: if it were unjust
for God to punish men's sins, how could he be the judge of the human race?
This argument carries a lot of weight with a Jew, because, being familiar with
the Old Testament, he knows that God will in fact judge all men (cf. Amos 5:18;
Joel 4:12ff). Finally, St Paul replies that if his questioner's false reasoning is
pushed to its logical conclusion one would need to do evil in order to achieve
good. Anyone who says that is clearly wrong.

8. St Paul's adversaries accuse him of having said that evil had to be
committed for good, that is, God's truth and justice, to be made manifest. But
this is a misrepresentation, which the Apostle energetically rejects, although he
does not stop here to reply to his accusers. St Paul is not saying that a Christian

83

All are sinners — Jews and Gentiles both

9What then? Are we Jews any better off?c No, not at all;
for Id have already charged that all men, both Jews and
Ps 14:1-3
Ps 53:2-4
Greeks, are under the power of sin, 10as it is written:
"None is righteous, no, not one;
11no one understands, no one seeks for God.

---

non sicut blasphemamur et sicut aiunt nos quidam dicere: "Faciamus mala, ut
veniant bona?" Quorum damnatio iusta est. 9 Quid igitur? Praecellimus eos?
Nequaquam! Antea enim causati sumus Iudaeos et Graecos omnes sub peccato
esse, 10sicut scriptum est: *"Non est iustus quisquam,* 11*non est intellegens, non*

---

should follow evil ways for a good end: that would be to blur the difference
between good and evil, and to argue that the end justifies the means.

Christian moral teaching requires that one do right even if oneself or others
are hurt by that action: the end does not justify the means and an action can
only be fully good when all its elements are good – object, end and circumstances; and it will be bad if any one of these elements is bad. Therefore,
no morally bad action may be done for any reason, even for an apparently good
reason, or even with a supposedly good intention. If one were to act using wrong
standards, it would mean undermining the laws and mores of society (cf. St
Augustine, *Contra mendacium*, chaps. 1 and 7).

Faced with people's constant tendency to justify their actions by appealing
to circumstances, the Magisterium of the Church has reminded us of the basic
principles governing moral behaviour: "God desires us always to have, above
all, an upright intention, but that is not enough. He also requires that the action
be a good action [. . .]. It is not permissible to do evil in order to achieve a good
end" (Pius XII, *Address*, 18 April 1952).

9-18. The general meaning of this passage is quite clear but some points are
obscure. St Paul provides quotations from Sacred Scripture which prove that
the Jews are blameworthy, so much so that they no longer have any grounds
for personal congratulation, even though they still enjoy the special privileges
with which God endowed their nation.

After a short introduction (v. 9) St Paul goes on to describe the universal
apostasy which the psalmist already spoke about (vv. 10-12). He then lists the
sins against which the prophets fulminated so often (cf. Is 5:8-25; 59:2-8; Jer
8:8; Amos 5:21; Mal 2:8) – sins of word (vv. 13-14) as well as of deed (v. 15).
Finally he spells out the punishment which will be meted out to those guilty of
such sins.

Both the passages in the Old Testament and the use St Paul makes of them
seem to refer not only to the Jews but to a worldwide phenomenon.

10-12. These verses show us the sorry state of affairs resulting from original

cOr *at any disadvantage?* dGreek *we.*

¹²All have turned aside, together they have gone wrong;
no one does good, not even one."
¹³"Their throat is an open grave, Ps 5:10
Ps 140:4
they use their tongues to deceive."
"The venom of asps is under their lips."
¹⁴"Their mouth is full of curses and bitterness." Ps 10:7

---

est requirens Deum. ¹²*Omnes declinaverunt, simul inutiles facti sunt; non est qui faciat bonum, non est usque ad unum.* ¹³*Sepulcrum patens est guttur eorum, linguis suis dolose agebant, venenum aspidum sub labiis eorum,* ¹⁴*quorum os*

---

sin and from personal sin. In various places in the Old Testament we find this kind of bitter complaint: man's wickedness has spread all over the earth, his every thought is evil (cf. Gen 6:5-7). What is particularly depressing is the unfaithfulness of the Jewish people, when they abandon the true God and become idolaters (cf. 1 Kings 19:14, 18), forsake the fountain of living waters for broken cisterns (cf. Jer 2:13) and fail to repent of their wickedness (cf. Jer 8:6). This does not happen just in one particular epoch: from the time of Noah – the only just man in a wicked world – up to the present day God has always been opposed (cf. the lamentations in Ps 12:2; 55:11-12; etc.).

At the same time there have always been faithful servants who "have not bent the knee to Baal"; these have been the vehicle used for the spreading of salvation. What then is to be made of St Paul's assertion that "none is righteous, not one"? These words should not be taken as referring to absolutely everyone. We do know that, in addition to the sacred human nature of Jesus, the Blessed Virgin was exempted from the stain of all sin, even venial sin (cf. Third Council of Constantinople, *De duabus in Christo voluntatibus et operationibus*; Council of Trent, *De iustificatione*, can. 23), and also that even before Christ there were just and devout people like Noah, Abraham, Moses etc., who received divine grace and were enabled to do good works by virtue of the future merits of Christ.

13-18. God sent the prophets to make the Israelites see that they had sinned and to have them repent. St Paul is doing the same kind of thing here: he uses passages from the Old Testament to stir the consciences of his fellow Jews and indeed all those who read his letter.

A person's goodness and holiness does not lie in not knowing about evil or in adopting an attitude of naive optimism, forgetting that sin is the only evil really harmful to man and which therefore needs to be countered at every step. So, when someone's heart becomes hardened and he has made a private pact with sin, all that one can do is act the way Christ did: "sometimes in his preaching all seems very sad, because he is hurt by the evil men do. However, if we watch him closely, we will note immediately that his anger comes from love. It is a further invitation for us to leave infidelity and sin behind" (J. Escrivá, *Christ is passing by*, 162).

Is 59:7-8
Prov 1:16
¹⁵"Their feet are swift to shed blood,

¹⁶in their paths are ruin and misery,

¹⁷and the way of peace they do not know."

Ps 36:2
¹⁸"There is no fear of God before their eyes."

Gal 3:22
¹⁹Now we know that whatever the law says it speaks to those who are under the law, so that every mouth may be stopped, and the whole world may be held accountable to
Ps 143:2
Gal 2:16
God. ²⁰For no human being will be justified in his sight by
Rom 7:7
works of the law, since through the law comes knowledge of sin.

Righteousness, a free gift through faith in Christ

²¹But now the righteousness of God has been manifested apart from law, although the law and the prophets bear
Rom 1:16
witness to it, ²²the righteousness of God through faith in

---

maledictione et amaritudine plenum est; ¹⁵*veloces pedes eorum ad effundendum sanguinem,* ¹⁶*contritio et infelicitas in viis eorum,* ¹⁷*et viam pacis non cognoverunt.* ¹⁸*Non est timor Dei ante oculos eorum."* ¹⁹Scimus autem quoniam, quaecumque lex loquitur, his, qui in lege sunt, loquitur, ut omne os obstruatur, et obnoxius fiat omnis mundus Deo; ²⁰quia ex operibus legis *non iustificabitur omnis caro coram illo,* per legem enim cognitio peccati. ²¹Nunc autem sine lege iustitia Dei manifestata est, testificata a Lege et Prophetis, ²²iustitia autem Dei per fidem Iesu Christi, in omnes qui credunt. Non enim est

---

13. "Their throat is an open grave": a reference to the fact that impious people speak words which bring death (cf. Jer 5:16) and reflect the filth and corruption they carry within, for they "are like white-washed tombs, which outwardly appear beautiful, but within they are full of dead men's bones and all uncleanness" (Mt 23:27).

19-20. These verses act as a kind of summary of what the Apostle has been saying about the position of Jews and Gentiles vis-à-vis the righteousness of God.

21-22. The doctrinal richness of this text and of the whole passage (vv. 21-26) is here condensed in a way very typical of St Paul's style. He explains how justification operates: God the Father, the source of all good, by his redemptive decree is the "efficient cause" of our salvation; Jesus Christ, by shedding his blood on the Cross, merits this salvation for us; faith is the instrument by which the Redemption becomes effective in the individual person.

The righteousness of God is the action by which God makes people righteous, or just (cf. St Augustine, *De spiritu et littera,* IX, 15). This righteousness was

Jesus Christ for all who believe. For there is no distinction; [23]since all have sinned and fall short of the glory of God, [24]they are justified by his grace as a gift, through the

Gal 2:8

---

distinctio: [23]omnes enim peccaverunt et egent gloria Dei, [24]iustificati gratis per

---

originally proclaimed in the books of the Old Testament – the Law and the Prophets – but it has now been made manifest in Christ and in the Gospel. Salvation does not depend on fulfilment of the Mosaic Law, for that Law is not sufficient to justify anyone: only faith in Jesus Christ can work salvation. "If anyone says that, without divine grace through Jesus Christ, man can be justified before God by his own works, whether they were done by his natural powers or by the light of the teaching of the Law: let him be anathema" (Council of Trent, *De iustificatione*, can. 1).

It is not the law, then, which saves, but "faith in Jesus Christ". This expression should be interpreted in line with the unanimous and constant teaching of the Church, which is that "faith is the beginning of human salvation", and a person's will must cooperate with faith to prepare the ground for the grace of justification (cf. *ibid.*, chap. 8 and can. 9).

23-26. The Apostle first describes the elements that go to make up the mystery of faith (vv. 23-25): all men need to be liberated from sin; God the Father has a redemptive plan, which is carried out by the atoning and bloody sacrifice of Christ's death; faith is a necessary condition for sharing in the Redemption wrought by Christ; the sacrifice of the Cross is part and parcel of the History of Salvation: before the Incarnation of the Word, God patiently put up with men's sins; in the fullness of time he chose – through Christ's sacrifice – to require full satisfaction for those sins so that men might be enabled to become truly righteous in God's eyes and God's perfections become more manifest.

"The Cross of Christ, on which the Son, consubstantial with the Father, renders full justice to God, is also a radical revelation of mercy, that is, of the love that goes against what constitutes the very root of evil in the history of man – against sin and death" (John Paul II, *Dives in misericordia*, 8).

23. "Fall short of the glory of God": this shows the position man is in when he is in a state of sin. Because he has not the life of grace in him, he is not properly orientated towards his supernatural end, is deprived of the right to heaven that sanctifying grace confers, and consequently does not have these divine perfections which supernatural life gives him.

24. All have been justified, that is, all have been made "righteous" (cf. 1:17). This justification is the result of a gratuitous gift of God which St Paul describes in a way which reinforces his point ("grace", "as a gift"): this identifies the source of the gift as God's loving-kindness and it also shows the new state in

87

which justification places a person. So important is this statement – that grace is a gift which God gives without merit on our part – that the Council of Trent, when using this text from St Paul, made a point of explaining what it meant: that is, that nothing which precedes justification (whether it be faith, or morals) *merits* the grace by which man is justified (cf. Rom 11:16; Council of Trent, *De iustificatione*, chap. 8).

This new kind of life, whose motor is grace, requires free and active cooperation on man's part; by that cooperation a person in the state of grace obtains merit through his actions: "For such is God's goodness to men that he wills that his gifts be our merits, and that he will grant us an eternal reward for what he has given us" (*Indiculus*, chap. 9). The fact that grace is a gratuitous gift of God does not mean that man does not have an obligation to respond to it: we are not justified by keeping the Law or by a decision of our free will; however, justification does not happen without our cooperation; grace strengthens our will and helps it freely to keep the Law (cf. St Augustine, *De spiritu et littera*, IX, 15).

Justification by grace is attained "through the redemption which is in Jesus Christ". The Council of Trent teaches that when a sinner is justified there is "a passing from the state in which man is born a son of the first Adam, to the state of grace and adoption as sons of God through the second Adam, Jesus Christ our Saviour" (*De iustificatione*, chap. 4). This has been made possible because our Lord saved us by giving himself up as our ransom. The Greek word translated as "redemption" refers to the ransom money paid to free a person from slavery. Christ has freed us from the slavery of sin, paying the necessary ransom (cf. Rom 6:23). By sacrificing himself for us, Christ has become our master or owner, who mediates between the Father and the whole human race: "Let us all take refuge in Christ; let us have recourse to God to free us from sin: let us put ourselves up for sale in order to be redeemed by his blood. For the Lord says, 'You were sold for nothing, and you shall be redeemed without money' (Is 52:3); without spending a penny of your inheritance, for I have paid on your behalf. This is what the Lord says: He paid the price, not with silver but with his blood" (St Augustine, *In Ioann. Evang.*, 41, 4).

Our very creation means that we belong totally to God the Father and therefore also to Christ, insofar as he is God, but "as man, he is also for many reasons appropriately called 'Lord'. First, because he is our Redeemer, who delivered us from sin, he deservedly acquired the power by which he truly is and is called our Lord" (*St Pius V Catechism*, I, 3, 11).

And so, through the Incarnation, whose climax was Christ's redemptive sacrifice, "God gave human life the dimension that he intended man to have from his first beginning; he has granted that dimension definitively [. . .] and he has granted it also with the bounty that enables us, in considering the original sin and the whole history of the sins of humanity, and in considering the errors of the human intellect, will and heart, to repeat with amazement the words of the sacred Liturgy: 'O happy fault . . . which gained us so great a Redeemer!'" (John Paul II, *Redemptor hominis*, 1).

redemption which is in Christ Jesus, [25]whom God put 2 Cor 5:19
1 Jn 2:2
forward as an expiation by his blood, to be received by faith.
This was to show God's righteousness, because in his Lev 16
Acts 17:30
Is 53:11
divine forbearance he had passed over former sins; [26]it was
to prove at the present time that he himself is righteous and
that he justifies him who has faith in Jesus.

---

gratiam ipsius per redemptionem, quae est in Christo Iesu; [25]quem proposuit
Deus propitiatorium per fidem in sanguine ipsius ad ostensionem iustitiae suae,
cum praetermisisset praecedentia delicta [26]in sustentatione Dei, ad ostensionem
iustitiae eius in hoc tempore, ut sit ipse iustus et iustificans eum, qui ex fide est

---

25. The "expiation" was the cover or mercy seat of the Ark, which stood in
the centre of the Holy of Holies in the Temple (cf. Exod 25:17-22). It was made
of beaten gold and had a cherub at either end, each facing the other. It had two
functions: one was to act as God's throne (cf. Ps 80:2; 99:1), from which he
spoke to Moses during the time of the exodus from Egypt (cf. Num 7:89; Exod
37:6); the other was to entreat God to pardon sin through a rite of expiatory
sacrifice on the feast of the Day of Atonement (cf. Lev 16): on that day the High
Priest sprinkled the mercy seat with the blood of animals sacrificed as victims,
to obtain forgiveness of sins for priest and people.

St Paul asserts that God has established Jesus as the true expiation, of which
the mercy seat in the Old Testament was merely a figure.

No angel or man could ever atone for the immense evil that sin is – an offence
to the infinite majesty of God. The Blessed Trinity decided "that the Son of
God, whose power is infinite, clothed in the weakness of our flesh, should
remove the infinite weight of sin and reconcile us to God in his Blood" (*St Pius
V Catechism*, I, 3, 3).

This expiatory sacrifice, prefigured in the bloody sacrificial rites of the Old
Testament (cf. Lev 16:1ff), was announced by John the Baptist when he pointed
to Jesus as the Lamb of God (cf. Jn 1:29 and note); and Jesus himself referred
to the sacrifice of the Cross when he said that the Son of man had come "to
give his life as a ransom for many" (Mt 20:28).

This sacrifice is renewed daily in the Holy Mass, one of the purposes of which
is atonement, as the Liturgy itself states: "Lord, may this sacrifice once offered
on the cross to take away the sins of the world now free us from our sins"
(*Roman Missal*, Feast of the Triumph of the Cross, prayer over the gifts).

26. In the time prior to Christ's coming the sins of mankind remained
unatoned for: neither the rites designed by man to placate God's anger, nor
those established by God himself in the Old Law, were in any way equal to
atoning for the offence offered to God by sin. Therefore, the just of the Old
Testament were really justified by virtue of their faith in the future Messiah, a
faith which expressed itself in observance of the rites established by God.

During all this period the Lord kept deferring punishment ("passing over

Rom 2:17; 4:2-3;
5:2, 8; 11:18
Gal 6:13-14
Eph 2:8
1 Cor 1:31
²⁷Then what becomes of our boasting? It is excluded. On what principle? On the principle of works? No, but on the principle of faith. ²⁸For we hold that a man is justified by faith apart from works of law. ²⁹Or is God the God of Jews only? Is he not the God of Gentiles also? Yes, of Gentiles also, ³⁰since God is one; and he will justify the circumcised on the ground of their faith and the uncircumcised through
Mt 5:17 their faith.³¹Do we then overthrow the law by this faith? By no means! On the contrary, we uphold the law.

Iesu. ²⁷Ubi est ergo gloriatio? Exclusa est. Per quam legem? Operum? Non, sed per legem fidei. ²⁸Arbitramur enim iustificari hominem per fidem sine operibus legis. ²⁹An Iudaeorum Deus tantum? Nonne et gentium? Immo et gentium, ³⁰quoniam quidem unus Deus, qui iustificabit circumcisionem ex fide et praeputium per fidem. ³¹Legem ergo destruimus per fidem? Absit, sed legem statuimus.

---

former sins"). This time of "God's forbearance" lasted until the messianic era, "the present time", that is, the period between the first and second comings of Christ. On the righteousness of God and God as the Justifier of man, see note on Rom 1:17.

27-31. These words are addressed to the same imaginary interlocutor as appeared at the beginning of the chapter. Although he is Lord of all nations, God showed special preference for the people of Israel. Relying on this, the Jews wrongly thought that only they could attain blessedness because only they enjoyed God's favour. This led them to look down on other peoples. After the coming of Christ, they no longer have any basis for this pride: St John Chrysostom explains that it had simply become outdated, superseded (cf. *Hom. on Rom*, 7), for God had set up a single way of salvation for all men – the "principle of faith" which the Apostle refers to. This new way means that Jews must forget their ancient pride and become humble, for God has opened the gates of salvation to all mankind.

Consequently, no one – not even the Jew – is justified by works of the Law. What justifies a person is faith: not faith alone, as Luther wrongly argued, but the faith which works through charity (cf. Gal 5:6); faith which is not presumptuous self-confidence in one's own merits, but a firm and ready acceptance of all that God has revealed, faith which moves one to place one's hope in Christ's merits and to repent of one's sins. Therefore it will be "by faith" – not by circumcision – that the Jews will be justified, and it will be "through their faith" that the uncircumcised will attain salvation. From this it might appear as though the Law had been revoked; but that is not the case: faith ratifies the Law, gives it its true meaning and raises it to perfection. For, through being a preparation for the Gospel, the Mosaic Law receives from Christ the fulness it

4

The example of Abraham

¹What then shall we say about^e Abraham, our forefather according to the flesh? ²For if Abraham was justified by works, he has something to boast about, but not before God. ³For what does the scripture say? "Abraham believed God,

Gal 3:6-9
Jas 2:20-24
Gen 12:1

Gen 15:6

---

¹Quid ergo dicemus invenisse Abraham progenitorem nostrum secundum carnem? ²Si enim Abraham ex operibus iustificatus est, habet gloriam, sed non apud Deum. ³Quid enim Scriptura dicit? *"Credidit autem Abraham Deo, et*

---

was lacking: the precept of charity reveals the meaning which God gave the law but which lay hidden until Christ made it manifest, for "love is the fulfilling of the law" (Rom 13:10). St Paul in a way summarizes all this teaching in v. 28, which is the key statement in the passage.

1-25. Here St Paul finishes the exposition which began in 1:18: righteousness or justification comes neither through nature nor through the Law, but through faith – which is described as "the righteousness of faith".

The Apostle quotes Scripture to support what he says, putting before us the example of Abraham, who was not justified by works of the Law, but rather by faith (vv. 1-8), as it says in Gen 15:6 and as David confirms in the psalms (cf. vv. 6-8).

The Apostle also stresses (vv. 9-12) that Abraham's righteousness was not the result of circumcision, because it happened prior to circumcision (Gen 17). Therefore, according to God's plan circumcision was only an external sign of justification, not its cause.

He then goes on (vv. 13-17a) to explore the relationship between the focus of Abraham's faith – namely, the promise which God made him that he would be the father of many nations and that in his descendants all the nations of the earth would be blessed (cf. Gen 12:1-3; 15:5-6) – and works of the Law, actions done in obedience to the Law; by doing so he shows that the promise God makes is completely gratuitous, completely God's initiative. He concludes (17b-22) by praising the great faith of the Father of all believers, who put his trust in a promise which from the human point of view seemed impossible to fulfil.

Abraham's faith is a model for Christians. The promise made to him is fulfilled in us when we believe in Christ, who died and arose for our sakes (vv. 22-25).

3. The words of Gen 15:5-6 which God addresses to Abraham ("Look towards heaven, and number the stars, if you are able to number them [. . .]. So

^eOther ancient authorities read *was gained by.*

Rom 11:6 and it was reckoned to him as righteousness." ⁴Now to one
who works, his wages are not reckoned as a gift but as his
due. ⁵And to one who does not work but trusts him who
justifies the ungodly, his faith is reckoned as righteousness.

---

reputatum est illi ad iustitiam." ⁴Ei autem, qui operatur, merces non reputatur
secundum gratiam sed secundum debitum; ⁵ei vero, qui non operatur, sed credit

---

shall your descendants be") provide the answer to a question implicit in the
preceding verses of the letter and are also an introduction to the account of
Abraham's life of faith which follows. There is indeed good reason to ask what
was the meaning of the Patriarch's life, and what was it that was "reckoned to
him" who is the father of the chosen people in the flesh and in faith, when he
obeyed God's call. The "boast" of Abraham, who stands out above all
generations of the people of Israel (cf. Sir 44:19; Jn 8:33, 39, 53), is not mere
human pride: he *can* boast "before God" (cf. v. 2). When the Patriarch, already
an old man, saw himself close to death and without offspring (cf. Gen 15:2-3),
Yahweh told him to look up and count the stars, if he could, and then made a
solemn promise that his descendants would be as numerous as the stars. At that
moment Abraham "believed the Lord" and God reckoned it to him "as
righteousness" (Gen 15:6): he rewarded Abraham's faith by granting him
righteousness or justification.

This "reckoning" casts God in the role of a Master who notes credits and
debits in a ledger, the credits and debits being the merits and demerits of his
servants. However, in the case of Abraham, God, in the merit column, noted
not his works but his faith, which is why this faith was reckoned to him as
righteousness: righteousness was like a payment owed to him on account of
faith. The gratuitous character of righteousness or justification is in fact
emphasized here, because in Abraham's case faith was reckoned as
righteousness entirely due to God's grace and favour. The entire story of
Abraham, especially the episode where God makes him the promise, is an
example of how God goes about things: he draws the human soul out of its state
of ignorance, and then leads it on towards faith and moves it to accept a
supernatural mission of unimagined scope. "Scripture tells us again and again
that God is not a respecter of persons. When he invites a soul to live a life fully
in accordance with the faith, he does not set store by merits of fortune, nobility,
blood or learning. God's call precedes all merits. . . . Vocation comes first, God
loves us before we even know how to go toward him, and he places in us the
love with which we can respond to his call. God's fatherly goodness comes out
to meet us" (J. Escrivá, *Christ is passing by*, 33).

5. The act of faith is the first step towards obtaining justification (=
salvation). The Magisterium of the Church teaches that, usually, those who are
making their way towards faith predispose themselves in this sense: moved and
helped by divine grace they freely direct themselves towards God because they

⁶So also David pronounces a blessing upon the man to whom God reckons righteousness apart from works:

⁷"Blessed are those whose iniquities are forgiven; and whose sins are covered;

⁸blessed is the man against whom the Lord will not reckon his sin."

⁹Is this blessing pronounced only upon the circumcised, or also upon the uncircumcised? We say that faith was reckoned to Abraham as righteousness. ¹⁰How then was it reckoned to him? Was it before or after he had been circumcised? It was not after, but before he was circumcised. ¹¹He received circumcision as a sign or seal of the righteousness which he had by faith while he was still uncircumcised. The purpose was to make him the father of all who believe without being circumcised and who thus have righteousness reckoned to them, ¹²and likewise the father

---

in eum, qui iustificat impium, reputatur fides eius ad iustitiam, ⁶sicut et David dicit beatitudinem hominis, cui Deus reputat iustitiam sine operibus: ⁷"*Beati, quorum remissae sunt iniquitates et quorum tecta sunt peccata. ⁸Beatus vir, cui non imputabit Dominus peccatum.*" ⁹Beatitudo ergo haec in circumcisione an etiam in praeputio? Dicimus enim: "*Reputata est Abrahae fides ad iustitiam.*" ¹⁰Quomodo ergo reputata est? In circumcisione an in praeputio? Non in circumcisione sed in praeputio: ¹¹et signum accepit circumcisionis, signaculum iustitiae fidei, quae fuit in praeputio, ut esset pater omnium credentium per

---

believe in the truth of Revelation and, above all, believe that God, in his grace, justifies the sinner "through the redemption which is in Christ Jesus" (Rom 3:24). This first act of faith moves the person to recognize and repent of his sins; to put his trust in God's mercy and to love him above all things; and to desire the sacraments and resolve to live a holy life (cf. Council of Trent, *De iustificatione*, chap. 6). God reckons this faith "as righteousness", that is to say, as something which deserves to be rewarded. It is not, therefore, good works that lead to justification; rather, justification renders works good and meritorious of eternal life. Faith opens up for us whole new perspectives.

9-12. God prescribed circumcision as the seal of his Covenant with Abraham and his descendants: "And God said to Abraham, 'As for you, you shall keep my covenant, you and your descendants after you throughout their generations. This is my covenant, which you shall keep, between me and you and your descendants after you: Every male among you shall be circumcised. You shall be circumcised in the flesh of your foreskins, and it shall be a sign of the covenant between me and you'" (Gen 17:9-11).

Gal 3:16-18, 29
Gen 12:3, 7;
18:18; 22:15-18

Rom 3:20; 5:13,
20; 7:7-11
Gal 3:10, 19-22

Gen 17:5
Is 48:13
Heb 11:17-19

Gen 15:5

of the circumcised who are not merely circumcised but also follow the example of the faith which our father Abraham had before he was circumcised.

13The promise to Abraham and his descendants, that they should inherit the world, did not come through the law but through the righteousness of faith. 14If it is the adherents of the law who are to be the heirs, faith is null and the promise is void. 15For the law brings wrath, but where there is no law there is no transgression.

16That is why it depends on faith, in order that the promise may rest on grace and be guaranteed to all his descendants — not only to the adherents of the law but also to those who share the faith of Abraham, for he is the father of us all, 17as it is written, "I have made you the father of many nations" — in the presence of the God in whom he believed, who gives life to the dead and calls into existence the things that do not exist. 18In hope he believed against hope, that he

---

praeputium, ut reputetur illis iustitia, 12et pater circumcisionis his non tantum, qui ex circumcisione sunt, sed et qui sectantur vestigia eius, quae fuit in praeputio, fidei patris nostri Abrahae. 13Non enim per legem promissio Abrahae aut semini eius, ut heres esset mundi, sed per iustitiam fidei; 14si enim, qui ex lege heredes sunt, exinanita est fides et abolita est promissio. 15Lex enim iram operatur; ubi autem non est Lex nec praevaricatio. 16Ideo ex fide, ut secundum gratiam, ut firma sit promissio omni semini, non ei, qui ex lege est solum sed et ei, qui ex fide est Abrahae — qui est pater omnium nostrum, 17sicut scriptum

---

Circumcision acquires a very special significance in the chosen people, although other ancient peoples and modern societies also follow this practice. And it symbolized the purification and justification which Christian Baptism would effect in the fulness of time.

13-14. God made this promise to Abraham about his having countless descendants (cf. Gen 15:5-6) centuries before the Mosaic Law was given to the people of Israel through Moses. Therefore, the promise made to Abraham was not linked to the Law but rather to the Patriarch's faith. That is why the heirs of the promise are those who follow the faith of Abraham.

15. The Old Law, giving man a more exact knowledge of the natural law, without giving him special help (grace) to keep the law, "brings [God's] wrath": sin is committed when one simply breaks the natural law, but it takes on the character of "transgression" because one is flying in the face of an explicit law of God.

should become the father of many nations; as he had been told, "So shall your descendants be." [19]He did not weaken in faith when he considered his own body, which was as good as dead because he was about a hundred years old, or when he considered the barrenness of Sarah's womb. [20]No distrust made him waver concerning the promise of God, but he grew strong in his faith as he gave glory to God, [21]fully convinced that God was able to do what he had promised. [22]That is why his faith was "reckoned to him as righteousness." [23]But the words, "it was reckoned to him," were written not for his sake alone, [24]but for ours also. It will be reckoned to us who believe in him that raised from the dead Jesus our Lord, [25]who was put to death for our trespasses and raised for our justification.

Gen 17:1, 17

Heb 11:8-12
Lk 1:37

Rom 4:3
Gen 15:6
1 Cor 10:6

Is 53:4-6
1 Cor 15:17
1 Pet 1:21

---

est: "*Patrem multarum gentium posui te*" — ante Deum, cui credidit, qui vivificat mortuos et vocat ea, quae non sunt, quasi sint; [18]qui contra spem in spe credidit, ut fieret *pater multarum gentium*, secundum quod dictum est: "*Sic erit semen tuum.*" [19]Et non infirmatus fide consideravit corpus suum iam emortuum, cum fere centum annorum esset, et emortuam vulvam Sarae; [20]in repromissione autem Dei non haesitavit diffidentia, sed confortatus est fide, dans gloriam Deo, [21]et plenissime sciens quia, quod promisit, potens est et facere. [22]Ideo et *reputatum est illi ad iustitiam.* [23]Non est autem scriptum tantum propter ipsum: *reputatum est illi,* [24]sed et propter nos, quibus reputabitur, credentibus in eum, qui suscitavit Iesum Dominum nostrum a mortuis, [25]qui traditus est propter delicta nostra et suscitatus est propter iustificationem nostram.

24-25. The faith of which St Paul is speaking includes among its basic truths the redemptive Death of Christ and his Resurrection, two events which are indissolubly linked, two ways in which God's justice and mercy are manifested.

5

SALVATION AND THE CHRISTIAN LIFE

Rom 3:22-24;
3:28
Eph 3:12
2 Cor 12:9-10
1 Cor 13:13
Jas 1:2-4
1 Pet 1:5-7;
4:13-14
Rev 1:9

Reconciliation through Christ's sacrifice, the basis of our hope

¹Therefore, since we are justified by faith, we[f] have peace with God through our Lord Jesus Christ. ²Through him we have obtained access[g] to this grace in which we stand, and we[h] rejoice in our hope of sharing the glory of God. ³More than that, we[h] rejoice in our sufferings, knowing that suffering produces endurance, ⁴and endurance produces char-

---

¹Iustificati igitur ex fide, pacem habemus ad Deum per Dominum nostrum Iesum Christum, ²per quem et accessum habemus fide in gratiam istam, in qua stamus et gloriamur in spe gloriae Dei. ³Non solum autem, sed et gloriamur in

---

1-5. In this very moving passage God helps us see "the divine interlacing of the three theological virtues which form the backing upon which the true life of every Christian man or woman has to be woven" (J. Escrivá, *Friends of God*, 205). Faith, hope and charity act in us in turn, causing us to grow in the life of grace. Thus, faith leads us to know and be sure of the things we hope for (cf. Heb 11:1); hope ensures that we shall attain them, and enlivens our love of God; charity, for its part, gives us energy to practise the other two theological virtues. The definitive outcome of this growth in love, faith and hope is the everlasting peace that is of the essence of eternal life.

As long as we are in this present life we do have peace to some degree – but with tribulation. Therefore, the peace attainable in this life does not consist in the contentment of someone who wants to have no problems, but rather in the resoluteness full of hope ("character") of someone who manages to rise above suffering and stays faithful through endurance. Suffering is necessary for us, because it is the normal way to grow in virtue (cf. Jas 1:2-4; 1 Pet 1:5-7); that is why it is providential (cf. Phil 1:19; Col 1:24) and leads to joy and happiness (1 Thess 1:6).

"A person who hopes for something and strives eagerly to attain it is ready to endure all kinds of difficulty and distress. Thus, for example, a sick person, if he is eager to be healthy, is happy to take the bitter medicine which will cure him. Therefore, one sign of the ardent hope that is ours thanks to Christ is that we glory not only in the hope of future glory, but also in the afflictions which we suffer in order to attain it" (St Thomas Aquinas, *Commentary on Romans*, *ad loc.*).

A person who lives by faith, hope and charity realizes that suffering is not something meaningless but rather is designed by God for our perfecting.

[f]Other ancient authorities read *let us.*   [g]Other ancient authorities add *by faith.*   [h]Or *let us.*

acter, and character produces hope, ⁵and hope does not disappoint us, because God's love has been poured into our hearts through the Holy Spirit who has been given to us.

acter, and character produces hope, [5]and hope does not disappoint us, because God's love has been poured into our hearts through the Holy Spirit who has been given to us.

[6]While we were yet helpless, at the right time Christ died for the ungodly. [7]Why, one will hardly die for a righteous man – though perhaps for a good man one will dare even to die. [8]But God shows his love for us in that while we were yet sinners Christ died for us. [9]Since, therefore, we are now justified by his blood, much more shall we be saved by him from the wrath of God. [10]For, if while we were enemies we were reconciled to God by the death of his Son, much more, now that we are reconciled, shall we be saved by his life. [11]Not only so, but we also rejoice in God through our Lord

Rom 8:4-16
Gal 4:4-6

Rom 3:26
1 Pet 3:18
Jn 15:13

Rom 8:32
Jn 3:16
1 Jn 4:9-10, 19
1 Thess 1:10

2 Cor 5:18

---

tribulationibus, scientes quod tribulatio patientiam operatur, [4]patientia autem probationem, probatio vero spem; [5]spes autem non confundit, quia caritas Dei diffusa est in cordibus nostris per Spiritum Sanctum, qui datus est nobis. [6]Adhuc enim Christus, cum adhuc infirmi essemus, secundum tempus pro impiis mortuus est. [7]Vix enim pro iusto quis moritur; nam pro bono forsitan quis et audeat mori. [8]Commendat autem suam caritatem Deus in nos, quoniam, cum adhuc peccatores essemus, Christus pro nobis mortuus est. [9]Multo igitur magis iustificati nunc in sanguine ipsius, salvi erimus ab ira per ipsum! [10]Si enim cum

---

Perfection consists "in the bringing of our wills so closely into conformity with the will of God that, as soon as we realize he wills anything, we desire it ourselves with all our might, and take the bitter with the sweet, knowing that to be His Majesty's will [. . .]. If our love is perfect, it has this quality of leading us to forget our own pleasure in order to please him whom we love. And that is indeed what happens" (St Teresa of Avila, *Book of Foundations*, chap. 5).

5. The love which St Paul speaks of here is, at one and the same time, God's love for us – manifested in his sending the Holy Spirit – and the love which God places in our soul to enable us to love him. The Second Council of Orange, quoting St Augustine, explains this as follows: "To love God is entirely a gift of God. He, without being loved, loves us and enabled us to love him. We were loved when we were still displeasing to him, so that we might be given something whereby we might please him. So it is that the Spirit of the Father and the Son, whom we love with the Father and the Son, pours charity into our hearts" (Second Council of Orange, *De gratia*, can. 25; cf. St Augustine, *In Ioann. Evang.*, 102, 5).

6-11. The friendship which reigned in paradise between God and man was followed by the enmity created by Adam's sin. By promising a future redeemer, God once more offered mankind his friendship. The scale of God's love for us

Jesus Christ, through whom we have now received our
reconciliation.

Adam's original sin

¹²Therefore as sin came into the world through one man
and death through sin, and so death spread to all men

---

inimici essemus reconciliati sumus Deo per mortem Filii eius, multo magis
reconciliati salvi erimus in vita ipsius; ¹¹non solum autem, sed et gloriamur in
Deo per Dominum nostrum Iesum Christum, per quem nunc reconciliationem
accepimus. ¹²Propterea, sicut per unum hominem peccatum in hunc mundum

---

can be seen in the "reconciliation" which the Apostle speaks about, which took
place on the Cross, when Christ did away with this enmity, making our peace
with God and reconciling us to him (cf. Eph 2:15-16).

The petition in the Our Father, "Forgive us our trespasses as we forgive those
that trespass against us", is an invitation to imitate the way God treats us,
because by loving our enemies "there shines forth in us some likeness to God
our Father, who, by the death of his Son, ransomed from everlasting perdition
and reconciled to himself the human race, which before was most unfriendly
and hostile to him" (*St Pius V Catechism*, IV, 14, 19).

12-21. Four important teachings are discernible in this passage: 1) Adam's
sin and its consequences, which include, particularly, death (vv. 12-14);   2)
the contrast between the effects of original sin and those of the Redemption
wrought by Christ (vv. 15-19);   3) the role of the Law of Moses in relation to
sin (especially vv. 13, 20), anticipating what is explained more elaborately in
chapter 7;   4) the final victory of the reign of grace (vv. 20-21). These
teachings are closely connected by one single idea: only Jesus Christ can justify
us and bring us to salvation. The Apostle refers to Adam as a "type of the one
who was to come", that is, Jesus, the Messiah, who is the true head of the human
race; and he also stresses that Christ, by his obedience and submission to the
Father's will, counters the disobedience and rebellion of Adam, restoring to us
– superabundantly – the happiness and eternal life which we lost through the
sin of our first parents.

Here we can see the clash of the two kingdoms – the kingdom of sin and death
and the kingdom of righteousness and grace. These two kingdoms were
established, the first by Adam and the second by Christ, and spread to all
mankind.

Because the superabundance of Christ's grace is the more important factor,
Adam's sin is referred to in no great detail. St Paul takes it as something
everyone is familiar with. All Christians have read about or been told about the
account of the fall in Genesis (Gen 3) and they are familiar with many passages
in Sacred Scripture which confirm and explain something which is self-evident
– that all men are mortal and that the human race is subject to a whole series

because all men sinned – [13]sin indeed was in the world
before the law was given, but sin is not counted where there
is no law. [14]Yet death reigned from Adam to Moses, even
over those whose sins were not like the transgression of
Adam, who was a type of the one who was to come.

Rom 3:23; 4:15; 7:7-10

---

intravit et per peccatum mors, et ita in omnes homines mors pertransiit, eo quod
omnes peccaverunt. [13]Usque ad legem enim peccatum erat in mundo; peccatum
autem non imputatur, cum lex non est, [14]sed regnavit mors ab Adam usque ad
Moysen etiam in eos, qui non peccaverunt in similitudine praevaricationis

---

of afflictions (cf. Sir 25:33; Wis 2:23-24; Ps 51:7; Job 14:4; Gen 8:21; etc.).

12-14. This passage can be elaborated on as follows: just as sin entered the
world through the action of a single individual man, so righteousness is attained
for us by one man – Jesus Christ. Adam, the first man, is a type of the "new
Adam": Adam contained within himself all mankind, his offspring; the "new
Adam" is "the first-born of all creation" and "the head of the body, the church"
(Col 1:15, 18) because he is the redeeming Word Incarnate. To Adam we are
linked by flesh and blood, to Christ by faith and the sacraments.

When, in his infinite goodness, he raised Adam to share in the divine life,
God also decreed that our first parent would pass on to us his human nature and
with it all the various gifts that perfected it and the grace that sanctified it. But
Adam committed a sin by breaking God's commandment and as a result he
immediately lost the holiness and righteousness in which he had been installed,
and because of this disloyalty he incurred God's wrath and indignation and, as
a consequence, death – as God had warned him. By becoming mortal and falling
under the power of the devil, Adam "was changed for the worse", in both body
and soul (cf. Council of Trent, *De peccato originali*, can. 1). From then on
Adam and his descendants pass on a human nature deprived of supernatural
gifts, and men are in a state of enmity with God, which means that they cannot
attain eternal beatitude.

The fact of original sin is a truth of faith. This has been stated once again
solemnly by Paul VI: "We believe that in Adam all have sinned. From this it
follows that, on account of the original offence committed by him, human
nature, which is common to all men, is reduced to that condition in which it
must suffer the consequences of that fall [. . .]. Consequently, fallen human
nature is deprived of the economy of grace which it formerly enjoyed. It is
wounded in its natural powers and subjected to the dominion of death which is
transmitted to all men. It is in this sense that every man is born in sin. We hold,
therefore, in accordance with the Council of Trent, that original sin is transmitted along with human nature, *not by imitation but by propagation*, and is,
therefore, incurred by each person individually" (*Creed of the People of God*,
16).

Our own experience bears out what divine Revelation tells us: when we

1 Tim 2:5 ¹⁵But the free gift is not like the trespass. For if many died through one man's trespass, much more have the grace of God and the free gift in the grace of that one man Jesus Christ abounded for many. ¹⁶And the free gift is not like the effect of that one man's sin. For the judgment following one trespass brought condemnation, but the free gift following many trespasses brings justification. ¹⁷If, because of one man's trespass, death reigned through that one man, much more will those who receive the abundance of grace and the free gift of righteousness reign in life through the one man Jesus Christ.

Adae, qui est figura futuri. ¹⁵Sed non sicut delictum, ita et donum; si enim unius delicto multi mortui sunt, multo magis gratia Dei et donum in gratia unius hominis Iesu Christi in multos abundavit. ¹⁶Et non sicut per unum, qui peccavit, ita et donum; nam iudicium ex uno in condemnationem, gratia autem ex multis delictis in iustificationem. ¹⁷Si enim unius delicto mors regnavit per unum,

---

examine our conscience we realize that we have this inclination towards evil and we are conscious of being enmeshed in evils which cannot have their source in our holy Creator (cf. Vatican II, *Gaudium et spes*, 13). The obvious presence of evil in the world and in ourselves convinces us of the profound truth contained in Revelation and moves us to fight against sin.

"So much wretchedness! So many offences! Mine, yours, those of all mankind. . . .

"*Et in peccatis concepit me mater mea!* In sin did my mother conceive me! (Ps 51:5). I, like all men, came into the world stained with the guilt of our first parents. And then . . . my own sins: rebellions, thought about, desired, committed. . . .

"To purify us of this rottenness, Jesus chose to humble himself and take on the form of a slave (cf. Phil 2:7), becoming incarnate in the spotless womb of our Lady, his Mother, who is also your Mother and mine. He spent thirty years in obscurity, working like everyone else, at Joseph's side. He preached. He worked miracles. . . . And we repaid him with a cross.

"Do you need more motives for contrition?" (J. Escrivá, *The Way of the Cross*, IV, 2).

13-14. Both the commandment imposed by God on Adam, and the Mosaic Law, threatened the transgressor with death; but the same cannot be said of the period between Adam and Moses. In that period also people did sin against the natural law written on every person's heart (cf. 2:12ff). However, their sins "were not like the transgression of Adam", because the natural law did not explicitly bind under pain of death. If, nevertheless, they in fact had to die, this proves, the Apostle concludes, that death is due not to personal sins but to

100

[18]Then as one man's trespass led to condemnation for all men, so one man's act of righteousness leads to acquittal and life for all men. [19]For as by one man's disobedience many were made sinners, so by one man's obedience many will be made righteous. [20]Law came in, to increase the trespass; but where sin increased, grace abounded all the more, [21]so that, as sin reigned in death, grace also might reign through righteousness to eternal life through Jesus Christ our Lord.

Is 53:11

Rom 3:23; 4:15; 5:13; 7:7-10 Gal 3:19 Rom 11:32

multo magis, qui abundantiam gratiae et donationis iustitiae accipiunt, in vita regnabunt per unum Iesum Christum. [18]Igitur sicut per unius delictum in omnes homines in condemnationem, sic et per unius iustitiam in omnes homines in iustificationem vitae; [19]sicut enim per inoboedientiam unius hominis peccatores constituti sunt multi, ita et per unius oboeditionem iusti constituentur multi. [20]Lex autem subintravit, ut abundaret delictum; ubi autem abundavit peccatum, superabundavit gratia, [21]ut sicut regnavit peccatum in morte, ita et gratia regnet per iustitiam in vitam aeternam per Iesum Christum Dominum nostrum.

original sin. It is also proved, the Fathers of the Church usually add, by the fact that some people die before reaching the use of reason, that is, before they are capable of sinning.

Death is a consequence of original sin, because that sin brought with it the loss of the "preternatural" gift of immortality (cf. Gen 2:17; 3:19). Adam incurred this loss when, through a personal act of his, he broke an explicit, specific command of God. Later, under the Mosaic Law, there were also certain precepts which involved the death penalty if broken (cf., for example, Exod 21:12ff; Lev 24:16). In the period from Adam to Moses there was no law which stated: If you sin, you shall die. However, people in that period were all subject to death, even those who committed no sin "like the transgression of Adam", that is, what is termed "actual sin".

Therefore, death is due to a sin – original sin – which attaches to each man, woman and child, yet which is not an "actual sin". This original sin is the cause of death, and the fact that everyone dies is the proof that everyone is affected by original sin. The Second Vatican Council sums up this teaching as follows: "The Church, taught by divine Revelation, declares that God has created man in view of a blessed destiny that lies beyond the limits of his sad state on earth. Moreover, the Christian faith teaches that bodily death, from which man would have been immune had he not sinned (cf. Wis 1:13; 2:23-24; Rom 5:21; 6:23; Jas 1:15), will be overcome when that wholeness which he lost through his own fault will be given once again to him by the almighty and merciful Saviour. For God has called man, and still calls him, to cleave with all his being to him in sharing for ever a life that is divine and free from all decay" (*Gaudium et spes*, 18).

6

Baptism

Rom 3:5-8
Col 2:12-13
Tit 3:5-7
1 Pet 3:21-22

[1]What shall we say then? Are we to continue in sin that grace may abound? [2]By no means! How can we who died to sin still live in it? [3]Do you not know that all of us who have been baptized into Christ Jesus were baptized into his

---

[1]Quid ergo dicemus? Permanebimus in peccato, ut gratia abundet? [2]Absit! Qui enim mortui sumus peccato, quomodo adhuc vivemus in illo? [3]An ignoratis quia, quicumque baptizati sumus in Christo Iesu, in mortem ipsius baptizati sumus? [4]Consepulti ergo sumus cum illo per baptismum in mortem, ut quemadmodum suscitatus est Christus a mortuis per gloriam Patris, ita et nos in novitate

---

1-11. The universal dominion of sin, which began with the sin of Adam, is not the only event to be reckoned with. When sin reached its full extent, the grace brought by Jesus Christ came in superabundance. Through Baptism this grace reaches each of us and frees us from the control of sin. When we receive this sacrament we die: that is to say, our blameworthiness is destroyed, we renounce sin once and for all, and are born again into a new life.

"The Lord", St Ambrose tells the newly baptized, "who wanted his benefactions to endure, the serpent's plans to be turned to naught, and the harm done to be put right, delivered a sentence on mankind: 'You are dust, and to dust you shall return' (Gen 3:19), and made man subject to death [. . .]. The remedy was given him: man would die and rise again [. . .]. You ask me how? [. . .] Pay attention. So that in this world too the devil's snare would be broken, a rite was instituted whereby man would die, being alive, and rise again, being alive [...]. Through immersion in water the sentence is blotted out: 'You are dust, and to dust you shall return'" (*De Sacramentis*, II, 6).

This passage of the epistle, which reveals the key truths concerning Baptism, also reminds us of the profound meaning of this rite which Christ established, its spiritual effects in Christians and its far-reaching effects with respect to the Christian life. Thus, we can apply to Baptism what St Thomas Aquinas says about all the sacraments: "Three aspects of sanctification may be considered – its very cause, which is Christ's Passion; its form, which is grace and the virtues; and its ultimate end, which is eternal life. And all these are signified by the sacraments. Consequently, a sacrament is a sign which is both a reminder of the past, that is, of the Passion of Christ, and an indication of what is effected in us by Christ's Passion, and a foretelling and pledge of future glory" (*Summa theologiae*, III, q. 60, a. 3).

In the specific case of Baptism, the various things which the sacrament implies carry a special nuance – a new birth which presupposes a symbolic death. It reproduces in us not only the Passion, Death and burial of Christ, symbolized by immersion in water (vv. 3-4, 6) but also new life, the life of

death? ⁴We were buried therefore with him by baptism into
death, so that as Christ was raised from the dead by the glory
of the Father, we too might walk in newness of life.

vitae ambulemus. ⁵Si enim complantati facti sumus similitudini mortis eius,

grace which pours into the soul, enabling the person to share in the Resurrection
of Christ (vv. 4-5). This sharing in Christ's Resurrection to immortal life is a
kind of seed which will ultimately produce the glorious resurrection of our
bodies.

The baptized person is, therefore, someone newly created, someone born into
a new life, someone who has moved out of darkness into light. The white
garment used at Baptism symbolizes innocence and grace; the burning candle,
the light of Christ – two symbols the Church uses in the baptismal liturgy to
signify what is happening.

Thus, in Baptism, God "removes every trace of sin, whether original or
personal" (*The Rite of Baptism*, Introduction, 5) and also remits the penalties
that these sins incur. On being baptized in the name of the three divine Persons,
the Christian is shown God the Father's love for him (a love he has not merited),
is given a share in the paschal mystery of the Son, and to him is communicated
new life in the Spirit (cf. *Instruction on Infant Baptism*, 20 October 1980, 9).
Baptism, which is also described as "the door of the spiritual life", unites a
person to Christ and to the Church by means of grace, which makes us children
of God and heirs to heaven. Finally, in addition to the infused virtues and
supernatural gifts, the person is given "the graces necessary to live in a
Christian way, and on his soul is impressed the sacramental character which
makes him a Christian for evermore" (*St Pius X Catechism*, 250).

Baptism, which confers a "character", that is, a kind of seal confirming our
Christian calling, gives us a share in Christ's priesthood and makes us capable
of receiving the other sacraments.

4. It is easier to grasp the symbolism of burial and resurrection if one
remembers that in earlier times, and particularly in the apostolic period,
Baptism was usually administered by immersion in water – in some cases by
total immersion, up to three times, with one Person of the Blessed Trinity being
invoked each time. "They asked you, 'Do you believe in God the Father
almighty?' You said, 'I believe', and you were immersed, that is, you were
buried. Again they asked you, 'Do you believe in our Lord Jesus Christ and in
his Cross?' You said, 'I believe', and you were again immersed. This time you
have been buried with Christ, and he who is buried with Christ rises with Christ.
For a third time you were asked, 'Do you believe in the Holy Spirit?' You said,
'I believe', and for a third time you were immersed, so that by this three-fold
confession you might be loosed of your many attachments to your past life"
(St Ambrose, *De sacramentis*, II, 7).

Today Baptism is normally administered by pouring water over the head – a

Eph 2:4-7
Col 2:12

Rom 8:11
Phil 3:10-11

Gal 5:24
Col 3:3-4, 9-10
Rom 6:14
1 Pet 4:1

Acts 13:33-34
1 Cor 15:26
Heb 2:14
Rev 1:18

⁵For if we have been united with him in a death like his, we shall certainly be united with him in a resurrection like his. ⁶We know that our old self was crucified with him so that the sinful body might be destroyed, and we might no longer be enslaved to sin. ⁷For he who has died is freed from sin. ⁸But if we have died with Christ, we believe that we shall also live with him. ⁹For we know that Christ being raised from the dead will never die again; death no longer has dominion over him. ¹⁰The death he died he died to sin,

---

sed et resurrectionis erimus; ⁶hoc scientes quia vetus homo noster simul crucifixus est, ut destruatur corpus peccati, ut ultra non serviamus peccato. ⁷Qui enim mortuus est, iustificatus est a peccato. ⁸Si autem mortui sumus cum Christo, credimus quia simul etiam vivemus cum eo; ⁹scientes quod Christus suscitatus ex mortuis iam non moritur, mors illi ultra non dominatur. ¹⁰Quod

---

method also used in apostolic times and which gradually came into general use because it was found more convenient.

5. Just as the ingraft and the plant form a single thing and make a single principle of life, Christians by being grafted onto or incorporated into Christ through Baptism form one single thing with him and begin to draw on his divine life. We are also "united with him in a death like his": Christ suffered physical death; we, in Baptism, die spiritually to the life of sin. St John Chrysostom explains this as follows: "Baptism is for us what the Cross and burial were for Christ; but with this difference: the Saviour died physically, he was physically buried, whereas we ought to die spiritually. That is why the Apostle does not say we are 'united with him in his death', but 'in a death *like his*'" (*Hom. on Rom*, 10).

9-10. Jesus Christ chose to bear all the consequences of sin, even though he was sinless. His voluntary Death on the Cross and his glorious Resurrection broke the bonds of death, for himself and for all his own. Death no longer shall have dominion: "[Christ died] that through death he might destroy him who has the power of death, that is, the devil, and deliver all those who through fear of death were subject to lifelong bondage" (Heb 2:14-15). And as a consequence he won, for his own human nature and for us, a new life.

In all those who have been baptized these same events in Christ's life are in some way reproduced. "Our past sins have been wiped out by the action of grace. Now, so as to stay dead to sin after Baptism, personal effort is called for, although God's grace continues to be with us, providing us with great help" (Chrysostom, *Hom. on Rom*, 11). This personal effort might be encapsulated in a resolution: "May we never die through sin; may our spiritual resurrection be eternal" (J. Escrivá, *Holy Rosary*, first glorious mystery).

once for all, but the life he lives he lives to God. [11]So you also must consider yourselves dead to sin and alive to God in Christ Jesus.

Gal 2:19
Heb 7:27; 9:28
1 Pet 2:24; 3:18
2 Cor 5:15

Liberation from sin

[12]Let not sin therefore reign in your mortal bodies, to make you obey their passions. [13]Do not yield your members to sin as instruments of wickedness, but yield yourselves to God as men who have been brought from death to life, and your members to God as instruments of righteousness. [14]For sin will have no dominion over you, since you are not under law but under grace.

Rom 7:14-24
Gen 4:7
Rom 12:1

1 Jn 3:6

[15]What then? Are we to sin because we are not under law but under grace? By no means! [16]Do you not know that if you yield yourselves to any one as obedient slaves, you are slaves of the one whom you obey, either of sin, which leads to death, or of obedience, which leads to righteousness? [17]But thanks be to God, that you who were once slaves of sin have become obedient from the heart to the standard of teaching to which you were committed, [18]and, having been

Rom 6:1
Jn 8:34
2 Pet 2:19

Jn 8:34-36
Gal 5:13

---

enim mortuus est, peccato mortuus est semel; quod autem vivit, vivit Deo. [11]Ita et vos existimate vos mortuos quidem esse peccato, viventes autem Deo in Christo Iesu. [12]Non ergo regnet peccatum in vestro mortali corpore, ut oboediatis concupiscentiis eius, [13]neque exhibeatis membra vestra arma iniustitiae peccato, sed exhibete vos Deo tamquam ex mortuis viventes et membra vestra arma iustitiae Deo. [14]Peccatum enim vobis non dominabitur; non enim sub lege estis sed sub gratia. [15]Quid ergo? Peccabimus, quoniam non sumus sub lege sed sub gratia? Absit! [16]Nescitis quoniam, cui exhibetis vos servos ad oboedientiam, servi estis eius, cui oboeditis, sive peccati ad mortem, sive oboeditionis ad iustitiam? [17]Gratias autem Deo quod fuistis servi peccati,

---

12-13. Our body, while forming one substance with our soul, is also an instrument (like a pen in the hand of a writer) which can be used either to do works of justice and piety or to enter into combat against the spirit. True, it is a "mortal body", but, St John Chrysostom comments, "It is not in any sense an evil thing, because it can be a weapon of holiness and righteousness [. . .]. Our body stands between vice and virtue. It is a weapon we can freely put to one use or the other. The soldier who fights to defend his country uses the same weapons as the criminal who makes an attempt on the life of his fellow citizens [. . .]. And so the body can be an instrument of good or evil depending on what the soul chooses: it is not naturally disposed to either course" (*Hom. on Rom*, 11).

1 Pet 1:14-16 set free from sin, have become slaves of righteousness. [19]I am speaking in human terms, because of your natural limitations. For just as you once yielded your members to impurity and to greater and greater iniquity, so now yield your members to righteousness for sanctification.

[20]When you were slaves of sin, you were free in regard to Rom 7:5; 8:6, 13 righteousness. [21]But then what return did you get from the things of which you are now ashamed? The end of those Jn 15:8, 16 things is death. [22]But now that you have been set free from sin and have become slaves of God, the return you get is Rom 5:12, 21
Gal 6:7-9
Jas 1:15 sanctification and its end, eternal life. [23]For the wages of sin is death, but the free gift of God is eternal life in Christ Jesus our Lord.

7

The Christian is not bound by the Law

[1]Do you not know, brethren – for I am speaking to those who know the law – that the law is binding on a person only 1 Cor 7:39 during his life? [2]Thus a married woman is bound by law to her husband as long as he lives; but if her husband dies she is discharged from the law concerning the husband.

---

oboedistis autem ex corde in eam formam doctrinae, in quam traditi estis, [18]liberati autem a peccato servi facti estis iustitiae. [19]Humanum dico propter infirmitatem carnis vestrae. Sicut enim exhibuistis membra vestra servientia immunditiae et iniquitati ad iniquitatem, ita nunc exhibete membra vestra servientia iustitiae ad sanctificationem. [20]Cum enim servi essetis peccati, liberi eratis iustitiae. [21]Quem ergo fructum habebatis tunc, in quibus nunc erubescitis? Nam finis illorum mors! [22]Nunc vero liberati a peccato, servi autem facti Deo, habetis fructum vestrum in sanctificationem, finem vero vitam aeternam! [23]Stipendia enim peccati mors, donum autem Dei vita aeterna in Christo Iesu Domino nostro.

[1]An ignoratis, fratres – scientibus enim legem loquor – quia lex in homine dominatur, quanto tempore vivit? [2]Nam quae sub viro est mulier, viventi viro

---

1-4. St John Chrysostom says that the comparison which St Paul makes here shows great respect for the Mosaic Law: "Paul speaks of the Law as a husband, and of the faithful as a wife. But his conclusion is not consistent with what he said earlier, bcause he should go on to conclude: the Law will rule you no more, because the Law is dead. However, [. . .] in order not to provoke the Jews he simply says, 'You have died to the Law'" (*Hom. on Rom*, 12). Prior to the Resurrection, St Paul and those he is addressing were subject to the Law

³Accordingly, she will be called an adulteress if she lives with another man while her husband is alive. But if her husband dies she is free from that law, and if she marries another man she is not an adulteress.

⁴Likewise, my brethren, you have died to the law through the body of Christ, so that you may belong to another, to him who has been raised from the dead in order that we may bear fruit for God. ⁵While we were living in the flesh, our sinful passions, aroused by the law, were at work in our members to bear fruit for death. ⁶But now we are discharged

Rom 6:5-7
Col 2:13-14
Gal 2:19
Jn 15:8

Rom 7:7, 10;
8:6, 13

Rom 6:4
2 Cor 3:6
Mt 9:16-17

---

alligata est lege; si autem mortuus fuerit vir, soluta est a lege viri. ³Igitur vivente viro vocabitur adultera, si fuerit alterius viri; si autem mortuus fuerit vir, libera est a lege, ut non sit adultera, si fuerit alterius viri. ⁴Itaque, fratres mei, et vos mortificati estis legi per corpus Christi, ut sitis alterius, eius qui ex mortuis suscitatus est, ut fructificaremus Deo. ⁵Cum enim essemus in carne, passiones peccatorum quae per legem sunt operabantur in membris nostris, ut fructificarent morti; ⁶nunc autem soluti sumus a lege, mortui ei, in qua detinebamur,

---

(represented by the husband). Once they have been given a share in the death of Christ, through Baptism (cf. 6:3-4), they are "dead", and therefore they are free of the Law – free, however, to do good, to yield the fruit of a holy life, that is, to "bear fruit" for God, by being united to Christ.

4. In his epistles St Paul describes the Church as a "body" and even goes as far as to call it "the body of Christ", to explain the profound relationship between the Church and Christ and also the mutual dependence of Christians. On this concept of the Church as "body of Christ", cf. "Introduction to the 'Theology' of St Paul", above, pp. 44-6.

5. In this as in other Pauline texts, the term "flesh" refers to human weakness and therefore to man's condition after original sin, the origin of his concupiscence, that is, the disordered passions which encourage him to sin (cf. "Introduction to the 'Theology' of St Paul", p. 30).

6. The grace of Christ liberates man from the tyranny of sin. After Adam's original sin, no one, without grace, could avoid sin completely. With the help of grace a person can aspire to serve God of his own free will, not out of fear of punishment but out of filial love (cf. 2 Cor 3:6), not because of the threats contained in the Old Testament but with the new energy bestowed by divine filiation. This is the freedom of spirit which Christians practise: they do what God wants because they too want it: "We [. . .] hold that man's will is helped by God to act correctly in many ways, because man, in addition to having been created with free will and having doctrine which teaches him how he ought to

107

from the law, dead to that which held us captive, so that we serve not under the old written code but in the new life of the Spirit.

The Law and covetousness

Rom 3:20; 4:15; 5:13, 20

⁷What then shall we say? That the law is sin? By no means! Yet, if it had not been for the law, I should not have known sin. I should not have known what it is to covet if the law had not said, "You shall not covet." ⁸But sin, finding opportunity in the commandment, wrought in me all kinds of covetousness. Apart from the law sin lies dead. ⁹I was once alive apart from the law, but when the commandment came, sin revived and I died; ¹⁰the very commandment which promised life proved to be death to me.

Ex 20:17
Deut 5:21
Jas 1:14-15
1 Cor 15:56
Gen 2:17;
3:19, 22
Lev 18:5
Heb 3:13-19

ita ut serviamus in novitate Spiritus et non in vetustate litterae. ⁷Quid ergo dicemus? Lex peccatum est? Absit! Sed peccatum non cognovi nisi per legem, nam concupiscentiam nescirem nisi lex diceret: "*Non concupisces.*" ⁸Occasione autem accepta, peccatum per mandatum operatum est in me omnem concupiscentiam; sine lege enim peccatum mortuum erat. ⁹Ego autem vivebam sine lege aliquando, sed, cum venisset mandatum, peccatum revixit, ¹⁰ego autem mortuus sum, et inventum est mihi mandatum, quod erat ad vitam, hoc

live, has also been given the Holy Spirit. The Spirit inspires his soul with love for highest and immutable Good, that is God, [...] so that with this grace, which is as it were a pledge of the future free gift, he might be stirred to unite himself to his Creator and have a burning desire to share in the true light. And so he will receive his fulfilment from him who gave him his life" (St Augustine, *De spiritu et littera*, III, 5).

7-13. The newness of the Christian life contrasts with the letter of the Law of Moses. The Law brought on death (v. 5), even though it was not in itself bad (cf. Rom 3:20; 4:15; 5:13, 20). The Apostle mentions two other factors along with the Law – sin and man himself. He shows how these interconnect: the "Law" is the Law of Moses, although it can also refer to the commandment God gave our first parents (v. 11); "sin" is presented as a seducer (v. 11), opposed to God (v. 13), and it can also mean Adam's original sin and all that flowed from it, especially covetousness – evil desires, or concupiscence (vv. 7-8); the "I" in vv. 7-13 can be taken as meaning Paul himself before his conversion, or mankind in general before the Redemption, or Jews subject to the Mosaic Law.

The Law is not bad; on the contrary, it is holy, just and good (cf. v. 12). It is, St John Chrysostom suggests, like a doctor who forbids a sick person to eat something harmful: if despite this the sick person eats it, it is not the doctor

¹¹For sin, finding opportunity in the commandment, deceived me and by it killed me. ¹²So the law is holy, and the commandment is holy and just and good.

---

esse ad mortem; ¹¹nam peccatum, occasione accepta, per mandatum seduxit me et per illud occidit. ¹²Itaque lex quidem sancta, et mandatum sanctum et iustum

---

who is to be blamed (cf. *Hom. on Rom*, 12). The Law is good because it is a gift from God, it is directed towards him, it reveals the right order established by divine wisdom, it prohibits all evils, it helps man to see where his duty lies and, above all, it prepares the way for the coming of the Redeemer (Rom 3:19f; 5:20; Gal 3:19, 24). However, the Law is not enough: it does not equip a person to conquer sin. This inadequacy of the Law paradoxically shows up its value: it leads us to have recourse to Christ's grace and supernatural resources.

In this connexion the Fathers of the Church insist that the Law only brings on sin by making people realize the gravity of their actions, thereby increasing their guilt. "Before the Law", St John Chrysostom comments, "sinners well knew that they were sinning; but after the Law they know it much better [. . .]. Thus, one is much more at fault when one sins not only against the light of reason, but also against that light and against the Law, which adds a still greater clarity to the light of reason" (*Hom. on Rom*, 12). But this should not make us feel pessimistic. In spite of everything the consciousness of the evil of sin which the Law provides leads us to seek the grace of God. "By this promise, that is, through the help of divine grace", St Augustine says, "the Law is perfectly obeyed [. . .]. The Law was given so that grace might be sought; and grace was given so that the Law might be obeyed" (*De spiritu et littera*, XIX, 34).

11. After our first parents' transgression of the precept, God asks, first Adam and then Eve, why they committed it. Eve replies: "The serpent beguiled me, and I ate" (Gen 3:13). This original sin involved deception on the devil's part: he made evil – disobedience and pride – take the appearance of good: "You will not die. For God knows that when you eat of it [the forbidden fruit] your eyes will be opened, and you will be like God, knowing good and evil" (Gen 3:4-5). "Satan", John Paul II comments, "promises man divine omnipotence and omniscience, that is, absolute self-sufficiency and independence. But man is not man except insofar as he can 'choose' God, in whose likeness he has been created. However, the first Adam chooses himself instead of God; he yields to temptation and finds himself wretched, fragile, weak, 'naked', 'the slave of sin' (cf. Jn 8:34)" (*Homily*, 8 March 1981).

"In original sin and in every sin man refuses to recognize the gift and the Love which God offers him in Creation. Refusing to recognize, in his heart, the deepest meaning of this gift, that is, of the love which is the specific agent of Creation and of the original Covenant (cf. Gen 3:5), man turns his back on God-Love, on the 'Father'. In a certain sense he casts him out of his heart. By so doing he separates his heart and almost cuts it off from everything that comes

¹³Did that which is good, then, bring death to me? By no means! It was sin, working death in me through what is good, in order that sin might be shown to be sin, and through the commandment might become sinful beyond measure.

Interior struggle

Job 14:4
Ps 51:7
Jn 3:6

¹⁴We know that the law is spiritual; but I am carnal, sold under sin. ¹⁵I do not understand my own actions. For I do not do what I want, but I do the very thing I hate. ¹⁶Now if I do what I do not want, I agree that the law is good. ¹⁷So then it is no longer I that do it, but sin which dwells within me. ¹⁸For I know that nothing good dwells within me, that

Gen 6:5; 8:21
Rom 3:10-18

---

et bonum. ¹³Quod ergo bonum est, mihi factum est mors? Absit! Sed peccatum, ut appareat peccatum, per bonum mihi operatum est mortem; ut fiat supra modum peccans peccatum per mandatum. ¹⁴Scimus enim quod lex spiritalis est; ego autem carnalis sum, venumdatus sub peccato. ¹⁵Quod enim operor, non intellego; non enim, quod volo, hoc ago, sed quod odi, illud facio. ¹⁶Si autem, quod nolo, illud facio, consentio legi quoniam bona. ¹⁷Nunc autem iam non ego operor illud, sed, quod habitat in me, peccatum. ¹⁸Scio enim quia non habitat

---

from the Father, and is left with what comes from the world" (John Paul II, *General audience*, 30 April 1980).

Reflection on the terrible consequences of sin helps us appreciate, by contrast, the infinite mercy of God, which is manifested in Christ. Man can "be like God" only if he is born of God as a son in the Only-begotten Son.

14-25. As can be seen from the use of the present tense, the "I" in vv. 14-25 is no longer Paul before his conversion, but rather after it: and it also stands for all mankind redeemed by Christ's grace. Here we have a vivid description of the interior struggle which everyone experiences, Christians included. These words are in line with something we are all well aware of: in our bodies there is a "law", an inclination, which fights against the law of our spirit (cf. v. 23), that is, against the spiritual good which God's grace causes us to desire. The very expression "the law of sin which dwells in my members" emphasizes how strenuously our senses, appetites and passions try to reject the dictates of the spirit; however, the spirit can gain the upper hand. The Church's teaching is that Baptism does not take away a person's inclination to sin (*fomes peccati*), concupiscence: he or she still experiences a strong desire for earthly or sensual pleasure. "Since it [concupiscence] is left to provide a trial, it has no power to injure those who do not consent and who, by the grace of Christ Jesus, manfully resist" (Council of Trent, *De peccato originali*, can. 5).

The Jews were able to keep the Law of Moses only through the help of divine grace granted them in anticipation of the merits of Christ. Without grace they

is, in my flesh. I can will what is right, but I cannot do it.
¹⁹For I do not do the good I want, but the evil I do not want
is what I do. ²⁰Now if I do what I do not want, it is no longer
I that do it, but sin which dwells within me.

---

in me, hoc est in carne mea, bonum; nam velle adiacet mihi, operari autem
bonum, non! ¹⁹Non enim, quod volo bonum, facio, sed, quod nolo malum, hoc
ago. ²⁰Si autem, quod nolo, illud facio, iam non ego operor illud, sed, quod

---

were like slaves, "sold under sin" (v. 14). After Christ, a person who rejects
the Redemption is in a similar position, for "in the state of corrupt nature man
needs grace to heal his nature and enable him to avoid sin entirely. In this present
life this healing is brought about in his mind [the spiritual part of man]: the
carnal appetite is not completely healed. Hence the Apostle (Rom 7:25) says
of the person healed by grace, 'I serve the law of God with my mind, but with
my flesh I serve the law of sin'. In this state a person can avoid mortal sin [...]
but he cannot avoid all venial sin, due to the corruption of his sensual appetite"
(St Thomas Aquinas, *Summa theologiae*, I-II, q. 109, a. 8).

Hence our need for God's help if we are to persevere in virtue; hence also
our need to make a genuine personal effort to be faithful. The *St Pius V
Catechism*, when dealing with the fact that even after Baptism man is subject
to various disabilities, including concupiscence, explains that God has willed
that death and suffering, which originate in sin, remain part of our lot, thereby
enabling us to attain mystical and real union with Christ, who chose to undergo
suffering and death; and, likewise, we still have concupiscence, and experience
bodily weakness etc. "that in them we may have the seed and material of virtue
from which we shall hereafter receive a more abundant harvest of glory and
more ample rewards" (II, 2, 48). "'*Infelix ego homo!, quis me liberabit de
corpore mortis huius?* Unhappy man that I am! Who will deliver me from this
body of death?' The cry is Saint Paul's – Courage: he too had to fight" (J.
Escrivá, *The Way*, 138).

14. After original sin, man was subject to his passions and exposed to the
continuous assault of concupiscence – "sold under sin". Healed by Christ's
grace in Baptism, he is free of this slavery, but not totally so: there is still this
inclination to sin, and his enslavement grows the more he sins. On the other
hand, if he responds to grace, he becomes ever more free. "Just think: the
Almighty, who through his Providence rules the whole universe, does not want
the forced service of slaves; he prefers to have children who are free. Although
we are born *proni ad peccatum*, inclined to sin, due to the fall of our first
parents, he has placed in the soul of each and every one of us a spark of infinite
intelligence, an attraction towards the good, a yearning for everlasting peace.
And he brings us to understand that we will attain truth, happiness and freedom
if we strive to make this seed of eternal life grow in our hearts" (J. Escrivá,
Friends of God, 33).

Eph 3:18

Gal 5:17
Jas 1:14
1 Pet 2:11

1 Cor 15:57
Rom 5:21; 6:23

²¹So I find it to be a law that when I want to do right, evil lies close at hand. ²²For I delight in the law of God, in my inmost self, ²³but I see in my members another law at war with the law of my mind and making me captive to the law of sin which dwells in my members. ²⁴Wretched man that I am! Who will deliver me from this body of death? ²⁵Thanks be to God through Jesus Christ our Lord! So then, I of myself serve the law of God with my mind, but with my flesh I serve the law of sin.

8

Life in the Spirit

Rom 7:23, 24; 3:27

¹There is therefore now no condemnation for those who are in Christ Jesus. ²For the law of the Spirit of life in Christ

---

habitat in me, peccatum.²¹Invenio igitur hanc legem volenti mihi facere bonum, quoniam mihi malum adiacet. ²²Condelector enim legi Dei secundum interiorem hominem; ²³video autem aliam legem in membris meis repugnantem legi mentis meae et captivantem me in lege peccati, quae est in membris meis. ²⁴Infelix ego homo! Quis me liberabit de corpore mortis huius? ²⁵Gratias autem Deo per Iesum Christum Dominum nostrum! Igitur ego ipse mente servio legi Dei, carne autem legi peccati.

¹Nihil ergo nunc damnationis est his, qui sunt in Christo Iesu; ²lex enim

---

1-13. After original sin man is pulled in two different directions: either he seeks God above all things and contends, with God's grace, against the inclinations of his own concupiscence; or else he lets himself be overwhelmed by the disordered passions of the flesh. The former lifestyle is "life in the Spirit", the latter, life "according to the flesh". "There are only two possible ways of living on this earth: either we live a supernatural life, or we live an animal life" (J. Escrivá, *Friends of God*, 200).

Sanctifying grace is the source of life "according to the Spirit". It is not a matter of simply being in the state of grace or of performing a number of regular pious practices. Life according to the Spirit – spiritual or supernatural life – means a living-according-to-God which influences everything a Christian does: he is constantly trying to bring his thoughts, yearnings, desires and actions into line with what God is asking of him; in everything he does he tries to follow the inspirations of the Holy Spirit.

Life according to the flesh, on the other hand, has its source in the triple concupiscence which is a consequence of original sin – "all that is in the world, the lust of the flesh, and the lust of the eyes and the pride of life" (1 Jn 2:16). In this present life it is not possible to kill concupiscence at its root: it is forever

Jesus has set me free from the law of sin and death. ³For
God has done what the law, weakened by the flesh, could
not do: sending his own Son in the likeness of sinful flesh
and for sin,ⁱ he condemned sin in the flesh, ⁴in order that
the just requirement of the law might be fulfilled in us, who
walk not according to the flesh but according to the Spirit.
⁵For those who live according to the flesh set their minds
on the things of the flesh, but those who live according to
the Spirit set their minds on the things of the Spirit. ⁶To set
the mind on the flesh is death, but to set the mind on the
Spirit is life and peace. ⁷For the mind that is set on the flesh
is hostile to God; it does not submit to God's law, indeed it
cannot; ⁸and those who are in the flesh cannot please God.

Acts 13:38-39;
15:10-11
2 Cor 5:21
Jn 1:14
Phil 2:7
Heb 2:14-18;
4:15
Rom 10:4

Gal 5:16-23
Rom 6:21
Gal 6:8

Jas 4:4
1 Jn 2:15-16

Spiritus vitae in Christo Iesu liberavit te a lege peccati et mortis. ³Nam, quod
impossibile erat legi, in quo infirmabatur per carnem, Deus Filium suum
mittens in similitudine carnis peccati et pro peccato, damnavit peccatum in
carne, ⁴ut iustitia legis impleretur in nobis, qui non secundum carnem
ambulamus, sed secundum Spiritum. ⁵Qui enim secundum carnem sunt, quae
carnis sunt, sapiunt; qui vero secundum Spiritum, quae sunt Spiritus. ⁶Nam
sapientia carnis mors, sapientia autem Spiritus vita et pax; ⁷quoniam sapientia
carnis inimicitia est in Deum, legi enim Dei non subicitur, nec enim potest. ⁸Qui

producing new growths. The Christian is freed from original sin through
Baptism (chap. 6); the coming of Christ has set aside the ritualistic precepts of
the Mosaic Law (chap. 7); but his life in Jesus Christ is threatened by concupiscence even after Baptism, which places him under the Law of the Spirit.
"We need to submit to the spirit, to wholeheartedly commit ourselves and strive
to keep the flesh in its place. By so doing our flesh will become spiritual again.
Otherwise, if we give in to the easy life, this will lower our soul to the level of
the flesh and make it carnal again" (St John Chrysostom, *Hom. on Rom*, 13).

3. Man was unable to free himself from sin through his own efforts or even
with the help of the Old Law. But what is impossible for man is possible for
God. God in fact freed man from sin by sending his own Son, who became man
and conquered sin through his death. If we unite ourselves to the merits of Christ
and obtain a share in his Resurrection, we too can overcome sin.

By assuming human nature the Second Person of the Blessed Trinity chose
to take on the likeness of sinful flesh, but not sin itself. He could have assumed
a glorious body, but "since man has three states – namely, innocence, sin, and
glory – Christ assumed from the state of glory the beatific vision; from the state
of innocence, freedom from sin; and from the state of sin, the necessity of being
subject to the penalties of this life" (St Thomas Aquinas, *Summa theologiae*,

ⁱOr *and as a sin offering.*

Jn 3:5-6
1 Cor 3:16;
12:3
1 Cor 3:23
Gal 2:20
Phil 1:21
1 Pet 4:6
Rom 6:4, 8-11

⁹But you are not in the flesh, you are in the Spirit, if the Spirit of God really dwells in you. Any one who does not have the Spirit of Christ does not belong to him. ¹⁰But if Christ is in you, although your bodies are dead because of sin, your spirits are alive because of righteousness. ¹¹If the Spirit of him who raised Jesus from the dead dwells in you, he who raised Christ Jesus from the dead will give life to your mortal bodies also through his Spirit who dwells in you.

---

autem in carne sunt, Deo placere non possunt. ⁹Vos autem in carne non estis, sed in spiritu, si tamen Spiritus Dei habitat in vobis. Si quis autem Spiritum Christi non habet, hic non est eius. ¹⁰Si autem Christus in vobis est, corpus quidem mortuum est propter peccatum, spiritus vero vita propter iustitiam. ¹¹Quod si Spiritus eius, qui suscitavit Iesum a mortuis, habitat in vobis, qui suscitavit Christum a mortuis, vivificabit et mortalia corpora vestra per

---

III, q. 13, a. 3, ad 2). These disabilities – hunger, fatigue, suffering and especially death – are what constitutes "sinful flesh". By making himself subject to them Christ became like us, thereby making it easier for us to know him and assuring us that he will not abandon us even when we experience these limitations.

10-11. Once he is justified the Christian lives in the grace of God and confidently hopes in his future resurrection; Christ himself lives in him (cf. Gal 2:20; 1 Cor 15:20-23). However, he is not spared the experience of death, a consequence of original sin (cf. Rom 5:12; 6:23). Along with suffering, concupiscence and other limitations, death is still a factor after baptism; it is something which motivates us to struggle and makes us to be like Christ. Almost all commentators interpret the expression "your bodies are dead because of sin" as referring to the fact that, due to sin, the human body is destined to die. So sure is this prospect of death that the Apostle sees the body as "already dead".

St John Chrysostom makes an acute observation: if Christ is living in the Christian, then the divine Spirit, the Third Person of the Trinity, is also present in him. If this divine Spirit is absent, then indeed death reigns supreme, and with it the wrath of God, rejection of his laws, separation from Christ, and expulsion of our Guest. And he adds: "But when one has the Spirit within, what can be lacking? With the Spirit one belongs to Christ, one possesses him, one vies for honour with the angels. With the Spirit, the flesh is crucified, one tastes the delight of an immortal life, one has a pledge of future resurrection and advances rapidly on the path of virtue. This is what Paul calls putting the flesh to death" (*Hom. on Rom*, 13).

Rom 6:6, 18
2 Cor 4:16
Gal 6:8

[12]So then, brethren, we are debtors, not to the flesh, to live according to the flesh – [13]for if you live according to the flesh you will die, but if by the Spirit you put to death the deeds of the body you will live.

Christians are children of God

Eph 4:22-24
Gal 4:4-7
Jn 1:12; 15:15
1 Jn 3:1; 4:18
Rom 5:5

[14]For all who are led by the Spirit of God are sons of God. [15]For you did not receive the spirit of slavery to fall back into fear, but you have received the spirit of sonship. When

inhabitantem Spiritum suum in vobis. [12]Ergo, fratres, debitores sumus, non carni, ut secundum carnem vivamus. [13]Si enim secundum carnem vixeritis, moriemini; si autem Spiritu opera corporis mortificatis, vivetis. [14]Quicumque enim Spiritu Dei aguntur, hi filii Dei sunt. [15]Non enim accepistis spiritum

14-30. The life of a Christian is sharing in the life of Christ, God's only Son. By becoming, through adoption, true children of God we have, so to speak, a right to share also in Christ's inheritance – eternal life in heaven (vv. 14-18). This divine life in us, begun in Baptism through rebirth in the Holy Spirit, will grow under the guidance of this Spirit, who makes us ever more like Christ (vv. 14, 26-27). So, our adoption as sons is already a fact – we already have the first-fruits of the Spirit (v. 23) – but only at the end of time, when our body rises in glory, will our redemption reach its climax (vv. 23-25). Meanwhile we are in a waiting situation – not free from suffering (v. 18), groans (v. 23) and weakness (v. 26) – a situation characterised by a certain tension between what we already possess and are, and what we yearn for. This yearning is something which all creation experiences; by God's will, its destiny is intimately linked to our own, and it too awaits its transformation at the end of the world (vv. 19-22). All this is happening in accordance with a plan which God has, a plan established from all eternity which is unfolding in the course of time under the firm guidance of divine Providence (vv. 28-30).

14-15 Monsignor Escrivá taught thousands of people about this awareness of divine filiation which is such an important part of the Christian vocation. Here is what he says, for example, in *The Way*, 267: "We've got to be convinced that God is always near us. We live as though he were far away, in the heavens high above, and we forget that he is also continually by our side.

"He is there like a loving Father. He loves each of us more than all the mothers in the world can love their children – helping us, inspiring us, blessing . . . and forgiving.

"How often we have misbehaved and then cleared the frowns from our parents' brows, telling them: I won't do it any more! – That same day, perhaps, we fall again . . . – And our father, with feigned harshness in his voice and serious face, reprimands us while in his heart he is moved, realizing our

Gal 3:26-29
Lk 24:26;
22:28-30
Phil 3:10-11
Rev 21:7
Rom 5:2-5
2 Cor 4:17
Col 3:3-4
1 Jn 3:2
we cry, "Abba! Father!" [16]it is the Spirit himself bearing witness with our spirit that we are children of God, [17]and if children, then heirs, heirs of God and fellow heirs with Christ, provided we suffer with him in order that we may also be glorified with him.

[18]I consider that the sufferings of this present time are not worth comparing with the glory that is to be revealed to us.

---

servitutis iterum in timorem, sed accepistis Spiritum adoptionis filiorum, in quo clamamus: "Abba, Pater!" [16]Ipse Spiritus testimonium reddit una cum spiritu nostro quod sumus filii Dei. [17]Si autem filii, et heredes: heredes quidem Dei, coheredes autem Christi; si tamen compatimur, ut et conglorificemur.

---

weakness and thinking: poor child, how hard he tries to behave well!

"We've got to be filled, to be imbued with the idea that our Father, and very much our Father, is God who is both near us and in heaven."

This awareness of God as Father was something which the first chancellor of the University of Navarre experienced with special intensity one day in 1931: "They were difficult times, from a human point of view, but even so I was quite sure of the impossible – this impossibility which you can now see as an accomplished fact. I felt God acting within me with overriding force, filling my heart and bringing to my lips this tender invocation – *Abba! Pater!* I was out in the street, in a tram: being out in the street is no hindrance for our contemplative dialogue; for us, the hustle and bustle of the world is a place for prayer" (S. Bernal, *Monsignor Josemaría Escrivá de Balaguer*, p. 214).

18. "Who is there then", St Cyprian comments, "who will not strive to attain so great a glory, by making himself God's friend, to rejoice immediately with Christ, to receive the divine rewards after the pains and sufferings of this life? If it is glorious for soldiers of this world to return to their fatherland victorious after defeating the enemy, how much greater and more pleasing glory will there not be, once the devil is overcome, to return victorious to heaven [...]; to bear with one the trophies of victory [. . .]; to sit at God's side when he comes to judge, to be a co-heir with Christ, to be made equal to the angels and to enjoy with the Patriarchs, with the Apostles and with the Prophets the possession of the Kingdom of heaven [. . .]. A spirit secure in these supernatural thoughts stays strong and firm, and is unmoved by the attacks of demons and the threats of this world, a spirit strengthened by a solid and confident faith in the future [. . .]. It leaves here with dignity and confidence, rejoicing in one moment to close its eyes which looked on men and the world, and to see God and Christ! [. . .]. These are the thoughts the mind should have, this is how it ought to reflect, night and day. If persecution finds God's soldier prepared in this manner, there will be no power capable of overcoming a spirit so equipped for the struggle" (*Epist. ad Fortunatum*, 13).

¹⁹For the creation waits with eager longing for the revealing of the sons of God; ²⁰for the creation was subjected to futility, not of its own will but by the will of him who subjected it in hope; ²¹because the creation itself will be set

Gen 3:17-19;
5:29
Eccles 1:2
Hos 4:3
2 Pet 3:12-13
Rev 21:1

---

¹⁸Existimo enim quod non sunt condignae passiones huius temporis ad futuram gloriam, quae revelanda est in nobis. ¹⁹Nam exspectatio creaturae revelationem filiorum Dei exspectat; ²⁰vanitati enim creatura subiecta est, non volens sed propter eum, qui subiecit, in spem, ²¹quia et ipsa creatura liberabitur a servitute

---

19-21. To make his point more vividly St Paul, in a metaphor, depicts the whole of creation, the material universe, as a living person, groaning in pain impatiently waiting for a future event, raising its head, straining to see something appear on the horizon.

The material world is indeed, through God's design, linked to man and his destiny. "Sacred Scripture teaches that man was created 'in the image of God,' as able to know and love his Creator, and as set by him over all earthly creatures that he might rule them, and make use of them, while glorifying God" (Vatican II, *Gaudium et spes*, 12). The futility to which creation is subject is not so much corruption and death as the disorder resulting from sin. According to God's plan material things should be resources which enable man to attain the ultimate goal of his existence. By using them in a disordered way, disconnecting them from God, man turns them into instruments of sin, which therefore are subject to the consequences of sin.

"Are we of the twentieth century not convinced of the overpoweringly eloquent words of the Apostle of the Gentiles concerning the 'creation (that) has been groaning in travail together until now' and 'waits with eager longing for the revealing of the sons of God', the creation that 'was subjected to futility'? Does not the previously unknown immense progress – which has taken place especially in the course of this century – in the field of man's dominion over the world itself reveal – to a previously unknown degree – that manifold subjection 'to futility'? [. . .] The world of the previously unattained conquests of science and technology – is it not also the world 'groaning in travail' that 'waits with eager longing for the revealing of the sons of God'?" (John Paul II, *Redemptor hominis*, 8).

Re-establishment of the order willed by God, bringing the whole world to fulfil its true purpose, is the particular mission of the Holy Spirit, the Giver of Life, the true Lord of history: "'The arm of the Lord has not been shortened.' God is no less powerful today than he was in other times; his love for man is no less true. Our faith teaches us that all creation, the movement of the earth and the other heavenly bodies, the good actions of creatures and all the good that has been achieved in history, in short everything, comes from God and is directed toward him.

"The action of the Holy Spirit may pass unnoticed because God does not reveal to us his plans, and because man's sin obscures the divine gifts. But faith

free from its bondage to decay and obtain the glorious liberty of the children of God. ²²We know that the whole creation has been groaning in travail together until now; ²³and not only the creation, but we ourselves, who have the first fruits of the Spirit, groan inwardly as we wait for adoption as sons, the redemption of our bodies. ²⁴For in this hope we were saved. Now hope that is seen is not hope. For who hopes for what he sees? ²⁵But if we hope for what we do not see, we wait for it with patience.

²⁶Likewise the Spirit helps us in our weakness; for we do not know how to pray as we ought, but the Spirit himself intercedes for us with sighs too deep for words. ²⁷And he who searches the hearts of men knows what is the mind of the Spirit, becausej the Spirit intercedes for the saints according to the will of God.

²⁸We know that in everything God works for goodk with those who love him,l who are called according to his pur-

2 Cor 5:2-7
Gal 5:5
Phil 3:20-21
Heb 11:1

Rom 5:5
1 Cor 2:10-13
Gal 4:6
Ps 139:1
Jer 11:20

Eph 1:4-14

---

corruptionis in libertatem gloriae filiorum Dei. ²²Scimus enim quod omnis creatura congemiscit et comparturit usque adhuc; ²³non solum autem, sed et nos ipsi primitias Spiritus habentes, et ipsi intra nos gemimus adoptionem filiorum exspectantes, redemptionem corporis nostri. ²⁴Spe enim salvi facti sumus; spes autem, quae videtur, non est spes; nam, quod videt quis, sperat? ²⁵Si autem, quod non videmus, speramus, per patientiam exspectamus. ²⁶Similiter autem et Spiritus adiuvat infirmitatem nostram; nam quid oremus, sicut oportet, nescimus, sed ipse Spiritus interpellat gemitibus inenarrabilibus; ²⁷qui autem scrutatur corda, scit quid desideret Spiritus, quia secundum Deum postulat pro sanctis. ²⁸Scimus autem quoniam diligentibus Deum omnia

---

tells us that God is always acting. He has created us and maintains us in existence, and he is leading all creation by his grace towards the glorious freedom of the children of God" (J. Escrivá, *Christ is passing by*, 130).

28. Awareness of God as Father helps us see all the events of our life as orchestrated by the lovable Will of God. Our Father gives us what is best for us and expects us to discover his paternal love in adverse as well as in favourable events. "Notice", St Bernard points out, "that he does not say that things suit our whims but that they work for our good. They serve not caprice but usefulness; not pleasure but salvation; not what we desire but what is good for us. In that sense everything works for our good, even death itself, even sin [...]. Is it not the case that sins do good to him who on their account becomes more

jOr *that.*
kOther ancient authorities read *in everything he works for good,* or *everything works for good.*
lGreek *God.*

118

pose. ²⁹For those whom he foreknew he also predestined to
be conformed to the image of his Son, in order that he might
be the first-born among many brethren. ³⁰And those whom
he predestined he also called; and those whom he called he
also justified; and those whom he justified he also glorified.

Acts 13:48
1 Cor 15:20-23
Phil 3:21
Col 1:18
Heb 1:6
1 Cor 13
Ps 118:6

cooperantur in bonum, his, qui secundum propositum vocati sunt. ²⁹Nam, quos
praescivit, et praedestinavit conformes fieri imaginis Filii eius, ut sit ipse
primogenitus in multis fratribus; ³⁰quos autem praedestinavit, hos et vocavit;

· humble, more fervent, more solicitous, more on guard, more prudent?" (*De
fallacia et brevitate vitae*, 6). If we have this optimistic, hopeful attitude, we
will overcome every difficulty we meet: "The whole world seems to be coming
down on top of you. Whichever way you turn you find no way out. This time,
it is impossible to overcome the difficulties.

"But, have you again forgotten that God is your Father? – all-powerful,
infinitely wise, full of mercy. He would never send you anything evil. That
thing that is worrying you is good for you, even though those earthbound eyes
of yours may not be able to see it now.

"*Omnia in bonum!* Lord, once again and always, may your most wise Will
be done!" (J. Escrivá, *The Way of the Cross*, IX, 4).

29. Christ is called the "first-born" for many reasons. He is "the first-born
of all creation" (Col 1:15) because he is eternally begotten and because "all
things were made through him" (Jn 1:3). He is also the new Adam and therefore
the head of the human race in the work of redemption (cf. 1 Cor 15:22, 45). He
is "the first-born from the dead" (cf. Col 1:18; Rev 1:5) and therefore is the
head of all those who have reached heaven and all who are awaiting their future
resurrection (1 Cor 15:20, 23). Finally, he is the "first-born among many
brethren" because, in the order of grace, he gives us a share in his divine
sonship: by means of habitual grace – "sanctifying" grace – we become
children of God and brothers and sisters of Jesus Christ. "For, just as God chose
to communicate to others his natural goodness, giving them a share in that
goodness, so that he might be not only good but also the author of good things;
so the Son of God chose to communicate to others a sonship like his own, so
that he might be not only a son, but the first-born of many sons" (St Thomas
Aquinas, *Commentary on Rom, ad loc.*).

This remarkable fact is what leads the Christian to imitate Christ: our divine
sonship moves us to reflect the words and gestures of his Only-begotten Son.

"Lord, help me decide to tear off, through penance, this pitiful mask I have
fashioned with my wretched doings. ... Then, and only then, by following the
path of contemplation and atonement, will my life begin to copy faithfully the
features of your life. We will find ourselves becoming more and more like you.

"We will be other Christs, Christ himself, *ipse Christus*" (J. Escrivá, *The
Way of the Cross*, VI).

Trust in God

³¹What then shall we say to this? If God is for us, who is against us? ³²He who did not spare his own Son but gave him up for us all, will he not also give us all things with

---

et quos vocavit, hos et iustificavit; quos autem iustificavit, illos et glorificavit. ³¹Quid ergo dicemus ad haec? Si Deus pro nobis, quis contra nos? ³²Qui Filio

---

31-39. The elect will emerge unscathed and victorious from all attacks, dangers and sufferings and will do so not through their own efforts but by virtue of the all-powerful aid of him who has loved them from all eternity and who did not hesitate to have his own Son die for their salvation. It is true that as long as we are on this earth we cannot attain salvation, but we are assured that we will attain it precisely because God will not withhold all the graces we need to obtain this happy outcome: all that is needed is that we desire to receive this divine help. Nothing that happens to us can separate us from the Lord – not fear of death or love of life, not the bad angels or devils, not the princes or the powers of this world, nor the sufferings we undergo or which threaten us nor the worst that might befall us. "Paul himself", St John Chrysostom reminds us, "had to contend with numerous enemies. The barbarians attacked him; his custodians laid traps for him; even the faithful, sometimes in great numbers, rose against him; yet Paul always came out victorious. We should not forget that the Christian who is faithful to the laws of his God will defeat both men and Satan himself" (*Hom. on Rom*, 15).

This is the attitude which enables us to live as children of God, who fear neither life nor death: "Our Lord wants us to be in the world and to love the world but without being worldly. Our Lord wants us to remain in this world – which is now so mixed up and where the clamour of lust and disobedience and purposeless rebellion can be heard – to teach people to live with joy [...]. Don't be afraid of the paganised world: our Lord has in fact chosen us to be leaven, salt and light in this world. Don't be worried. The world won't harm you unless you want it to. No enemy of our soul can do anything if we don't consent. And we won't consent, with the grace of God and the protection of our Mother in heaven" (S. Bernal, *Monsignor Josemaría Escrivá de Balaguer*, p. 213).

31. This exclamation of the Apostle vividly reveals the full extent of the love of God the Father, who not only listens to our prayers but anticipates our needs. God is with us, he is always by our side. This is a cry expressing confidence and optimism, despite our personal wretchedness; it is firmly based on our sense of divine sonship. "Clothed in grace, we can cross mountains (cf. Ps 103:10), and climb the hill of our Christian duty, without halting on the way. If we use these resources with a firm purpose and beg our Lord to grant us an ever increasing hope, we shall possess the infectious joy of those who know they are children of God: 'If God is for us, who is against us?' (Rom 8:31) Let us be optimists. Moved by the power of hope, we shall fight to wipe away the trail

him? [33]Who shall bring any charge against God's elect? It is God who justifies; [34]who is to condemn? Is it Christ Jesus, who died, yes, who was raised from the dead, who is at the right hand of God, who indeed intercedes for us?[m] [35]Who shall separate us from the love of Christ? Shall tribulation, or distress, or persecution, or famine, or nakedness, or peril, or sword? [36]As it is written,

"For thy sake we are being killed all the day long;
we are regarded as sheep to be slaughtered."

[37]No, in all these things we are more than conquerors through him who loved us. [38]For I am sure that neither death, nor life, nor angels, nor principalities, nor things present, nor things to come, nor powers, [39]nor height, nor depth, nor anything else in all creation, will be able to separate us from the love of God in Christ Jesus our Lord.

Is 50:8-9
Ps 109:1
Acts 2:23
Heb 1:3; 7:25; 12:2
1 Jn 2:1

Ps 44:12
1 Cor 15:30
2 Cor 411
2 Tim 3:12
Jn 16:33

---

suo non pepercit, sed pro nobis omnibus tradidit illum, quomodo non etiam cum illo omnia nobis donabit? [33]Quis accusabit adversus electos Dei? Deus, qui iustificat? [34]Quis est qui condemnet? Christus Iesus, qui mortuus est, immo qui suscitatus est, qui et est ad dexteram Dei, qui etiam interpellat pro nobis? [35]Quis nos separabit a caritate Christi? Tribulatio an angustia an persecutio an fames an nuditas an periculum an gladius? [36]Sicut scriptum est: *"Propter te mortificamur tota die, aestimati sumus ut oves occisionis."* [37]Sed in his omnibus supervincimus per eum, qui dilexit nos. [38]Certus sum enim quia neque mors neque vita neque angeli neque principatus neque instantia neque futura neque virtutes [39]neque altitudo neque profundum neque alia quaelibet creatura poterit nos separari a caritate Dei, quae est in Christo Iesu Domino nostro.

---

of filth and slime left by the sowers of hatred. We shall find a new joyful perspective to the world, seeing that it has sprung forth beautiful and fair from the hands of God. We shall give it back to him with that same beauty" (J. Escrivá, *Friends of God*, 219).

38-39. "Angels", "principalities": names of different angelic hierarchies (cf. Eph 1:21; 3:10); also a possible reference to fallen angels, demons (cf. 1 Cor 15:24; Eph 6:12). "Powers" can mean the same as "angels" and "principalities".

"Height" and "depth" may refer to cosmic forces which, in the culture of that time, were thought to have some influence over the lives of men.

By listing these powerful superior forces (real or imaginary) St Paul is making the point that nothing and nobody, no created thing, is stronger than God's love for us.

[m]Or *It is Christ Jesus . . . for us.*

9

GOD'S PLAN FOR THE CHOSEN PEOPLE

The privileges of Israel and God's fidelity

¹I am speaking the truth in Christ, I am not lying; my conscience bears me witness to the Holy Spirit, ²that I have great sorrow and unceasing anguish in my heart. ³For I could wish that I myself were accursed and cut off from Christ for the sake of my brethren, my kinsmen by race. ⁴They are Israelites, and to them belong the sonship, the

Ex 32:32

Ex 4:22
Deut 7:6; 14:1-2

---

¹Veritatem dico in Christo, non mentior, testimonium mihi perhibente conscientia mea in Spiritu Sancto, ²quoniam tristitia est mihi magna et continuus dolor cordi meo. ³Optarem enim ipse ego anathema esse a Christo pro fratribus meis, cognatis meis secundum carnem, ⁴qui sunt Israelitae, quorum adoptio est

---

Chaps. 9-11 In these chapters – as we indicate in the title given to this section of the letter – St Paul deals with "God's plan for the chosen people." The Apostle explains that Israel, as a people, in general has failed to accept the Gospel despite the fact that God's promises of salvation were made to the Jews in the first instance.

3. There is an apparent contradiction between what is said here – "I could wish that I myself was accursed and cut off from Christ' – and what is said earlier (cf. 8:31ff) about nothing being able to separate us from the love of Christ. The two ideas in fact complement one another. God's love moves us to love others so intensely that we are ready to suffer anything if it means the conversion of others to God. Paul is not referring to permanent separation from God, that is, eternal damnation, but to being ready to renounce any material or spiritual favour God might grant us. This means that we should be ready to bear public opprobrium and be taken for evildoers, as Jesus was. Some writers have interpreted the verse as meaning that the Apostle is even ready to renounce eternal happiness, but obviously what we have here is typical oriental exaggeration, rather like what Moses said when he interceded with God on behalf of those Israelites who had fallen into idolatry: "[If thou wilt not forgive their sin] blot me, I pray thee, out of thy book which thou hast written" (Ex 32:32). Both Moses and Paul know that God loves them and protects them and that the vision of God necessarily involves the indescribable happiness of heaven, but they want to make it plain that they put the salvation of the chosen people ahead of their own personal advantage.

4-6. The Israelites are the descendants of Jacob, to whom God gave the name

glory, the covenants, the giving of the law, the worship, and the promises; [5]to them belong the patriarchs, and of their race, according to the flesh, is the Christ, who is God over all, blessed for ever.[n] Amen.

[6]But it is not as though the word of God had failed. For not all who are descended from Israel belong to Israel, [7]and not all are children of Abraham because they are his descendants; but "Through Isaac shall your descendants be named." [8]This means that it is not the children of the flesh who are the children of God, but the children of the promise are reckoned as descendants. [9]For this is what the promise said, "About this time I will return and Sarah shall have a

Rom 1:3
Mt 1
Lk 3:23-34
Jn 1:1
Rom 3:3-4
Num 23:19
Is 55:10-11
Rom 2:28-29
Gen 21:12
Mt 3:9

Gen 18:10

---

filiorum et gloria et testamenta et legislatio et cultus et promissiones, [5]quorum sunt patres, et ex quibus Christus secundum carnem: qui est super omnia Deus benedictus in saecula. Amen. [6]Non autem quod exciderit verbum Dei. Non enim omnes, qui ex Israel, hi sunt Israel; [7]neque quia semen sunt Abrahae, omnes filii, sed: *"In Isaac vocabitur tibi semen."* [8]Id est, non qui filii carnis, hi filii Dei, sed qui filii sunt promissionis, aestimantur semen; [9]promissionis enim verbum hoc est: *"Secundum hoc tempus veniam, et erit Sarae filius."* [10]Non

---

Israel (cf. Gen 32:29). The fact that they are children of Israel is the basis of the privileges which God bestows on them in the course of Salvation History – firstly, their status as the people of God, chosen as the adoptive sons of Yahweh (cf. Ex 4:22; Deut 7:6); also their being given the "glory" of God who dwelt in their midst (cf. Ex 25:8; Deut 4:7; Jn 1:14); their good fortune in being able to offer worship proper to the one true God, and in receiving from him the Law of Moses, which spelt out the principles of the natural moral law and revealed other aspects of God's will; and, finally, their being the recipients of oft-repeated messianic promises.

The remarkable honour bestowed on the chosen people is to be seen most clearly in the fact that God himself chose to assume a human nature which had all the characteristics of the Israelite race. Jesus Christ, as true man, is an Israelite "according to the flesh", and he is true God because he is "God above all, blessed for ever."

Similar statements made in other epistles of St Paul about the mystery of the Incarnation manifest Christ's two natures and one Person (cf. Rom 1:3-4; Phil 2:6-7; Col 2:9; Tit 2:13-14).

In the present passage, this statement appears in the form of a "doxology" or paean of praise to God, one of the most solemn ways in which Yahweh is exalted in the Old Testament (cf. Ps 41:14; 72:19; 106:48; Neh 9:5; Dan 2:20; etc.). By calling Jesus Christ "God, blessed for ever" his divinity is being declared in a most explicit manner.

[n]Or *Christ. God who is over all be blessed for ever.*

Gen 25:21-23 son." [10]And not only so, but also when Rebecca had conceived children by one man, our forefather Isaac, [11]though they were not yet born and had done nothing either good or bad, in order that God's purpose of election might continue, not because of works but because of his call, [12]she was told, Mal 1:2-3 "The elder will serve the younger." [13]As it is written, "Jacob, I loved, but Esau I hated."

---

solum autem, sed et Rebecca ex uno concubitum habens, Isaac patre nostro; [11]cum enim nondum nati fuissent aut aliquid egissent bonum aut malum, ut secundum electionem propositum Dei maneret, [12]non ex operibus sed ex vocante dictum est ei: *"Maior serviet minori"*; [13]sicut scriptum est: *"Iacob*

10-13. Contrary to expectations and without reference to the law of primogeniture which applied in the time of the Patriarchs, God selected not Esau, the first-born, but his twin brother Jacob to be the heir of the promise made to Abraham and his descendants; what the Lord told their mother Rebecca – "the elder shall serve the younger" (Gen 25:23) – came about when Isaac blessed Jacob and made him master of his brother (cf. Gen 27:29). This election, made before the twins were born, demonstrates that the Patriarch's calling was entirely independent of anything Jacob might do to deserve it. According to the prophet Malachi (Mal 1:2-3) the fact that God gave preference to the second son should always serve as a reminder to the Jews (descendants of the same Jacob) that their calling to be the chosen people was a sign of Yahweh's love of predilection: "I have loved Jacob but I have hated Esau"; this should lead them to be grateful to God.

These examples taken from Sacred History help the Apostle explain to the Jews why they should not be surprised to see the Gentiles being called to the faith.

Commenting on this passage, St Thomas Aquinas points out the difference between the way we love and the way God loves: "Man's will is moved to love by the attraction of the good he finds in the thing loved; that is why he chooses it in preference to something else [. . .]. God's will, on the other hand, is the cause of every good to be found in a created thing [. . .]. Hence God does not love a person because he finds in him something which leads him to choose that person: he chooses him rather than others because he loves him" (*Commentary on Rom, ad loc*).

Our Lord showed the Apostles the gratuitous nature of vocation when he told them, "You did not choose me, but I chose you" (Jn 15:16).

In fact, the example of Jacob, the calling of the Apostles, St Paul's own vocation and that of so many others in the course of history show that God is pleased to select precisely those whom men might consider least suitable: "You realize you are weak. And so indeed you are. In spite of that – rather, just because of that – God has chosen you.

Israel's vocation

Deut 32:4
Ex 33:19
Ps 147:10-11
Eph 2:8
Ex 9:16

¹⁴What shall we say then? Is there injustice on God's part? By no means! ¹⁵For he says to Moses, "I will have mercy on whom I have mercy, and I will have compassion on whom I have compassion." ¹⁶So it depends not upon man's will or exertion, but upon God's mercy. ¹⁷For the scripture says to Pharaoh, "I have raised you up for the very purpose

---

dilexi, Esau autem odio habui." ¹⁴Quid ergo dicemus? Numquid iniustitia apud Deum? Absit! ¹⁵Moysi enim dicit: *"Miserebor, cuius misereor, et misericordiam praestabo, cui misericordiam praesto."* ¹⁶Igitur non volentis neque currentis, sed miserentis Dei. ¹⁷Dicit enim Scriptura pharaoni: *"In hoc ipsum excitavi te, ut ostendam in te virtutem meam, et ut annuntietur nomen meum in*

"He always uses inadequate instruments, so that the 'work' will be seen to be his. Of you, he only asks docility" (J. Escrivá, *The Way*, 475).

13. The expression "I have hated Esau" must be interpreted in the light of the constant teaching of Sacred Scripture: God loves everything that exists and does not hate anyone or anything he has made (cf. Wis 11:24). Therefore, God also loves Esau; but if we compare this love and his very special love for Jacob, the former looks like hatred. This is a very common Semitic way of speaking; our Lord uses it sometimes – for example, when he compares the love he is owed with the love one owes one's parents (cf. Mt 10:37 and Lk 14:26).

14-33. The selection of the people of Israel in preference to all other nations, the hardening of Pharaoh's heart and the punishment meted out to him, individual salvation or rejection as indicated by the vessel of clay: these are all examples which point to the profound mystery of predestination. Our faith teaches us that God, who is almighty and all-knowing, not only knows all future events but by his infallible will arranges them to achieve his design: divine Wisdom, Sacred Scripture tells us, "reaches mightily from one end of the earth to the other, and she orders all things well" (Wis 8:1).

God ordains from all eternity that rational creatures shall attain eternal bliss with the help of grace and with their own free cooperation. The essence of the mystery of predestination lies in the fact that our limited minds cannot fully understand how the inevitability of the success of God's plan fits in with human freedom. Human freedom must play its part "because the beverage of man's salvation certainly contains the power to benefit all, but if one does not drink it, one is not healed" (Council of Quierzy, A.D. 853, *Doctrina de libero arbitrio hominis et de praedestinatione*, chap. 4). Nor is it possible for us to understand the mystery of how God can allow some people to be rejected despite his desire that all should be saved.

Because we are free agents, we might think that salvation or repudiation is entirely dependent on ourselves; on the other hand, if God's will really is infallible, then salvation or rejection seems to depend entirely on his choice. In the process of dealing with these two erroneous positions, the Church has, over the centuries, spelt out its teaching in greater detail. Against those who over-emphasize the part played by human freedom, the Magisterium has stated that "the free will of man was made so weak and unsteady through the sin of the first man that, after the Fall, no one could love God as was required, or believe in God, or perform good works for God unless the grace of divine mercy anticipated him" (Second Council of Orange, *De gratia,* conclusion). Quoting St Augustine, that Council went on to say that when men freely follow the will of God, even when they do what they do voluntarily, their will nevertheless is the will of Him who is disposing and ordaining what they desire (cf. *ibid.*, can. 23; *In Ioann. Evang.*, 19, 19). To put it more graphically: loving God is a gift of God.

"Almighty God desires that all men without exception be saved (cf. 1 Tim 2:4), though not all may be saved. That some are saved is due to the gift given by Him who saves; that some perish, however, is because they deserved to perish" (Council of Quierzy, *Doctrina de libero arbitrio* . . . , chap. 3). Elsewhere the Magisterium teaches: "We confidently believe that the elect are predestined to life and the reprobate to death; but in this election of those to be saved, the mercy of God is prior to merit; whereas in those who will perish, the punishment they deserve [for their sins] precedes the just judgment of God. ... But that some are predestined to evil by God, that is, as if they could do nothing else, not only do we not believe, but if there are any who do hold that opinion, we, with the Council of Orange, heartily shun them" (Third Council of Valence, *De praedestinatione*, can. 3).

The mystery of predestination reveals three very encouraging truths. Firstly, the absolute freedom and generosity of God in granting us his grace without any merit on our part: all men are sinners against him (cf. 3:9ff), yet out of his goodness and mercy he offers them his love and justifies them (vv. 15-16). Secondly, God's salvific will extends to all mankind: "he desires all men to be saved" (1 Tim 2:4), and Christ, sent by the Father to effect our Redemption, died on the Cross for all mankind. Thirdly, God, in the work of our salvation, counts on our free cooperation and inspires us, through his grace, to cooperate. This means that man can always resist the grace God gives him. The work of our redemption, therefore, is a continuous interplay between divine grace, which takes the initiative, and man's response, with man's free decision being prepared by God. See also note on v. 18 below.

Therefore, we have no reason to fear God: he is a Father who has no desire to reject his children. St Augustine, after exploring this mystery, ends with an exhortation to hope and to prayer: "You, therefore, ought to hope that this same perseverance in obedience will come to you from the Father of lights (cf. Jas 1:17), from whom comes every good endowment and every perfect gift, and you should ask for this in your prayers each day, and when doing so you should be confident that you are not far from the predestination of his people, for he it is who enables you to do as you are doing" (*De dono perseverantiae*, 22, 62).

126

Rom 9:21

of showing my power in you, so that my name may be
proclaimed in all the earth. ¹⁸So then he has mercy upon
whomever he wills, and he hardens the heart of whomever
he wills.

¹⁹You will say to me then, "Why does he still find fault?
For who can resist his will?" ²⁰But who are you, a man, to
answer back to God? Will what is moulded say to its
moulder, "Why have you made me thus?" ²¹Has the potter

Is 29:16; 45:9;
64-7
Jer 18:1-6
Wis 12:12; 15:7
Sir 33:12-13

---

universa terra." ¹⁸Ergo, cuius vult, miseretur, et quem vult, indurat. ¹⁹Dices
itaque mihi: "Quid ergo adhuc queritur? Voluntati enim eius quis restitit?" ²⁰O
homo, sed tu quis es, qui respondeas Deo? *Numquid dicet figmentum ei, qui se
finxit*: "Quid me fecisti sic?" ²¹An non habet potestatem *figulus luti* ex eadem

---

18. In freely distributing his grace unequally among men, God desires this
variety to contribute to the beauty and perfection of creation. This unequal
distribution of grace also includes the gift of final perseverance, which is not
something to which man has a right: God gives it to whomever he chooses.
However, God grants everyone the grace of conversion and repentance and
opens to all the gates of salvation; if a person in the exercise of his freedom
rejects these gifts, God respects this human decision.

Only in the sense that he allows it to happen can one say that God is the cause
of resistance to grace; strictly speaking, the sinner is entirely responsible for
his hardness of heart. St Thomas Aquinas uses this comparison to explain the
matter: "Although the sun, for its part, enlightens all bodies, if it encounters an
obstacle in a body it leaves the body in darkness, as happens to a house whose
window-shutters are closed. Clearly, the sun is not the cause of the house being
darkened, since it does not act of its own accord in failing to light up the interior
of the house; the cause of the darkness is the person who closed the shutters.
So God chooses not to give [the light of] grace to those who put an obstacle in
its way" (*Summa theologiae*, I-II, q. 79, a.3).

The coincidence in God of infinite justice and infinite mercy is another
unfathomable mystery. All that we really need to remember is that God always
offers man the opportunity to change and repent. The Church invites us,
therefore, not to close our heart to God's invitations: "O that today you would
hearken to his voice! Harden not your hearts" (Ps 95:8).

20-23. This image of the potter making vessels for different uses is to be
found in a number of places in Sacred Scripture. Every Jew was very familiar
with it. In the Prophets it refers to God's power over human events: the potter
is God and the vessel the chosen people (cf. Is 29:16; 45:9; Jer 18:6ff). In the
Wisdom Books the same idea is applied to the individual Israelite, who is
subject to God in the same way as clay is to the hands of the potter, because
"all men are from the ground, and Adam was created of the dust. In the fullness

127

Rom 2:4
Prov 16:4

Eph 2:1-7
Rom 8:29

Hos 2:1, 25
1 Pet 2:10

Hos 1:9

Is 10:22-23
Rom 11:5

no right over the clay, to make out of the same lump one vessel for beauty and another for menial use? [22]What if God, desiring to show his wrath and to make known his power, has endured with much patience the vessels of wrath made for destruction, [23]in order to make known the riches of his glory for the vessels of mercy, which he has prepared beforehand for glory, [24]even us whom he has called, not from the Jews only but also from the Gentiles? [25]As indeed he says in Hosea,

"Those who were not my people
I will call 'my people',
and her who was not beloved
I will call 'my beloved'."

[26]And in the very place where it was said to them 'You are not my people',
they will be called 'sons of the living God'."

[27]And Isaiah cries out concerning Israel: "Though the

---

massa facere aliud quidem vas in honorem, aliud vero in ignominiam? [22]Quod si volens Deus ostendere iram et notam facere potentiam suam sustinuit in multa patientia vasa irae aptata in interitum [23]et ut ostenderet divitias gloriae suae in vasa misericordiae, quae praeparavit in gloriam, [24]quos et vocavit nos non solum ex Iudaeis sed etiam ex gentibus? [25]Sicut et in Osee dicit: *Vocabo Non plebem meam Plebem meam et Non dilectam Dilectam.* [26]*Et erit: in loco, ubi dictum est eis: 'Non plebs mea vos', ibi vocabuntur filii Dei vivi."* [27]Isaias autem clamat pro Israel: *"Si fuerit numerus filiorum Israel tamquam arena maris,*

---

of his knowledge the Lord distinguished them and appointed their different ways [. . .]. As clay in the hand of the potter – for all his ways are as he pleases – so men are in the hand of him who made them, to give them as he decides" (Sir 33:10-13; cf. Wis 15:7). One cannot call God to account for his actions; his Will far exceeds man's capacity to grasp it. However, this does not mean that our personal freedom and responsibility are thereby lessened. We can rely on God not willing anything but our good.

Referring to the metaphor of the potter, St John Chrysostom comments: "By saying this the Apostle does not mean to deny free will: he simply wants to show that we need to be very obedient to God. As regards asking God to explain his actions, we should be like clay: we should not ask questions or even form them in our mind; instead we should have the pliability of clay which yields to the potter's touch and becomes what he wants it to become [. . .]. Worship God and be as docile as clay [. . .]. God never does anything blindly or in an arbitrary way, but you may not be able to discover the hidden and wise purpose of his actions" (*Hom. on Rom*, 16).

number of the sons of Israel be as the sand of the sea, only
a remnant of them will be saved; [28]for the Lord will execute
his sentence upon the earth with rigour and dispatch." [29]And
as Isaiah predicted,

Is 1:9

"If the Lord of hosts had not left us children,
we would have fared like Sodom and been made like
Gomorrah."

[30]What shall we say, then? That Gentiles who did not
pursue righteousness have attained it, that is, righteousness
through faith; [31]but that Israel who pursued the righteousness which is based on law did not succeed in fulfilling that
law. [32]Why? Because they did not pursue it through faith,
but as if it were based on works. They have stumbled over
the stumbling stone, [33]as it is written,

Rom 10:20-21;
11:7

Is 8:14-15

Is 28:16-17
Ps 118:22-23
Mt 21:42, 44
Eph 2:20
1 Pet 2:6-8

"Behold, I am laying in Zion a stone that will make men
stumble,
a rock that will make them fall;
and he who believes in him will not be put to shame."

---

*reliquiae salvae fient. [28]Verbum enim consummans et brevians faciet Dominus
super terram." [29]Et sicut praedixit Isaias: "Nisi Dominus Sabaoth reliquisset
nobis semen, sicut Sodoma facti essemus et sicut Gomorra similes fuissemus."
[30]Quid ergo dicemus? Quod gentes, quae non sectabantur iustitiam, appre-
henderunt iustitiam, iustitiam autem, quae ex fide est; [31]Israel vero sectans
legem iustitiae in legem non pervenit. [32]Quare? Quia non ex fide sed quasi ex
operibus; offenderunt in lapidem offensionis, [33]sicut scriptum est: "Ecce pono
in Sion lapidem offensionis et petram scandali; et qui credit in eo, non
confundetur."*

30-33. The true Israel is not in fact those descended from Abraham
"according to the flesh" (cf. Rom 9:7), who seek to justify themselves through
works rather than through faith; the true Israel is the "remnant" of which the
prophets spoke, that portion of Israel which, following Abraham's example,
lives by faith, and those Gentiles who – like the "remnant" of Israel – accept
the Gospel of Jesus Christ. Thus, the Church, made up of one portion of Israel
and another of Gentiles, is the true Israel, which from the time of Christ onwards
is constituted not by links of human descent but by spiritual ties.

10

Israel's infidelity

¹Brethren, my heart's desire and prayer to God for them is
that they may be saved. ²I bear them witness that they have
a zeal for God, but it is not enlightened. ³For, being ignorant
of the righteousness that comes from God, and seeking to
establish their own, they do not submit to God's righteousness. ⁴For Christ is the end of the law, that everyone who
has faith may be justified.

⁵Moses writes that the man who practises the righteousness which is based on the law shall live by it. ⁶But the
righteousness based on faith says, Do not say in your heart,
"Who will ascend into heaven?" (that is, to bring Christ
down) ⁷or "Who will descend into the abyss?" (that is, to
bring Christ up from the dead). ⁸But what does it say? The
word is near you, on your lips and in your heart (that is, the

Acts 22:3

*Rom 9:31-32
Phil 3:9*

*Mt 5:17
Jn 1:17-18
Gal 3:24*

*Lev 18:5
Gal 3:12*

*Deut 9:4;
30:12-14
Eph 4:7-10*

1 Pet 3:19

¹Fratres, voluntas quidem cordis mei et obsecratio ad Deum pro illis in salutem.
²Testimonium enim perhibeo illis quod aemulationem Dei habent, sed non
secundum scientiam; ³ignorantes enim Dei iustitiam et suam iustitiam
quaerentes statuere, iustitiae Dei non sunt subiecti; ⁴finis enim legis Christus
ad iustitiam omni credenti. ⁵Moyses enim scribit de iustitia, quae ex lege est:
"Qui fecerit homo, vivet in eis." ⁶Quae autem ex fide est iustitia, sic dicit: *"Ne
dixeris* in corde tuo: *Quis ascendet in caelum?"*, id est Christum deducere; ⁷aut:
"Quis descendet in abyssum?", hoc est Christum ex mortuis revocare. ⁸Sed quid
dicit? *"Prope te est verbum, in ore tuo et in corde tuo"*; hoc est verbum fidei,
quod praedicamus. ⁹Quia si confitearis in ore tuo: *"Dominum Iesum!"*, et in

6-8. St Paul here quotes and applies some words from Deuteronomy: "This
commandment," Moses tells the people of Israel, "which I command you this
day is not too hard for you, neither is it far off. It is not in heaven, that you
should say, 'Who will go up for us to heaven, and bring it to us, that we may
hear it and do it? [. . .] Who will go over the sea for us, and bring it to us, that
we may hear it and do it?' But the word is very near you; it is in your mouth
and in your heart, so that you can do it" (Deut 30:11-14). The law which God
handed to Moses, then, clearly revealed his will and made it much easier to
fulfil. By the Incarnation, the Word of God became flesh and dwelt among us
and showed us the way to God. For the Christian the life and teaching of the
Word made flesh are divine precepts and commandments. Through his
Incarnation Jesus Christ brought us grace and truth; by rising from the dead he
conquered death; and by ascending into heaven and, with the Father, sending
the Holy Spirit, he perfected his work of redemption.

word of faith which we preach); [9]because, if you confess
with your lips that Jesus is Lord and believe in your heart
that God raised him from the dead, you will be saved. [10]For
man believes with his heart and so is justified, and he
confesses with his lips and so is saved. [11]The scripture says,
"No one who believes in him will be put to shame." [12]For
there is no distinction between Jew and Greek; the same
Lord is Lord of all and bestows his riches upon all who call
upon him. [13]For, "every one who calls upon the name of
the Lord will be saved."
[14]But how are men to call upon him in whom they have

1 Cor 12:3
Mk 9:38-40
Acts 2:36-39

Is 26:16
Rom 1:16
Gal 3:26-28
Acts 10:34-36;
15:7-9

Joel 3:5
Acts 2:14-21

Heb 11:6
Acts 8:31

corde tuo credideris quod Deus illum excitavit ex mortuis, salvus eris. [10]Corde
enim creditur ad iustitiam, ore autem confessio fit in salutem. [11]Dicit enim
Scriptura: "Omnis, *qui credit in illo, non confundetur.*" [12]Non enim est
distinctio Iudaei et Graeci, nam idem Dominus omnium, dives in omnes, qui
invocant illum: [13]*Omnis* enim, *quicumque invocaverit nomen Domini, salvus*

9. At least from the third century B.C. we have documentary evidence that,
out of respect, the Jews did not utter the name "Yahweh" but generally referred
to God instead as "Lord". The first Christians, by giving Christ the title of
"Lord", were making a profession of faith in the divinity of Jesus.

10. To make the act of faith, human free will must necessarily be involved,
as St Thomas explains when commenting on this passage: "He very rightly
says that man believes with his heart. Because everything else to do with
external worship of God, man can do it against his will, but he cannot believe
if he does not want to believe. So, the mind of a believer is not obliged to adhere
to the truth by rational necessity, as is the case with human knowledge: it is
moved by the will" (*Commentary on Rom, ad loc.*)

However, in order to live by faith, in addition to internal assent external
profession of faith is required; man is made up of body and soul and therefore
he tends by nature to express his inner convictions externally; when the honour
of God or the good of one's neighbour requires it, one even has an obligation
to profess one's faith externally. For example, in the case of persecution we are
obliged to profess our faith, even at the risk of life, if, on being interrogated
about our beliefs, our silence would lead people to suppose that we did not
believe or that we did not hold our faith to be the true faith and our bad example
would cause others to fall away from the faith. However, external profession
is an obligation not only in extreme situations of that kind. In all situations –
be they ordinary or exceptional – God will always help us to confess our faith
boldly (cf. Mt 10:32-33; Lk 12:8).

14-21. To sum up what the Apostle is saying: the Jews have no excuse for

131

not believed? And how are they to believe in him of whom they have never heard? And how are they to hear without a preacher? [15]And how can men preach unless they are sent? As it is written, "How beautiful are the feet of those who preach good news!" [16]But they have not all heeded the gospel; for Isaiah says, "Lord, who has believed what he has heard from us?" [17]So faith comes from what is heard, and what is heard comes by the preaching of Christ.

---

erit. [14]Quomodo ergo invocabunt, in quem non crediderunt? Aut quomodo credent ei, quem non audierunt? Quomodo autem audient sine praedicante? [15]Quomodo vero praedicabunt nisi mittantur? Sicut scriptum est: *"Quam speciosi pedes evangelizantium bona."* [16]Sed non omnes oboedierunt evangelio; Isaias enim dicit: *"Domine, quis credidit auditui nostro?"* [17]Ergo fides ex

---

not invoking Christ as Lord, for if they do not believe in him it is due to their rebelliousness, for the Good News has indeed been preached to them.

14-17. The Church's work of evangelization is aimed at eliciting faith, moving people to conversion and reception of its sacraments, in fulfilment of the Lord's commandment, "Go into all the world and preach the Gospel to the whole of creation. He who believes and is baptized will be saved; but he who does not believe will be condemned" (Mk 16:15-16). The Acts of the Apostles give us a great deal of information about this first period of evangelization, which was marked by many miracles worked by the Apostles through the power Jesus gave them.

On the very day of Pentecost we can already see how vibrant was St Peter's preaching and the miracles which accompanied it: "The men and women who have come to the city from all parts of the world listen with amazement [. . .]. These wonders, which take place before their very eyes, lead them to listen to the preaching of the Apostles. The Holy Spirit himself, who is acting through our Lord's disciples, moves the hearts of their listeners and leads them to the faith" (J. Escrivá, *Christ is passing by*, 127). It is God himself who works these miracles through the Apostles; it is he who, through the preaching of Peter and the Eleven, is revealing the mysteries; and, finally, it is he who is moving the hearts of the people. This triple divine action leads to the hearers' act of faith. "Two things are required for faith", says St Thomas. "First, the things which are of faith have to be proposed [. . .]; second, the assent of the believer to the things which are proposed to him" (*Summa theologiae*, II-II, q. 6, a. 1, c).

He goes on to say later that, as regards the first of these two things, faith comes from God, who reveals truths either directly, as in the case of the Apostles and the Prophets, or else indirectly through preachers of the faith sent by Him (cf. Rom 10:15). Speaking of the second, he says that in the individual's assent to the truths of faith factors come into play which are external to the

¹⁸But I ask; have they not heard? Indeed they have; for   Ps 19:4-5
"Their voice has gone out to all the earth,
and their words to the ends of the world."
¹⁹Again I ask, did Israel not understand? First Moses says,   Deut 32:21
"I will make you jealous of those who are not a nation;   Rom 11:11
with a foolish nation I will make you angry."

---

auditu, auditus autem per verbum Christi. ¹⁸Sed dico: Numquid non audierunt? Quin immo, *in omnem terram exiit sonus eorum, et in fines orbis terrae verba eorum.* ¹⁹Sed dico: Numquid Israel non cognovit? Primus Moyses dicit: *"Ego ad aemulationem vos adducam per Non gentem: per gentem insipientem ad iram vos provocabo."* ²⁰Isaias autem audet et dicit: *"Inventus sum in non*

---

person – for example, miracles, and preaching which expounds the truth of faith. But none of these factors is sufficient: even though they witness the same miracle or hear the same preaching, some believe and others do not. There must therefore be something which moves the person *interiorly*; although the person's free will must play a part, it cannot account for the act of faith, because that act is a supernatural one; therefore, it must be that God moves the will interiorly, by means of grace (cf. *Summa theologiae, ibid.*).

Following Jesus' example, "every catechist must constantly endeavour to transmit by his teaching and behaviour the teaching and life of Jesus [. . .]. Every catechist should be able to apply to himself the mysterious words of Jesus: 'My teaching is not mine, but his who sent me' (Jn 7:16)" (John Paul II, *Catechesi tradendae*, 6).

Good example is not enough: apostolic action, through the spoken word, is called for. We have a mission to speak in God's name: his disciples "should everywhere on earth bear witness and give an answer to everyone who asks a reason for the hope of an eternal life which is theirs" (Vatican II, *Lumen gentium*, 10).

This was what the first Christians did. "Whenever we read the Acts of the Apostles, we are moved by the audacity, the confidence in their mission and the sacrificing joy of the disciples of Christ. They do not ask for multitudes. Even though the multitudes come, they address themselves to each particular soul, to each person, one by one. Philip, to the Ethiopian (cf. Acts 8:24-40); Peter, to the centurion Cornelius (cf. Acts 10:1- 48); Paul, to Sergius Paulus (cf. Acts 13:6-12)" (J. Escrivá, *Homily* entitled "Loyalty to the Church").

Those who accept the Gospel message feel drawn towards it when those who proclaim it also bear witness to it. "It is therefore primarily by her conduct and by her life that the Church will evangelize the world [. . .]. This law once laid down by the Apostle Paul maintains its full force today. Preaching, the verbal proclamation of a message, is indeed always indispensable [. . .]. The word remains ever relevant, especially when it is the bearer of the power of God (cf. 1 Cor 2:1-5)" (Paul VI, *Evangelii nuntiandi*, 41-42).

²⁰Then Isaiah is so bold as to say,
"I have been found by those who did not seek me;
I have shown myself to those who did not ask for me."

²¹But of Israel he says, "All day long I have held out my hands to a disobedient and contrary people."

11

Part of Israel will be saved

¹ I ask, then, has God rejected his people? By no means! I myself am an Israelite, a descendant of Abraham, a member of the tribe of Benjamin. ²God has not rejected his people

---

quaerentibus me; palam apparui his, qui me non interrogabant." ²¹Ad Israel autem dicit: *"Tota die expandi manus meas ad populum non credentem et contradicentem."*

¹Dico ergo: Numquid reppulit Deus populum suum? Absit! Nam et ego Israelita sum, ex semine Abraham, tribu Beniamin. ²*Non reppulit Deus plebem*

20-21.   Even one's capacity to respond to divine grace is itself a free gift of God. As the Magisterium teaches: "If anyone says that the grace of God can be conferred through human invocation, and that it is not grace that prompts us to pray, he contradicts the prophet Isaiah or the Apostle who says the same thing: 'I have been found by those who did not seek me; I have shown myself to those who did not ask for me' (Rom 10:20; cf. Is 65:1)" (Second Council of Orange, *De gratia*, can. 3).

We find the source of God's mercy in his love for mankind, a love vividly described in the parable of the prodigal son. "We read, in fact, that when the father saw the prodigal son returning home 'he had *compassion*, ran to meet him, threw his arms around his neck and kissed him' [. . .]. One can therefore say that the love for the son, the love that springs from the very essence of fatherhood, in a way obliges the father to be concerned about his son's dignity. This concern is the measure of his love [. . .]. This love is able to reach down to every prodigal son, to every human misery, and especially to every form of moral misery, to sin" (John Paul II, *Dives in misericordia*, 6).

2-5.   When Israel fell into idolatry, God raised up the prophet Elijah, who confronted the king with the sins of the people, who were worshipping idols and listening to false prophets (cf. 1 Kings 19:9-18). The king, instead of listening to Elijah, persecuted him; he had to flee to Mount Horeb. There he complained to God about Israel, and God in reply told him that he would punish them: the sons of Israel would die by the sword, but not all of them. God would preserve seven thousand of them, who had remained faithful to him. St Paul

whom he foreknew. Do you not know what the scripture says of Elijah, how he pleads with God against Israel? ³"Lord, they have killed thy prophets, they have demolished thy altars, and I alone am left, and they seek my life." ⁴But what is God's reply to him? "I have kept for myself seven thousand men who have not bowed the knee to Baal." ⁵So too at the present time there is a remnant, chosen by grace. ⁶But if it is by grace, it is no longer on the basis of works; otherwise grace would no longer be grace.

⁷What then? Israel failed to obtain what it sought. The elect obtained it, but the rest were hardened, ⁸as it is written,

"God gave them a spirit of stupor,

eyes that should not see and ears that should not hear,

down to this very day."

⁹And David says,

"Let their feast become a snare and a trap,

1 Kings 19:18

Is 10:20-21
Rom 9:27
Rom 4:4
Gal 2:16
Eph 2:8

Deut 29:3
Is 6:9; 29:10
Mt 13:13-15
Jn 12:40
Acts 28:26

Ps 69:23-24;
35:8
Rom 10:19

---

suam, quam praescivit. An nescitis in Elia quid dicit Scriptura? Quemadmodum interpellat Deum adversus Israel: ³*"Domine, prophetas tuos occiderunt, altaria tua suffoderunt, et ego relictus sum solus, et quaerunt animam meam."* ⁴*Sed quid dicit illi responsum divinum? "Reliqui* mihi *septem milia virorum, qui non curvaverunt genu Baal."* ⁵Sic ergo et in hoc tempore reliquiae secundum electionem gratiae factae sunt. ⁶Si autem gratia, iam non ex operibus, alioquin gratia iam non est gratia. ⁷Quid ergo? Quod quaerit Israel, hoc non est consecutus, electio autem consecuta est; ceteri vero excaecati sunt, ⁸sicut scriptum est: *"Dedit illis Deus spiritum soporis, oculos, ut non videant et aures, ut non audiant, usque in hodiernum diem."* ⁹Et David dicit: *"Fiat mensa eorum in laqueum et in captionem et in scandalum et in retributionem illis.*

---

recalls this episode as an example of God intervening in Salvation History through men he has specially chosen. Even in times when sinfulness was rampant the Lord kept certain individuals faithful; these acted as his instruments to revive and extend people's grasp of true teaching and love of his laws, and to render due worship to the Creator: for example, he chose Noah and his family when the world was full of wickedness (Gen 6:5-8), and Abraham, when men had forgotten the true God (Josh 24:2ff), and he did the same when the people of Israel fell into idolatry.

The Prophets describe those who stay faithful to Yahweh as "the remnant of Israel", or words to that effect (cf. Jer 3:14; Ezek 9:8; Amos 3:12; Is 4:2-3; Mic 4:7; Zeph 2:7, 9), and prophesy that this "remnant" will be found, first, among those deported to Babylonia, later among the repatriated exiles and, finally, after the exile, among the servants of God, after the still unfaithful people are decimated and purified.

a pitfall and a retribution for them;

Acts 13:46-48
Mt 8:11-12;
21:43-46
Deut 32:21
[10]let their eyes be darkened so that they cannot see,
and bend their backs for ever."

Acts 9:15
Gal 2:9
[11]So I ask, have they stumbled so as to fall? By no means! But through their trespass salvation has come to the Gentiles, so as to make Israel jealous. [12]Now if their trespass means riches for the world, and if their failure means riches for the Gentiles, how much more will their full inclusion mean!

1 Cor 9:19-23
The new chosen people

[13]Now I am speaking to you Gentiles. Inasmuch then as I am an apostle to the Gentiles, I magnify my ministry [14]in order to make my fellow Jews jealous, and thus save some of them. [15]For if their rejection means the reconciliation of the world, what will their acceptance mean but life from the

---

[10]*Obscurentur oculi eorum, ne videant, et dorsum illorum semper incurva!"* [11]Dico ergo: Numquid sic offenderunt, ut caderent? Absit! Sed illorum casu salus gentibus, ut illi ad aemulationem adducantur. [12]Quod si casus illorum divitiae sunt mundi et deminutio eorum divitiae gentium, quanto magis plenitudo eorum! [13]Vobis autem dico gentibus: Quantum quidem ego sum gentium apostolus, ministerium meum honorifico, [14]si quo modo ad aemulandum provocem carnem meam et salvos faciam aliquos ex illis. [15]Si enim amissio eorum reconciliatio est mundi, quae assumptio nisi vita ex mortuis? [16]Quod si primitiae

---

The same thing is happening, St Paul explains, now that the Gospel is being preached. The people of Israel in general are not accepting it and are not becoming part of the Church; only a small number of Jews have believed, and these are the "remnant" of Israel, chosen by God so that in them the promises might be kept. The conversion of Paul himself is an example and an earnest of this return of the people of Israel to their God, in line with the invitation that Hosea addressed to them: "Return, O Israel, to the Lord your God, for you have stumbled because of your iniquity" (Hos 14:2).

Throughout the history of the Church lapses of this type have occurred, with a consequent breakdown in morality. Whenever this happens, those Christians who stay true to the faith may, like Elijah, feel inclined to despair; but they should react with a realistic and vigilant optimism and not indulge in useless lamentation. In the presence of God, they should reflect on the fact that God actually wants to use them and their holy lives to turn the situation around: "A secret, an open secret: these world crises are sanctity crises. God wants a handful of men 'of his own' in every human activity. And then ... 'pax Christi in regno Christi* – the peace of Christ in the kingdom of Christ'" (J. Escrivá, *The Way*, 301).

dead? [16]If the dough offered as first fruits is holy, so is the whole lump; and if the root is holy, so are the branches.

[17]But if some of the branches were broken off, and you, a wild olive shoot, were grafted in their place to share the richness[o] of the olive tree, [18]do not boast over the branches. If you do boast, remember it is not you that support the root, but the root that supports you. [19]You will say, "Branches were broken off so that I might be grafted in." [20]That is true.

Num 15:17-21

Eph 2:11-18

Rom 3:27-28;
9:1-5; 14:1-5
1 Cor 1:31
Jn 4:22

---

sanctae sunt, et massa; et si radix sancta, et rami. [17]Quod si aliqui ex ramis fracti sunt, tu autem, cum oleaster esses, insertus es in illis et consocius radicis pinguedinis olivae factus es, [18]noli gloriari adversus ramos; quod si gloriaris, non tu radicem portas, sed radix te. [19]Dices ergo: "Fracti sunt rami, ut ego inserar." [20]Bene; incredulitate fracti sunt, tu autem fide stas. Noli altum sapere,

---

16-24. "The Church is a cultivated field, the tillage of God. On that land the ancient olive tree grows whose holy roots were the prophets and in which the reconciliation of Jews and Gentiles has been brought about and will be brought about again (cf. Rom 11:13-26)" (Vatican II, *Lumen gentium*, 6).

The good olive tree represents the faithful of the Old Testament, and in its turn the new Israel of God, the Church. The natural branches which remain are those Jews who have been converted to Christianity; the broken-off branches are the unbelieving Jews who have rejected Christ; the branches from the wild tree, grafted on to the cultivated tree, are the Gentiles who have come to take the place of the Jews unfaithful to grace, thereby sharing in the same faith as the Patriarchs and Prophets and in the promised blessings.

This comparison does not fit in with what normally happens in gardening, where it is usually the branch of a good tree that is grafted onto a wild one. St Paul intentionally ignores this, in order to stress that God acts as he so pleases to effect his design.

God wants to have a fully developed tree; he wants his house to be filled (cf. Lk 14:23). And so the place left vacant by the Jews has been filled by the Gentiles, for the house does not belong to the Israelites – although they were the first to live in it – but to God, who had planned that the Jewish people would invite the Gentiles to fill his house. "This teaching", St John Chrysostom comments, "is not just from Paul's lips, for it is given us by our Lord Jesus Christ's parables in the Gospel: a king is celebrating the wedding of his son; the guests refuse his invitation to the banquet, and then the ruler calls in everyone from the cross-roads to take their place. A man has a vineyard and he lets it out to some husbandmen; they kill his son and heir and the vineyard is given to others [. . .]. From these examples it is plain to see that the natural order of things demanded that the Jews should be the first to enter the Church and that the Gentiles should come after them" (*Hom. on Rom*, 19).

[o]Other ancient authorities read *rich root*.

Lk 23:31

Jn 15:2
Heb 3:14-15

They were broken off because of their unbelief, but you stand fast only through faith. So do not become proud, but stand in awe. [21]For if God did not spare the natural branches, neither will he spare you. [22]Note then the kindness and the severity of God: severity towards those who have fallen, but God's kindness to you, provided you continue in his kindness; otherwise you too will be cut off. [23]And even the others, if they do not persist in their unbelief, will be grafted in, for God has the power to graft them in again. [24]For if you have been cut from what is by nature a wild olive tree, and grafted, contrary to nature, into a cultivated olive tree, how much more will these natural branches be grafted back into their own olive tree.

---

sed time: [21]Si enim Deus naturalibus ramis non pepercit, ne forte nec tibi parcat. [22]Vide ergo bonitatem et severitatem Dei: in eos quidem, qui ceciderunt, severitatem, in te autem bonitatem Dei si permanseris in bonitate, alioquin et tu excideris. [23]Sed et illi, si non permanserint in incredulitate, inserentur; potens est enim Deus iterum inserere illos! [24]Nam si tu ex naturali excisus es oleastro et contra naturam insertus es in bonam olivam, quanto magis hi, qui secundum naturam sunt, inserentur suae olivae. [25]Nolo enim vos ignorare, fratres, mysterium hoc, ut non sitis vobis ipsis sapientes, quia caecitas ex parte contigit in Israel, donec plenitudo gentium intraret, [26]et sic omnis Israel salvus fiet, sicut

---

The comparison has a two-fold purpose: on the one hand, to check boasting by Christians of Gentile background, for if the natural, selected branches have been cut off, this can much more easily happen with those which are mere grafts; on the other hand, Paul wants to raise the Jews' spirits and encourage them to hope: the branches of the wild olive have been successfully grafted on against nature, so it will be much easier for the natural branches to be reunited with the source from which they come.

All these who have been baptized should feel humble and grateful for their Christian calling; they have no reason for resentment or presumption.

"That is how we too should act if we desire to be saved and to keep the grace of God until we die, placing all our trust in him alone [. . .]. The demon tempts us now to presumption, now to despair; when he assures us that we have no reason to fear falls, that is when we must fear, for if the Lord should cease even for an instant to aid us with his grace, that is when we would be lost. And when he tempts us to despair, we must, looking up to God, say: 'In thee, O Lord, do I seek refuge; let me never be put to shame' (Ps 31:2), or be deprived of your grace. These acts of self-distrust and of trust in God we should be making until the very last moment of our life, forever praying the Lord to give us holy humility" (St Alphonsus Mary Liguori, *The love of Jesus Christ reduced to practice*, chap. 9).

The conversion of the Jews

²⁵Lest you be wise in your own conceits, I want you to understand this mystery, brethren: a hardening has come upon part of Israel, until the full number of the Gentiles come in, ²⁶and so all Israel will be saved; as it is written,

"The Deliverer will come from Zion,

he will banish ungodliness from Jacob";

²⁷"and this will be my covenant with them

when I take away their sins."

²⁸As regards the gospel they are enemies of God, for your sake; but as regards election they are beloved for the sake of their forefathers. ²⁹For the gifts and the call of God are

Prov 3:7
Rom 12:16;
16:25-27
Lk 21:24

Is 59:20-21
Ps 14:7
Jer 31:31-33
Mt 23:39

Heb 6:17-18
Num 23:19
1 Sam 15:29

---

scriptum est: *"Veniet ex Sion, qui eripiat, avertet impietates ab Iacob;* ²⁷*et hoc illis a me testamentum, cum abstulero peccata eorum."* ²⁸Secundum evangelium quidem inimici propter vos, secundum electionem autem carissimi propter patres; ²⁹sine paenitentia enim sunt dona et vocatio Dei! ³⁰Sicut enim

---

25-32. We all yearn for the fulfilment of these words – threatening yet consoling – which Christ addressed to the scribes and Pharisees: "For I tell you, you will not see me again, until you say 'Blessed is he who comes in the name of the Lord'" (Mt 23:39). "Together with the prophets and the Apostle, the Church awaits the day, known to God alone, when all peoples will call on God with one voice and 'serve him with one accord' (Zeph 3:9)" (Vatican II, *Nostra aetate*, 4). The conversion of the Jews is a secret – a mystery, the text says (v. 25) – hidden in the future, which will come about when the Incarnation of the Word achieves its ultimate purpose.

This conversion will follow on that of the Gentiles, which will be as it were a prelude to it. Jesus has foretold that "Jerusalem will be trodden down by the Gentiles, until the times of the Gentiles are fulfilled" (Lk 21:24; cf. note on same), which in some way suggests that the Jews will be converted at the end of time.

However, when the Church in its preaching touches on the main signs of the end of the world, it only refers to the proclamation of the Gospel throughout the world, to apostasy and to the Antichrist, but it has nothing to say about the conversion of the Jews (cf. *St Pius V Catechism*, I, 8, 7). What the Church does do, and what we should do, is to pray the Lord to listen to its prayers "that the people you first made your own may arrive at the fulness of redemption" (*Roman Missal*, Good Friday Liturgy, prayer of the faithful).

29. God never goes back on anything he promises; therefore he continues to call the Jews to enter the chosen people. He does not take account of their disobedience or their sins: he will love them with an everlasting love, as he promised the patriarchs and in line with the merits accruing to them for their

irrevocable. [30]Just as you were once disobedient to God but now have received mercy because of their disobedience, [31]so they have now been disobedient in order that by the mercy shown to you they also may[p] receive mercy. [32]For God has consigned all men to disobedience, that he may have mercy upon all.

Gal 3:22
Ezek 18:23-32
1 Tim 2:4
Ps 139:6, 17-18
Job 11:6-8
Sir 1:1-3
Is 55:8-9
Is 40:13
Jer 23:18
1 Cor 2:11, 16
Wis 9:13

[33]O the depth of the riches and wisdom and knowledge of God! How unsearchable are his judgments and how inscrutable his ways!

[34]"For who has known the mind of the Lord,
or who has been his counsellor?"

---

aliquando vos non credidistis Deo, nunc autem misericordiam consecuti estis propter illorum incredulitatem, [31]ita et isti nunc non crediderunt propter vestram misericordiam, ut et ipsi nunc misericordiam consequantur. [32]Conclusit enim Deus omnes in incredulitatem, ut omnium misereatur! [33]O altitudo divitiarum et sapientiae et scientiae Dei! Quam incomprehensibilia sunt iudicia eius et investigabiles viae eius! [34]*Quis* enim *cognovit sensum Domini? Aut quis*

---

fidelity (cf. Rom 9:4-5). It is this very immutability of God's love that makes it possible for "all Israel" (v. 26) to be saved. God's calling, which is eternal, cannot cease; but we for our part can reject his call. The immutability of God's plan is reassuring to us: it means that even if we abandon him at any point, we can always return to our earlier fidelity: he is still there, waiting for us.

33-36. God's admirable goodness, to both Jews and Gentiles, permitting them to disobey and then taking pity on them in their wretchedness, causes the Apostle to pour out his heart in words reminiscent of the Book of Isaiah: "For my thoughts are not your thoughts, neither are your ways my ways, says the Lord. For as the heavens are higher than the earth, so are my ways higher than your ways, and my thoughts than your thoughts" (55:8-9). The designs of divine Providence may disconcert us, may be difficult to understand; but if we remember how great God is – he is beyond our comprehension – and how God's power and faithfulness overcome any obstacle man may place in God's way, we will realize that the very things which seem to frustrate his plans actually serve to forward them.

The correct attitude of man to the designs of God is one of humility. This will lead him to realize that the mysteries of God, which are intrinsically clear, seem obscure to us, simply because our mind's capacity is limited. Therefore, as Fray Luis de Granada reminds us, we must avoid saying that "something cannot be because we cannot understand it [. . .], for what is more in conformity with reason than to think in the highest way of him who is the All-High and to attribute to him the highest and best nature that our mind can conceive? [. . .]

[p]Other ancient authorities add *now*.

[35]"Or who has given a gift to him
that he might be repaid?"
[36]For from him and through him and to him are all things.
To him be glory for ever. Amen.

12

MORAL SECTION

LIVING IN CHARITY

HOW CHRISTIANS SHOULD CONDUCT THEMSELVES

Solidarity in the mystical Body

[1]I appeal to you therefore, brethren, by the mercies of God, to present your bodies as a living sacrifice, holy and accept-

---

consiliarius eius fuit? [35]*Aut quis prior dedit illi, et retribuetur ei?* [36]*Quoniam ex ipso et per ipsum et in ipsum omnia. Ipsi gloria in saecula. Amen.*
[1]*Obsecro itaque vos, fratres, per misericordiam Dei, ut exhibeatis corpora*

So it is that our failure to understand the sublimity of this mystery has a trace and scent of something divine, because, as we said, God being infinite must necessarily be beyond our comprehension" (*Introducción al símbolo de la fe*, part IV).

Chapters 12-15 These four chapters are what we might call the moral section of the Epistle to the Romans. On this, cf. pp. 50-1 above.

1. In the New Testament Christians are clearly called to offer sacrifices to God – no longer sacrifices of animals, as in the Old Law, but offerings of themselves. This new kind of worship must take a spiritual form, as Jesus told the Samaritan woman, rather than a purely material form: it must be something living, holy, not merely external and formal, and pleasing to God (cf. Jn 4:23). "It is by the apostolic preaching of the Gospel that the people of God is called together and gathered so that all who belong to this people, sanctified as they are by the Holy Spirit, may offer themselves 'a living sacrifice, holy and acceptable to God' (Rom 12:1)" (Vatican II, *Presbyterorum ordinis*, 2).
The basis of this priestly meaning of Christian life is to be found in the sacrament which makes us members of Christ's body: "Through Baptism all

141

able to God, which is your spiritual worship. ²Do not be conformed to this world^qbut be transformed by the renewal of your mind, that you may prove what is the will of God,

what is good and acceptable and perfect.^r

³For by the grace given to me I bid every one among you not to think of himself more highly than he ought to think,

but to think with sober judgment, each according to the measure of faith which God has assigned him. ⁴For as in one body we have many members, and all the members do

not have the same function, ⁵so we, though many, are one

---

vestra hostiam viventem, sanctam, Deo placentem, rationabile obsequium vestrum; ²et nolite conformari huic saeculo, sed transformamini renovatione mentis, ui probetis quid sit voluntas Dei, quid bonum et bene placens et perfectum. ³Dico enim per gratiam, quae data est mihi, omnibus, qui sunt inter vos, non altius sapere quam oportet sapere, sed sapere ad sobrietatem, unicuique sicut Deus divisit mensuram fidei. ⁴Sicut enim in uno corpore multa membra habemus, omnia autem membra non eundem actum habent, ⁵ita multi unum

---

of us have been made priests of our lives, 'to offer spiritual sacrifices acceptable to God through Jesus Christ' (1 Pet 2:5). Everything we do can be an expression of our obedience to God's will and so perpetuate the mission of the God-man" (J. Escrivá, *Christ is passing by*, 96).

Every day the Christian can and should offer himself along with Christ in the Holy Mass: "If the oblation whereby the faithful in this Sacrifice offer the divine victim to the heavenly Father is to produce its full effect [. . .] they must also offer themselves as victim, desiring intensely to make themselves as like as possible to Jesus Christ who suffered so much, and offering themselves as a spiritual victim with and through the High Priest himself" (Pius XII, *Mediator Dei*, 25). From this it follows that the whole Christian life and the struggle which it implies are imbued with deep priestly significance: "If I renounce everything I possess, if I carry the cross and follow Christ, I have offered a holocaust on the altar of God, or if I burn up my body in the fire of charity [. . .] I have offered a holocaust on the altar of God [. . .]; if I mortify my body and abstain from all concupiscence, if the world is crucified unto me and not me unto the world, then I have offered a holocaust on the altar of God and I am become a priest of my own sacrifice" (Origen, *In Lev. hom.*, 9, 9).

4-5. The variety which is to be found in every well-organized social structure is also, by God's will, a feature of the Church. This variety reflects the differing needs of the Christian community, which is not an amorphous grouping of people, each working separately for personal salvation, but an organized body. In that body each member has a defined role and functions for

^qGreek *age*.   ^rOr *what is the good and acceptable and perfect will of God.*

body in Christ, and individually members one of another.
⁶Having gifts that differ according to the grace given to us,
let us use them: if prophecy, in proportion to our faith; ⁷if
service, in our serving; he who teaches, in his teaching; ⁸he
who exhorts, in his exhortation; he who contributes, in
liberality; he who gives aid, with zeal; he who does acts of
mercy, with cheerfulness.

1 Pet 4:10-11

Mt 6:2-4
2 Cor 9:7

Tit 1:5-9
Amos 5:14-15
Is 1:17
1 Pet 1:22
Jn 13:12-17
1 Cor 13:13
Phil 2:3
Col 4:2

Charity towards all

⁹Let love be genuine; hate what is evil, hold fast to what

---

corpus sumus in Christo, singuli autem alter alterius membra. ⁶Habentes autem
donationes secundum gratiam, quae data est nobis, differentes, sive prophetiam
secundum rationem fidei, ⁷sive ministerium in ministrando sive qui docet, in
doctrina ⁸sive qui exhortatur, in exhortando; qui tribuit in simplicitate, qui
praeest in sollicitudine, qui miseretur in hilaritate. ⁹Dilectio sine simulatione.

---

the benefit of all, while at the same time seeking personal spiritual advance-
ment. This variety is, moreover, consistent with and conducive to the carrying
out of God's desire to sanctify and save men, not one by one, as if they were
unconnected to each other, but rather constituting a people which is established
and governed on the basis of this wonderful variety. This distinction was
established by God in order to build up the Church. Therefore, for example,
pastors and people are of mutual supernatural help to one another (cf. Vatican
II, *Lumen gentium*, 9 and 32).

Each of us should feel called on to invigorate – through personal effort, virtue
– the entire Mystical Body of Christ (cf. "Introduction to the 'Theology' of St
Paul", pp. 44-6 above). It is inaccurate, therefore, to make a distinction between
"personal virtues" and "social virtues".

"No virtue worthy of its name can foster selfishness. Every virtue necessarily
works to the good both of our own soul and to the good of those around us [...].
Ties of solidarity should bind us all and, besides, in the order of grace we are
united by the supernatural links of the Communion of Saints" (J. Escrivá,
Friends of God, 76).

6-8. "Gifts": also called charisms, these are special, transitory, divine
graces, granted not so much for the personal benefit of the recipient as for the
general good of the Church. This term (charism), we might note, was introduced
into the New Testament by St Paul.

9-21. "After speaking about those gifts which are not common to all, the
Apostle now teaches that charity is common to all" (St Thomas, *Commentary
on Rom, ad loc.*). True charity takes different forms depending on the needs
and capacity of each person; it always involves seeking good and avoiding evil

143

is good; [10]love one another with brotherly affection; outdo one another in showing honour. [11]Never flag in zeal, be aglow with the Spirit, serve the Lord. [12]Rejoice in your hope, be patient in tribulation, be constant in prayer.

Odientes malum, adhaerentes bono; [10]caritate fraternitatis invicem diligentes, honore invicem praevenientes, [11]sollicitudine non pigri, spiritu ferventes, Domino servientes, [12]spe gaudentes, in tribulatione patientes, orationi instantes,

---

(v. 9); it has to be exercised with those who are already Christians (vv. 10-16) and those who are not (vv. 17-21); indeed, the charity shown to the latter is instrumental in bringing them closer to the faith. However, it is not always possible to do to others all the good we would wish: we have limited resources, more pressing duties; there are problems of physical distance, etc. Only God, who is infinitely perfect and almighty, can do good to everyone all the time; this does not mean that he always gives everyone the same gifts: to some he gives more, to others less, according to the designs of his Wisdom.

Even bearing in mind our own limitations, our love for others should affect everything we do, everything we think and say. Obviously, one of the first consequences of charity is never to judge anyone, or speak badly about anyone, or scandalize them by what we say or do. Moreover, we should perform positive acts of this virtue; it would be impossible to give a complete list of the ways of being charitable but they certainly include, Fray Luis de Granada says, "among other things, these six – loving, counselling, assisting, suffering, forgiving and edifying. These are so closely connected to charity that the more one does them the more charity one has, and the less, less [. . .]. For, according to this order a person can check to see what he has and what he does not have as far as the perfection of that virtue is concerned. For we can say that he who loves is on the first step; he who loves and counsels, on the second; he who assists, on the third; he who suffers on the fourth; he who forgives and suffers, on the fifth; and he who builds on all this with his words and his good life, as is the task of perfect and apostolic men, on the highest step of all" (*Guide to Sinners*, I, II, chap. 16).

12. The love of God makes us joyful, strong and persevering. Therefore "one accepts tribulation with joy and hope, because one knows that what is promised in exchange is something much better" (Pseudo-Ambrose, *Comm. in Epist. ad Rom, ad loc.*)

This setting gives us every opportunity to derive supernatural benefit from suffering, which is quite a normal part of the Christian life: "A whole programme for a good course in the 'subject' of suffering is given to us by the Apostle: *spe gaudentes* – rejoicing in hope, *in tribulatione patientes* – patient in troubles, *orationi instantes* – persevering in prayer" (J. Escrivá, *The Way*, 209).

Joy in the midst of difficulties is in fact one of the clearest signs that love of

¹³Contribute to the needs of the saints, practise hospitality.

¹⁴Bless those who persecute you; bless and do not curse them. ¹⁵Rejoice with those who rejoice, weep with those who weep. ¹⁶Live in harmony with one another; do not be haughty, but associate with the lowly;ˢ never be conceited.¹⁷Repay no one evil for evil, but take thought for what is noble in the sight of all. ¹⁸If possible, so far as it depends upon you, live peaceably with all. ¹⁹Beloved, never avenge yourselves, but leave itᵗ to the wrath of God; for it is written, "Vengeance is mine, I will repay, says the Lord." ²⁰No, "if your enemy is hungry, feed him; if he is thirsty, give him drink; for by so doing you will heap burning coals upon his head." ²¹Do not be overcome by evil, but overcome evil with good.

Mt 5:38-48
Ps 35:13
1 Cor 12:26
Sir 7:34
Prov 3:7
Is 5:21

2 Cor 8:21
Prov 3:4 (LXX)
1 Thess 5:15
1 Pet 3:9
Mk 9:50
Heb 12:14
1 Cor 6:6-7
Deut 32:35
Lev 19:17-18
Prov 20:22
Mt 5:38-42
Heb 10:30
Prov 25:21-22
Mt 5:44

---

¹³necessitatibus sanctorum communicantes, hospitalitatem sectantes. ¹⁴Benedicite persequentibus; benedicite et nolite maledicere! ¹⁵Gaudere cum gaudentibus, flere cum flentibus. ¹⁶Idipsum invicem sentientes, non alta sapientes, sed humilibus consentientes. Nolite esse prudentes apud vosmetipsos. ¹⁷Nulli malum pro malo reddentes; *providentes bona coram* omnibus *hominibus*; ¹⁸si fieri potest, quod ex vobis est, cum omnibus hominibus pacem habentes; ¹⁹non vosmetipsos vindicantes, carissimi, sed date locum irae, scriptum est enim: "*Mihi vindicta, ego retribuam*", dicit Dominus. ²⁰Sed *si esurierit inimicus tuus, ciba illum; si sitit, potum da illi. Hoc enim faciens, carbones ignis congeres super caput eius.* ²¹Noli vinci a malo, sed vince in bono malum.

God is influencing everything we do, for, as St Augustine comments, "where one loves, either one does not feel the difficulty or else one loves the very difficulty [. . .]. The tasks of those who love are never laborious" (*De bono viduitatis*, 21, 26).

13. "For he who does not love his brother whom he has seen, cannot love God whom he has not seen" (1 Jn 4:20). Similarly, it can be said that Christians, that is "servants of the Lord", unless they serve their brethren whom they see before them, cannot serve God either. Serving God, in other words, ultimately means alleviating "the needs of the saints" and offering hospitality to strangers, after the example of the patriarchs Abraham and Lot (Gen 18:2-5; 19:2-3; cf. Heb 13:2).

21. As long as we live on this earth we will often experience the presence of evil – in the world around us, and in ourselves. Our first reaction can sometimes be like that of our Lord's disciples when the Samaritans refused to receive Christ: "Lord, do you want us to bid fire come down from heaven and

ˢOr *give yourselves to humble tasks.*   ᵗGreek *give place.*

13

Submission to authority

Mt 22:16-21
and par.
Jn 19:11
Tit 3:1
Heb 13:2
1 Pet 2:13-15
Prov 8:15-16

[1]Let every person be subject to the governing authorities. For there is no authority except from God, and those that exist have been instituted by God. [2]Therefore he who resists the authorities resists what God has appointed, and those who resist will incur judgment. [3]For rulers are not a terror to good conduct, but to bad. Would you have no fear of him who is in authority? Then do what is good, and you will

[1]Omnis anima potestatibus sublimioribus subdita sit. Non est enim potestas nisi a Deo; quae autem sunt, a Deo ordinatae sunt. [2]Itaque, qui resistit potestati, Dei ordinationi resistit; qui autem resistunt ipsi, sibi damnationem acquirent. [3]Nam principes non sunt timori bono operi sed malo. Vis autem non timere

consume them?" (Lk 9:54). But Jesus invites them to be gentle. "We have to understand everyone; we must live peaceably with everyone; we must forgive everyone. We shall not call injustice justice; we shall not say that an offence against God is not an offence against God, or that evil is good. When confronted by evil we shall not reply with another evil, but rather with sound doctrine and good actions – drowning evil in an abundance of good (cf. Rom 12:21). That is how Christ will reign in our souls and in the souls of the people around us" (J. Escrivá, *Christ is passing by,* 182).

1-7. Jesus himself declared in the presence of Pilate that all authority comes from God (Jn 19:11; cf. Prov 8:15-16; Wis 6:3). God, being the author of the social order, created man as needing to live and develop within a community, thereby enabling him to fulfil his purpose as perfectly and quickly as possible. "It is clear", Vatican II says, "that the political community and public authority are based on human nature, and therefore that they need belong to an order established by God; nevertheless, the choice of the political regime and the appointment of rulers are left to the free decisions of the citizens" (*Gaudium et spes,* 74).

Precisely because of its divine origin, civil authority – when it seeks the common good and is exercised within the limits of the moral order – should be obeyed in conscience. Failure to obey it is a transgression of the fourth commandment of the Decalogue, for, as St Thomas explains, "natural generation is not the only grounds for calling a person 'father'. There are all kinds of reasons why some should be given this title, and each of these kinds of fatherhood deserves corresponding respect [. . .]. Kings and princes are called fathers because they should look after the welfare of their people. Them also we honour with our obedience. And we do so not only out of fear but out of love; not only for reasons of human convenience but because our conscience

146

receive his approval, ⁴for he is God's servant for your good.
But if you do wrong, be afraid, for he does not bear the
sword in vain; he is the servant of God to execute his wrath
on the wrongdoer. ⁵Therefore one must be subject, not only
to avoid God's wrath but also for the sake of conscience.
⁶For the same reason you also pay taxes, for the authorities
are ministers of God, attending to this very thing. ⁷Pay all
of them their dues, taxes to whom taxes are due, revenue to
whom revenue is due, respect to whom respect is due,
honour to whom honour is due.

Mt 22:21
Mk 12:17
Lk 20:25

Mt 22:34-40
Jn 13:34-35
Gal 5:14
Col 3:14
1 Tim 1:5

Love, the fulfilling of the Law

⁸Owe no one anything, except to love one another; for he

---

potestatem? Bonum fac, et habebis laudem ex illa; ⁴Dei enim minister est tibi
in bonum. Si autem malum feceris, time; non enim sine causa gladium portat;
Dei enim minister est, vindex in iram ei, qui malum agit. ⁵Ideo necesse est
subditos esse, non solum propter iram sed et propter conscientiam. ⁶Ideo enim
et tributa praestatis; ministri enim Dei sunt in hoc ipsum instantes. ⁷Reddite
omnibus debita: cui tributum tributum, cui vectigal vectigal, cui timorem
timorem, cui honorem honorem. ⁸Nemini quidquam debeatis nisi ut invicem

---

tells us to act in this way. The reason for this is based on the fact, as the Apostle
says in this passage (Rom 13:1), that all authority comes from God; therefore,
one must give every one what is his due" (*On the two commandments of love
and the ten commandments of the Law*, IV). Among the things owed to authority
are: honour, respect, reverential fear, and the payment of taxes to contribute to
the support of services which allow citizens to live in peace and security, which
protect them from violence and civil disorder, and which guarantee them a more
civilized lifestyle.

From the very beginning Christians have striven to fulfil their social
obligations even if they are the victims of persecution (cf. Leo XIII, *Quod
apostolici; Diuturnum illud; Immortale Dei*). A moving example of the heroism
of the early Christians in practising these virtues is given us by St Justin Martyr,
around the middle of the second century (*First Apology*, 17). And Tertullian,
who so vehemently criticized the pagan world, wrote that the faithful, in their
assemblies, prayed for the emperor, his ministers and officials, and for temporal
well-being and peace (cf. *Apologeticum*, 39, 1ff). By acting in this way
Christians are keeping our Lord's commandment to "render to Caesar the
things that are Caesar's, and to God the things that are God's" (Mt 22:21).

8-10. To enable him to keep the Commandments of God perfectly, man
receives the interior influence of love of God and love of neighbour. For when
love motivates us we readily give what is due – and more besides – to him

147

Ex 20:13-17
Deut 5:17-21
Lev 18:19
Jas 2:8

1 Cor 13:4-7

1 Cor 7:29-31
Eph 5:14-16
Col 4:5
1 Thess 5:4-8
Eph 5:11-14
2 Tim 1:10

who loves his neighbour has fulfilled the law. ⁹The commandments, "You shall not commit adultery, You shall not kill, You shall not steal, You shall not covet," and any other commandment, are summed up in this sentence, "You shall love your neighbour as yourself." ¹⁰Love does no wrong to a neighbour; therefore love is the fulfilling of the law.

¹¹Besides this you know what hour it is, how it is full time now for you to wake from sleep. For salvation is nearer to us now than when we first believed; ¹²the night is far gone,

---

diligatis: qui enim diligit proximum, legem implevit. ⁹Nam: *Non adulterabis, Non occides, Non furaberis, Non concupisces*, et si quod est aliud mandatum, in hoc verbo recapitulatur: *Diliges proximum tuum tamquam teipsum.* ¹⁰Dilectio proximo malum non operatur; plenitudo ergo legis est dilectio. ¹¹Et hoc scientes tempus quia hora est iam vos de somno surgere, nunc enim propior est nobis salus quam cum credidimus. ¹²Nox processit, dies autem appropiavit.

---

whom we love. In his public preaching St John of Avila used to say, "Those of you who are unlettered should not think that this means you cannot enter paradise; study these two commandments, and when you have fulfilled them, realize that you have done everything laid down in the Law and the Prophets, and everything taught by the Gospel and by the Apostles and whatever you are admonished to do by all the countless books that have been written, for the Lord has sent his word to us in (this) manifold form (cf. Rom 9:28)" (*Sermons*, twelfth Sunday after Pentecost).

The relationship between the virtues of charity and justice is similar to that between love and the commandments of the Law. "Be convinced that justice alone is never enough to solve the great problems of mankind [. . .]. Charity must penetrate and accompany justice because it sweetens and deifies everything: 'God is love' (1 Jn 4:16). Our motive in everything we do should be the Love of God, which makes it easier for us to love our neighbour and which purifies and raises all earthly loves on to a higher level [. . .]. Charity, which is like a generous overflowing of justice, demands first of all the fulfilment of one's duty. The way to start is to be just; the next step is to do what is most equitable . . .; but in order to love, great refinement is required, and much thoughtfulness, and respect, and kindliness" (J. Escrivá, *Friends of God*, 172-3).

11-14. The Church uses this inspired text in the liturgy of Advent to help us prepare for the coming of the Lord. Christ came into the world by his Incarnation; he also comes to souls through grace; and at the end of time he will come as Judge. Rising like the sun, he dispelled the darkness when he came into the world, and he continues to dispel whatever darkness remains in souls the more he obtains mastery over the hearts of men.

the day is at hand. Let us then cast off the works of darkness and put on the armour of light; 13let us conduct ourselves becomingly as in the day, not in revelling and drunkenness, not in debauchery and licentiousness, not in quarrelling and jealousy. 14But put on the Lord Jesus Christ, and make no provision for the flesh, to gratify its desires.

Lk 21:34
Eph 5:18

Gal 3:27
Eph 4:24

Abiciamus ergo opera tenebrarum et induamur arma lucis. 13Sicut in die honeste ambulemus: non in comissationibus et ebrietatibus, non in cubilibus et impudicitiis, non in contentione et aemulatione; 14sed induite Dominum Iesum Christum et carnis curam ne feceritis in concupiscentiis.

The Christian needs to make an effort to stay awake: "There is a kind of sleep proper to the soul, and another proper to the body," St Augustine tells us. "The sleep of the soul consists in forgetting about God [. . .], whereas the soul who has stayed awake knows who its maker is [. . .]. But, just as he who sleeps [...], although the sun has already risen and the day is already hot, thinks it is still night, because he is not awake to see the new-born day, so there are some people who, even though Christ is here and the truth is being preached, are still asleep as far as their soul is concerned [. . .]. Your life, your behaviour, should be awake in Christ so that others – sleepy pagans – can see it and the sound of your watchfulness cause them to get up and throw off their sleepiness and begin to say with you in Christ: O God, my God, since dawn I have kept watch for you" (*Enarrationes in Psalmos*, 62, 4).

13-14. Souls who have become members of the Church through Baptism are always in need of conversion to a new life. Sometimes God uses Sacred Scripture to awaken people from their spiritual lethargy. In fact, he used these particular words of Scripture to move the heart of St Augustine and have him take the last step towards casting off the attachments of the flesh. "I felt myself still enslaved by my iniquities, and therefore did I groan to myself, 'How long? How long must I continue saying Tomorrow, tomorrow? Why not now? Why not, at one instant, make an end of all uncleanness?' [. . .] And behold I heard a voice, like that of a child in the house next door, repeating in a sing-song tone, 'Take up and read. Take up and read' [. . .]. I rose up [. . .] and returned to where I had left the book of the Apostle; I took it quickly into my hand, opened it and read in silence the first passage on which my eye happened to fall." Having transcribed the verses we are now commenting, Augustine continues: "I read no further, nor was there any need to; for with the end of this sentence, as by a clear and constant light infused into my heart, the darkness of all former doubts was immediately driven away" (*Confessions*, VII, 12, 28-29).

14. All Christians "put on" Christ in Baptism (cf. Gal 3:27). Starting with this initial configuration to Christ, they are steadily transformed into him by frequent reception of the sacraments, particularly the sacrament of Penance.

149

14

BEING UNDERSTANDING TOWARDS OTHERS

Seeing things from the other person's point of view

1 Cor 8:7-13; 10:14-33
Gen 1:29; 9:3
Col 2:16-17

¹As for the man who is weak in faith, welcome him, but not for disputes over opinions. ²One believes he may eat anything, while the weak man eats only vegetables. ³Let not him who eats despise him who abstains, and let not him who abstains pass judgment on him who eats; for God has

---

¹Infirmum autem in fide assumite, non in disceptationibus cogitationum. ²Alius enim credit manducare omnia; qui autem infirmus est, holus manducat. ³Is qui manducat, non manducantem non spernat; et qui non manducat, manducantem

---

"'*Induimini Dominum Iesum Christum*. Put on the Lord Jesus Christ', says St Paul to the Romans. It is in the Sacrament of Penance that you and I put on Jesus Christ and his merits" (J. Escrivá, *The Way*, 310).

1-3. In the Roman church there were some Christians who were influenced by Judaism to abstain from the types of food forbidden by the Old Law. Others, however, who were "strong" in the faith, knew that Christ had freed them from Mosaic observances such as avoidance of certain kinds of food, and from keeping to the Jewish calendar – sabbaths, full moons and other festivals. This second group were confirmed in their practice by the decrees of the Council of Jerusalem (cf. Acts 15:28-29). They regarded the others, who were fewer in number, as "weak" because they were tied down by the Mosaic precepts: they fasted on certain days, abstained from meat, did not drink wine, etc. (cf. Col 2:16, 20-22).

In themselves there was nothing wrong with those practices; for example, Eusebius the historian (*Ecclesiastical History*, 23, 5) tells us that James the Less, the bishop of Jerusalem, himself abstained from wine, spirits and meat, as a personal mortification (cf. also the rules for Nazirites: Lk 1:15). However, the "weak" were scandalized by the freedom of spirit of the others, and regarded them as sinners. And the "strong", for their part, looked down on the "weak" and did not mind causing them scandal. Both sets of Christians were sinning against charity. St Paul addresses them both in a fatherly way, exhorting the weak not to falsely judge the strong, and appealing to the strong not to despise the weak. In theory, the strong had right on their side, but in practice the main thing was not to give scandal (cf. v. 21 and 1 Cor 8:7-13).

4-12. These ideas and counsels addressed to the faithful at Rome provide the basis of the motto traditional in the Church, "Unity in essentials, freedom in doubtful matters, and in all things charity" (cf. John XXIII, *Ad Petri*

welcomed him. ⁴Who are you to pass judgment on the
servant of another? It is before his own master that he stands
or falls. And he will be upheld, for the Master is able to
make him stand.

⁵One man esteems one day as better than another, while
another man esteems all days alike. Let every one be fully
convinced in his own mind. ⁶He who observes the day,
observes it in honour of the Lord. He also who eats, eats in
honour of the Lord, since he gives thanks to God; while he
who abstains, abstains in honour of the Lord and gives

Mt 7:1
Jas 4:11-12
Rom 6:15

Gal 4:10

---

non iudicet, Deus enim illum assumpsit. ⁴Tu quis es, qui iudices alienum
servum? Suo domino stat aut cadit; stabit autem, potens est enim Dominus
statuere illum. ⁵Nam alius iudicat inter diem et diem, alius iudicat omnem diem;
unusquisque in suo sensu abundet. ⁶Qui sapit diem, Domino sapit; et qui
manducat, Domino manducat, gratias enim agit Deo; et qui non manducat,

---

Cathedram; Vatican II, *Unitatis redintegratio*, 4). They mark the limits within
which Christians should exercise their freedom – at one extreme, what is laid
down by lawful authority; at the other, the need to practise charity towards all.
The freedom of the "strong" ends where the demands of charity begin:
therefore, they should not scandalize the weak; and the mistake the weak make
is to regard as obligatory something which is not, something a person can do
or not as he pleases.

Love for freedom, properly understood, is never a danger to the faith: "The
only freedom that can assail the faith is a misinterpreted freedom, an aimless
freedom, one without objective principles, one that is lawless and irresponsible.
In a word, licence [. . .]. This is why it is inaccurate to speak of 'freedom of
conscience', thereby implying that it may be morally right for someone to reject
God [. . .]. I defend with all my strength 'freedom of consciences' (Leo XIII,
Enc. *Libertas praestantissimum*), which means that no one can licitly prevent
a man from worshipping God" (J. Escrivá, *Friends of God*, 32).

Freedom is "an exceptional sign of the image of God in man. For God willed
that man should 'be left in the hand of his own counsel' (Sir 15:14) so that he
might of his own accord seek his Creator and freely attain his full and blessed
perfection by cleaving to him. Man's dignity therefore requires him to act out
of conscious and free choice, as moved and drawn in a personal way from
within, and not by blind impulses in himself or by mere external constraint"
(Vatican II, *Gaudium et spes*, 17). Therefore, the exercise of freedom consists
in obeying a well formed conscience and thereby, with the help of grace,
attaining one's last end and the means necessary thereto. In fact, man will be
judged on his obedience or disobedience to the law written on his heart.
"Conscience is man's most secret core, and his sanctuary. There he is alone
with God" (*ibid.*, 16f). Its dictates must always be obeyed, even if they be

Rom 6:10-11
2 Cor 5:15
1 Thess 5:10
Lk 20:38
Acts 10:42

Mt 25:31
Acts 17:31
2 Cor 5:10
Rom 2:6-8
Is 45:23; 49:18
Phil 2:10-11

thanks to God. ⁷None of us lives to himself, and none of us dies to himself. ⁸If we live, we live to the Lord, and if we die, we die to the Lord; so then, whether we live or whether we die, we are the Lord's. ⁹For to this end Christ died and lived again, that he might be Lord both of the dead and of the living.

¹⁰Why do you pass judgment on your brother? Or you, why do you despise your brother? For we shall all stand before the judgment seat of God; ¹¹for it is written,

---

Domino non manducat et gratias agit Deo. ⁷Nemo enim nostrum sibi vivit et nemo sibi moritur; ⁸sive enim vivimus, Domino vivimus, sive morimur, Domino morimur. Sive ergo vivimus, sive morimur, Domini sumus. ⁹In hoc enim Christus et mortuus est et vixit, ut et mortuorum et vivorum dominetur. ¹⁰Tu autem quid iudicas fratrem tuum? Aut tu quare spernis fratrem tuum? Omnes enim stabimus ante tribunal Dei; ¹¹scriptum est enim: *"Vivo ego, dicit Dominus, mihi flectetur omne genu, et omnis lingua confitebitur Deo."* ¹²Itaque

---

mistaken, and others should always respect a person's conscience, for only God can read and judge the human heart, and he forbids us to judge the inner blameworthiness of others (cf. *ibid.*, 28).

"The just man, when he finds no way to excuse the action or the intention of someone whom he otherwise knows to be honest, not only does not judge him but rejects the very idea of doing so and leaves judgment to God. Our Lord on the Cross, not being able fully to excuse the sin of his crucifiers, at least lessened their malice saying that they did not know what they were doing. When we cannot excuse someone of sin, let us have pity on him, and try to find grounds for excusing him, such as ignorance or weakness" (St Francis de Sales, *Introduction to the Devout Life*, III, chap. 28).

7-9. We do not own ourselves, we are not our own masters. God, One and Three, has created us, and Jesus Christ has freed us from sin by redeeming us with his Blood. Therefore, he is our lord, and we his servants, committed to him body and soul. Just as the slave is not his own master, but he himself and all he does redounds to the benefit of his master, everything we are and everything we have are geared, in the last analysis, not to our own use and benefit: we have to live and die for the glory of God. He is lord of our life and of our death. Commenting on these words St Gregory the Great says: "The saints, therefore, do not live and do not die for themselves. They do not live for themselves, because in all that they do they strive for spiritual gain: by praying, preaching and persevering in good works, they seek the increase of the citizens of the heavenly fatherland. Nor do they die for themselves because men see them glorifying God by their death, hastening to reach him through death" (*In Ezechielem homiliae*, II, 10).

152

"As I live, says the Lord, every knee shall bow to me,
and every tongue shall give praise[u] to God."
[12]So each of us shall give account of himself to God.

Gal 6:5

Never make others stumble

[13]Then let us no more pass judgment on one another, but rather decide never to put a stumbling block or hindrance in the way of a brother. [14]I know and am persuaded in the Lord Jesus that nothing is unclean in itself; but it is unclean for any one who thinks it unclean. [15]If your brother is being injured by what you eat, you are no longer walking in love. Do not let what you eat cause the ruin of one for whom Christ died. [16]So do not let what is good to you be spoken of as evil. [17]For the kingdom of God does not mean food and drink but righteousness and peace and joy in the Holy Spirit; [18]he who thus serves Christ is acceptable to God and

Mt 15:1-20 and par.
Acts 10:15
1 Cor 10:25
1 Tim 4:3-4
Tit 1:15

1 Cor 8:10-13

Gal 5:22

Rom 12:17-18

---

unusquisque nostrum pro se rationem reddet Deo. [13]Non ergo amplius invicem iudicemus, sed hoc iudicate magis, ne ponatis offendiculum fratri vel scandalum. [14]Scio et certus sum in Domino Iesu quia nihil commune per seipsum, nisi ei, qui existimat quid commune esse, illi commune est. [15]Si enim propter cibum frater tuus contristatur, iam non secundum caritatem ambulas. Noli cibo tuo illum perdere, pro quo Christus mortuus est! [16]Non ergo blasphemetur bonum vestrum! [17]Non est enim regnum Dei esca et potus, sed iustitia et pax et gaudium in Spiritu Sancto; [18]qui enim in hoc servit Christo,

---

13-21. In everything we do we have an obligation to avoid causing others to stumble, causing scandal to others. However, this does not mean that we should omit to do what God commands, or act against our conscience. Jesus Christ preached the teaching his Father entrusted to him, even though this caused certain Pharisees to be scandalized (cf. Mt 15:14). Theirs was false scandal, which involves raising objections in order not to accept the truth – a phenomenon which also occurs frequently today. Genuine scandal can arise in connexion with actions which are in themselves morally indifferent but which can shock and even scandalize others, due to their spiritual immaturity or to their particular frame of mind: this was the context in which Jesus told St Peter to pay the half-shekel tax in order not to give offence (cf. Mt 17:27).

The situation dealt with in this passage is another example of the second kind of scandal. Although not distinguishing certain foods as unclean was lawful, some people might have seen that approach as wrong. In such cases it is, of course, not enough *not* to do evil: one must avoid even giving the appearance of doing evil: "I don't doubt your good intentions. I know that you act in the presence of God. But (and there is a 'but'), your actions are witnessed or may

[u]Or *confess*.

Tit 1:15

1 Cor 8:13

1 Cor 8:7
Jas 4:17

approved by men. [19]Let us then pursue what makes for peace and for mutual upbuilding. [20]Do not, for the sake of food, destroy the work of God. Everything is indeed clean, but it is wrong for any one to make others fall by what he eats; [21]it is right not to eat meat or drink wine or do anything that makes your brother stumble.[v] [22]The faith that you have, keep between yourself and God; happy is he who has no reason to judge himself for what he approves. [23]But he who

---

placet Deo et probatus est hominibus. [19]Itaque, quae pacis sunt, sectemur et quae aedificationis sunt in invicem. [20]Noli propter escam destruere opus Dei! Omnia quidem munda sunt, sed malum est homini, qui per offendiculum manducat. [21]Bonum est non manducare carnem et non bibere vinum neque id, in quo frater tuus offendit. [22]Tu, quam fidem habes, penes temetipsum habe coram Deo. Beatus, qui non iudicat semetipsum in eo quod probat. [23]Qui autem

---

be witnessed by men who judge by human standards. . . . And you must give them good example" (J. Escrivá, *The Way*, 275).

There is, as we have said, no obligation to avoid giving scandal where that is due to malice on the part of the observer – so-called pharisaical scandal.

22-23. When declaring all food to be clean, Jesus pointed out that "the things which come out of a man are what defile him" (Mk 7:15; cf. Mt 15:16-20). The Apostle will apply this teaching of Christ to the flesh of animals sacrificed to idols and to Jewish practices (cf. 1 Cor 8:8; Tit 1:15). Here specifically he says that "nothing is unclean in itself" (v. 14) and that "everything is indeed clean" (v. 20). Therefore, what the "strong" are doing is in principle morally neutral. However, it can become something bad if it causes brethren to fall (cf. vv. 20-21; 1 Cor 8:9-13), for the moral value of an action is determined also, though not principally, by the intention of the doer and by the circumstances of the situation.

Sometimes it can happen that a person is unaware that he is doing something wrong and in fact, acting in good faith, thinks he is doing something good. This is an instance of conscience being "certain" but not "right", because the dictate of conscience is not in line with the objective moral order. In connexion with this, the text says that "whatever does not proceed from faith is sin": here, "faith" refers to the certain conviction of the judgment of conscience which dictates that something is to be done or to be avoided.

Although conscience is what provides the immediate criterion for action, this does not mean that conscience is to be given total sway. Firstly, because, if it is wrong in what it directs, the person must first insofar as possible ensure that it accords with the truth and then embark on the right line of conduct; and, secondly, because one has an obligation to discover what God's will is and do

[v]Other ancient authorities add *or be upset or be weakened.*

has doubts is condemned, if he eats, because he does not act from faith; for whatever does not proceed from faith is sin.[w]

15

The example of Christ

[1] We who are strong ought to bear with the failings of the weak, and not to please ourselves; [2] let each of us please his neighbour for his good, to edify him. [3] For Christ did not please himself; but, as it is written, "The reproaches of

1 Cor 9:19, 22; 10:24, 33
Gal 6:2

Ps 69:10

discernit si manducaverit, damnatus est, quia non ex fide; omne autem, quod non ex fide, peccatum est.

[1] Debemus autem nos firmiores imbecillitates infirmorum sustinere, et non nobis placere. [2] Unusquisque nostrum proximo placeat in bonum ad aedificationem; [3] etenim Christus non sibi placuit, sed sicut scriptum est:

it. "To man in his ignorance and weakness, the Divine Saviour has brought his truth and his grace – the former to show him the way that will take him to his goal, the latter to give him the strength to reach that goal. What this means in practice is that one should accept the will and commandments of Christ and bring one's life into line with them – that is, all the internal and external acts involved in human decisions" (Pius XII, *Address*, 23 March 1952).

1-3. The rule which should govern Christian behaviour is that of mutual love. This love – charity – draws its inspiration from our Lord's own words, "A new commandment I give you, that you love one another; even as I have loved you, that you also love one another" (Jn 13:34; cf. note on Jn 13:34-35). Jesus set himself as the example we should follow: we should love each other as he loved us (cf. Jn 15:12-13; 1 Jn 3:16; 4:11; Eph 5:1-2); that is, even to the extent of giving our life through self-denial (Jn 15:13; 1 Jn 3:16; Rom 5:8). St Paul lays much stress on our Lord's abnegation: he bore our sins in his body and by his wounds we have been healed (cf. 1 Pet 2:24; Is 53:5-6); his sufferings were foretold in the Old Testament: "Zeal for thy house has consumed me, and the insults of those who insult thee have fallen on me [. . .]. They gave me poison for food, and for my thirst they gave me vinegar to drink" (Ps 69:9, 21; cf. Jn 2:17; Mt 27:34, 48).

This means that our charity should be inspired by Christ's own sentiments: "Turn your gaze constantly to Jesus who, without ceasing to be God, humbled himself and took the nature of a slave (cf. Phil 2:6-7), in order to serve us. Only by following in his direction will we find ideals that are worthwhile. Love seeks union, identification with the beloved. United to Christ, we shall be drawn to

[w] Other authorities, some ancient, insert here Ch 16:25-27.

1 Cor 6:6, 11
2 Tim 3:16
1 Mac 12:9

those who reproached thee fell on me." [4]For whatever was written in former days was written for our instruction, that by steadfastness and by the encouragement of the scriptures we might have hope. [5]May the God of steadfastness and encouragement grant you to live in such harmony with one another, in acccord with Christ Jesus, [6]that together you may with one voice glorify the God and Father of our Lord Jesus Christ.

Phil 2:1-4

[7]Welcome one another, therefore, as Christ has welcomed

"*Improperia improperantium tibi ceciderunt super me.*" [4]Quaecumque enim antea scripta sunt, ad nostram doctrinam scripta sunt, ut per patientiam et consolationem Scripturarum spem habeamus. [5]Deus autem patientiae et solacii det vobis idipsum sapere in alterutrum secundum Christum Iesum, [6]ut unanimes uno ore glorificetis Deum et Patrem Domini nostri Iesu Christi. [7]Propter quod suscipite invicem, sicut et Christus suscepit vos, in gloriam Dei. [8]Dico enim Christum ministrum fuisse circumcisionis propter veritatem Dei ad

---

imitate his life of dedication, his unlimited love and his sacrifice unto death. Christ brings us face to face with the ultimate choice: either we spend our life in selfish isolation, or we devote ourselves and all our energies to the service of others" (J. Escrivá, *Friends of God*, 236).

4. The excellence of Scripture and its sacred character derive from the fact that God is its author. This means that there is a consistency and unity running right through Sacred Scripture, a coherence which integrates both Testaments, Old and New: the Old Testament contains – prophetically and by way of prefigurement – what happens in the New; and in the New the prophecy and prefigurement of the Old are fulfilled. Since Scripture is the word of God, it is of the highest order: "All scripture is inspired by God and profitable for teaching, for reproof, for correction, and for training in righteousness, that the man of God may be complete, equipped for every good work" (2 Tim 3:16). This strength and authority of Scripture is useful not only for instruction in the faith but also for enlivening our hope and consoling us in every kind of trial, interior and exterior: the examples which we find in Scripture encourage us to be patient and also spur us on to fight. By reflecting on those examples we become convinced that if God asks sacrifice of "his own", he does so because he has a greater reward in store for them.

These truths led the Second Vatican Council to teach that in "the sacred books the Father who is in heaven comes lovingly to meet his children, and talks with them. And such is the force and power of the word of God that it can serve the Church as her support and vigour, and the children of the Church as strength for their faith, food for the soul, and a pure and lasting fount of spiritual life" (*Dei Verbum*, 21).

you, for the glory of God. ⁸For I tell you that Christ became
a servant to the circumcised to show God's truthfulness, in
order to confirm the promises given to the patriarchs, ⁹and
in order that the Gentiles might glorify God for his mercy.
As it is written,

Mt 15:24
Acts 3:25-26

Ex 34:6
Ps 89:2-3; 18:50

"Therefore I will praise thee among the Gentiles,
and sing to thy name";
¹⁰and again it is said,

Deut 32:43
(LXX)

"Rejoice, O Gentiles, with his people";
¹¹and again,

Ps 117:1

"Praise the Lord, all Gentiles,
and let all the peoples praise him";
¹²and further Isaiah says,

Is 11:10
Rev 5:5
Gen 49:10

"The root of Jesse shall come,
he who rises to rule the Gentiles;
in him shall the Gentiles hope."
¹³May the God of hope fill you with all joy and peace in

---

confirmandas promissiones patrum, ⁹gentes autem propter misericordiam glorificare Deum, sicut scriptum est: "*Propter hoc confitebor tibi in gentibus, et nomini tuo cantabo.*" ¹⁰Et iterum dicit: "*Laetamini, gentes, cum plebe eius.*" ¹¹Et iterum: "*Laudate, omnes gentes, Dominum, et magnificent eum omnes populi.*" ¹²Et rursus Isaias ait: "*Erit radix Iesse, et qui exsurget regere gentes: in eo gentes sperabunt.*" ¹³Deus autem spei repleat vos omni gaudio et pace in

---

8-13. "It was necessary that the word of God should be spoken first to you. Since you thrust it from you, and judge yourselves unworthy of eternal life, behold, we turn to the Gentiles. For so the Lord has commanded us" (Acts 13:46-47): this is what Paul and Barnabas said to Jews who opposed their preaching. Christ himself said that he had been sent only to seek out the lost sheep of the house of Israel, and that was the scope of the Apostles' first mission (cf. Mt 15:24; 10:5). However, God's plans never discriminated in favour of the Jews: they, once converted, were to preach the Good News to the Gentiles. After the Resurrection, Jesus sent his disciples to all nations (cf. Mt 28:18ff). Those who proclaimed the Gospel were Jews who had accepted Christ, and they addressed their preaching first to Jews and then to Gentiles.

This present passage refers to the fulfilment of God's designs through Christ. By becoming man God made good his promises to the Jews, kept faith with them. By the entry of the Gentiles into the Church his mercy towards all men is revealed, for his blessings are thereby extended to those who do not belong to Israel according to the flesh. Our Lord explained this very graphically in the parable of the two sons (Mt 21:28-32). He first calls the older son (the Gentiles), who refuses to obey him and afterwards repents and accepts his father's

believing, so that by the power of the Holy Spirit you may abound in hope.

E P I L O G U E

Paul's ministry

¹⁴I myself am satisfied about you, my brethren, that you yourselves are full of goodness, filled with all knowledge, and able to instruct one another. ¹⁵But on some points I have written to you very boldly by way of reminder, because of the grace given me by God ¹⁶to be a minister of Christ Jesus to the Gentiles in the priestly service of the gospel of God, so that the offering of the Gentiles may be acceptable, sanctified by the Holy Spirit. ¹⁷In Christ Jesus, then, I have reason to be proud of my work for God. ¹⁸For I will not venture to speak of anything except what Christ has wrought through me to win obedience from the Gentiles, by word and deed, ¹⁹by the power of signs and wonders, by the power of the Holy Spirit, so that from Jerusalem and as

Rom 1:5; 6:13
Rom 3:24-25;
11:13; 12:1
Phil 2:17
2 Cor 3:5-6

Mk 16:17
2 Cor 12:12
Acts 1:8
Col 1:25
2 Cor 10:15-16
1 Cor 3:10-12
Is 52:15

---

credendo, ut abundetis in spe in virtute Spiritus Sancti. ¹⁴Certus sum autem, fratres mei, et ego ipse de vobis, quoniam et ipsi pleni estis bonitate, repleti omni scientia, ita ut possitis et alterutrum monere. ¹⁵Audacius autem scripsi vobis ex parte, tamquam in memoriam vos reducens propter gratiam, quae data est mihi a Deo, ¹⁶ut sim minister Christi Iesu ad gentes, consecrans evangelium Dei, ut fiat oblatio gentium accepta, sanctificata in Spiritu Sancto. ¹⁷Habeo igitur gloriationem in Christo Iesu ad Deum; ¹⁸non enim audebo aliquid loqui eorum, quae per me non effecit Christus in oboedientiam gentium, verbo et factis, ¹⁹in virtute signorum et prodigiorum, in virtute Spiritus, ita ut ab

---

invitation and goes to work in the vineyard. The younger son (most of the Jewish people), on the other hand, seems to be ready to do his father's bidding but in fact does not. Many Jews were so hard of heart that not even the repentance and conversion of the Gentiles moved them to repent.

16. Christ "became a servant to the circumcised" (v. 8), that is, he directed his teaching to the Jews, proclaimed to them the Gospel of the Kingdom, in order to lead them to salvation. St Paul, within the context of the universal mission entrusted to the Apostles, was chosen to proclaim the Gospel of Christ to the Gentiles (cf. Rom 1:5). As well as preaching the Good News, the Apostle's mission included a strictly priestly commitment, which consisted in sanctifying the Gentiles in order to make them an offering pleasing to God (cf. Eph 3:6-9).

far round as Illyricum I have fully preached the gospel of Christ, [20]thus making it my ambition to preach the gospel, not where Christ has already been named, lest I build on another man's foundation, [21]but as it is written,

"They shall see who have never been told of him,
and they shall understand who have never heard of him."

Journeys planned

[22]This is the reason why I have so often been hindered from coming to you. [23]But now, since I no longer have any room for work in these regions, and since I have longed for many years to come to you, [24]I hope to see you in passing as I go to Spain, and to be sped on my journey there by you, once I have enjoyed your company for a little. [25]At present, however, I am going to Jerusalem with aid for the saints. [26]For Macedonia and Achaia have been pleased to make some contribution for the poor among the saints at Jerusalem; [27]they were pleased to do it, and indeed they are

Rom 1:13
1 Thess 2:18
Rom 1:10-12

1 Cor 16:6

Acts 11:29-30;
19:21; 20:22-23
1 Cor 16:1
2 Cor 8:1-6;
9:1-2
1 Cor 9:11
Gal 6:6

Ierusalem et per circuitum usque in Illyricum repleverim evangelium Christi, [20]sic autem contendens praedicare evangelium, non ubi nominatus est Christus, ne super alienum fundamentum aedificarem, [21]sed sicut scriptum est: *"Quibus non est annuntiatum de eo, videbunt, et qui non audierunt, intellegent."* [22]Propter quod et impediebar plurimum venire ad vos; [23]nunc vero ulterius locum non habens in his regionibus, cupiditatem autem habens veniendi ad vos ex multis iam annis, [24]cum in Hispaniam proficisci coepero, spero enim quod praeteriens videam vos et a vobis deducar illuc, si vobis primum ex parte fruitus fuero. [25]Nunc autem proficiscor in Ierusalem ministrare sanctis; [26]probaverunt enim Macedonia et Achaia communicationem aliquam facere in pauperes sanctorum, qui sunt in Ierusalem. [27]Placuit enim eis, et debitores sunt eorum; nam si spiritalibus eorum communicaverunt gentes, debent et in carnalibus

---

Previously only the Jewish people could be considered a holy people, a priestly people (cf. Ex 19:5-6). With the coming of Christ, the Gentiles also have become an "acceptable offering, sanctified by the Holy Spirit". All Christians who are part of this "offering of the Gentiles" should take to heart what St Augustine says: "You contain within you what you should offer. Draw from your heart, as from a treasure chest, the incense of praise; offer from the treasury of your conscience the sacrifice of faith. And with charity set fire to everything you offer. For within you are these offerings which you should sacrifice in praise of God" (*Enarrationes in Psalmos*, 55, 19). In other words, consciousness of being called to share in Christ's priesthood should help us to offer God our whole life: "Let the faithful, then, learn to appreciate the dignity to which they have been raised by the Sacrament of Baptism [. . .] and let them

159

in debt to them, for if the Gentiles have come to share in their spiritual blessings, they ought also to be of service to them in material blessings. [28]When therefore I have completed this, and have delivered to them what has been raised,[x] I shall go on by way of you to Spain; [29]and I know that when I come to you I shall come in the fulness of the blessing[y] of Christ.

[30]I appeal to you, brethren, by our Lord Jesus Christ and by the love of the Spirit, to strive together with me in your prayers to God on my behalf, [31]that I may be delivered from the unbelievers in Judea, and that my service for Jerusalem may be acceptable to the saints, [32]so that by God's will I may come to you with joy and be refreshed in your company. [33]The God of peace be with you all. Amen.

2 Cor 1:11
Phil 1:27
Col 4:2-3
2 Thess 3:1
Acts 20:3, 23;
21:10, 17, 27

1 Cor 14:33
2 Cor 13:11
Phil 4:9
1 Thess 5:23
2 Thess 3:16

---

ministrare eis. [28]Hoc igitur cum consummavero et assignavero eis fructum hunc, proficiscar per vos in Hispaniam; [29]scio autem quoniam veniens ad vos, in abundantia benedictionis Christi veniam. [30]Obsecro autem vos, fratres, per Dominum nostrum Iesum Christum et per caritatem Spiritus, ut concertemini mecum in orationibus pro me ad Deum, [31]ut liberer ab infidelibus, qui sunt in Iudaea, et ministerium meum pro Ierusalem acceptum sit sanctis, [32]ut veniens ad vos in gaudio per voluntatem Dei refrigerer vobiscum. [33]Deus autem pacis sit cum omnibus vobis. Amen.

---

not forget to offer themselves and their anxieties, their sorrows, their troubles, their miseries and their needs, in union with their divine Head crucified" (Pius XII, *Mediator Dei*, 25).

[x]Greek *sealed to them this fruit.*
[y]Other ancient authorities insert *of the gospel.*

16

Greetings and recommendations

¹I commend to you our sister Phoebe, a deaconess of the
church at Cenchreae, ²that you may receive her in the Lord
as befits the saints, and help her in whatever she may require
from you, for she has been a helper of many and of myself
as well.

Acts 18:18

---

¹Commendo autem vobis Phoebem sororem nostram, qua est ministra ecclesiae, quae est Cenchris, ²ut eam suscipiatis in Domino digne sanctis et assistatis

---

1-16. This long series of affectionate greetings which the Apostle sends the
Romans shows that the early Christians formed one great family, in which each
saw the rest as brothers and sisters (cf. Acts 15:23; Rom 1:13; 1 Cor 1:10; Jas
1:2; 2 Pet 1:10; 1 Jn 3:13; etc.). As we can see from the names given here, this
family contained people from many different parts of the Empire – Greeks:
Andronicus, Olympas, Asyncritus, Hermes; people from Asia Minor or the
Hellenic world: Epaenetus, Persis, Patrobas; Latins: Junias, Ampliatus, Prisca,
Julia, Urbanus; Jews: Herodion, Mary, Tryphaena, Tryphosa, etc. It also
included people of all types of social background; most of the people mentioned
probably were of humble condition or slaves or freed men, as can be deduced
from texts on funeral slabs; but there were others who had social positions of
some importance, like Prisca, who was a member of a noble Roman family,
Aristobulus and Narcissus, who belonged to a "a family", that is, a household
with many servants, Erastus, etc.

They all felt united by a bond of charity and a common calling to holiness,
as can be seen from references to "the saints" (cf. Rom 1:7; 1 Cor 1:2; Heb
13:24; Jude 3; etc.). They were not perfect; we are well aware that they had
their limitations (cf. the moral irregularities mentioned in chapter 13, and the
disagreements between the "strong" and the "weak" in chapter 14); but their
desire for sanctity and their charity inspired them to serve one another and to
put themselves and their possessions at the disposal of the Church. Their
commitment was such that they managed to spread their influence in a pagan
world and light it up with the light of salvation. They were families "who lived
in union with Christ and who made him known to others. Small Christian
communities which were centres for the spreading of the Gospel and its
message. Families no different from other families of those times, but living
with a new spirit, which spread to all those who were in contact with them. This
is what the first Christians were, and this is what we have to be – sowers of
peace and joy, the peace and joy that Jesus has brought to us" (J. Escrivá, *Christ
is passing by*, 30).

1-2. Phoebe was probably the bearer of this letter. She came from

Acts 18:2-3, 26
1 Cor 16:19
2 Tim 4:19
Col 4:15
Philem 2
1 Cor 16:15, 19

2 Cor 8:23

[3]Greet Prisca and Aquila, my fellow workers in Christ Jesus, [4]who risked their necks for my life, to whom not only I but also all the churches of the Gentiles give thanks; [5]greet also the church in their house. Greet my beloved Epaenetus, who was the first convert in Asia for Christ. [6]Greet Mary, who has worked hard among you. [7]Greet Andronicus and Junias, my kinsmen and my fellow prisoners; they are men of note among the apostles, and they were in Christ before me.[8]Greet Ampliatus, my beloved in the Lord. [9]Greet Urbanus, our fellow worker in Christ, and my beloved Stachys. [10]Greet Apelles, who is approved in Christ. Greet those who belong to the family of Aristobulus. [11]Greet my kinsman Herodion. Greet those in the Lord who belong to the family of Narcissus. [12]Greet those workers in the Lord,

---

ei in quocumque negotio vestri indiguerit, etenim ipsa astitit multis et mihi ipsi. [3]Salutate Priscam et Aquilam adiutores meos in Christo Iesu, [4]qui pro anima mea suas cervices supposuerunt, quibus non solus ego gratias ago, sed et cunctae ecclesiae gentium, [5]et domesticam eorum Ecclesiam. Salutate Epaenetum dilectum mihi, primitias Asiae in Christo. [6]Salutate Mariam, quae multum laboravit in vobis. [7]Salutate Andronicum et Iuniam cognatos meos et concaptivos meos, qui sunt nobiles in apostolis, qui et ante me fuerunt in Christo. [8]Salutate Ampliatum dilectissimum mihi in Domino. [9]Salutate Urbanum adiutorem nostrum in Christo et Stachyn dilectum meum. [10]Salutate Apellem probatum in Christo. Salutate eos, qui sunt ex Aristobuli. [11]Salutate Herodionem cognatum meum. Salutate eos, qui sunt ex Narcissi, qui sunt in Domino. [12]Salutate Tryphaenam et Tryphosam, quae laborant in Domino.

Cenchreae, the eastern port of Corinth. Paul refers to her being a *ministra ecclesiae*, a minister or servant of the church at Cenchreae, perhaps because she helped with the assistance given to the poor and needy and may have had an auxiliary role in the baptism of women. Pliny the Younger, in his letter to the emperor Trajan, makes reference to two such women who helped in the Christian community (*Letter 10*, 96).

4. Prisca and Aquila were a well-known married couple, as we can see from other passages in the New Testament (cf. Acts 18:2, 18; 1 Cor 16:19; 2 Tim 4:19). They probably came to the Apostle's aid in Ephesus at the time of the riot of the silversmiths (cf. Acts 19:23-40). Prisca or Priscilla, it has been suggested, was connected with a Roman family of senatorial rank, the Pudentes. According to an early tradition, St Paul stayed as a guest in their house in Rome.

5. Epaenetus was the "first-fruit" of Asia, that is, the first to be baptized in that eastern province of the Empire.

Tryphaena and Tryphosa. Greet the beloved Persis, who
has worked hard in the Lord. [13]Greet Rufus, eminent in the
Lord, also his mother and mine. [14]Greet Asyncritus,
Phlegon, Hermes, Patrobas, Hermas, and the brethren who
are with them. [15]Greet Philologus, Julia, Nereus and his
sister, and Olympas, and all the saints who are with them.
[16]Greet one another with a holy kiss. All the churches of
Christ greet you.
[17]I appeal to you, brethren, to take note of those who
create dissensions and difficulties, in opposition to the
doctrine which you have been taught; avoid them. [18]For
such persons do not serve our Lord Christ, but their own
appetites,[z] and by fair and flattering words they deceive the
hearts of the simple-minded. [19]For while your obedience is
known to all, so that I rejoice over you, I would have you
wise as to what is good and guileless as to what is evil;

Mk 15:21

1 Cor 16:20
2 Cor 13:12
1 Pet 5:14

Rom 6:17
1 Tim 1:3
2 Jn 10

Phil 3:19
Col 2:4
Tit 1:10

Rom 1:5, 8
Mt 10:16
1 Cor 14:20

Salutate Persidam carissimam, quae multum laboravit in Domino. [13]Salutate
Rufum electum in Domino et matrem eius et meam. [14]Salutate Asyncritum,
Phlegonta, Hermem, Patrobam, Hermam et qui cum eis sunt fratres. [15]Salutate
Philologum et Iuliam, Nereum et sororem eius et Olympam et omnes, qui cum
eis sunt, sanctos. [16]Salutate invicem in osculo sancto. Salutant vos omnes
ecclesiae Christi.[17]Rogo autem vos, fratres, ut observetis eos, qui dissensiones
et offendicula praeter doctrinam, quam vos didicistis, faciunt, et declinate ab
illis; [18]huiusmodi enim Domino nostro Christo non serviunt sed suo ventri, et
per dulces sermones et benedictiones seducunt corda innocentium. [19]Vestra
enim oboedientia ad omnes pervenit; gaudeo igitur in vobis, sed volo vos
sapientes esse in bono et simplices in malo. [20]Deus autem pacis conteret
Satanam sub pedibus vestris velociter. Gratia Domini nostri Iesu vobiscum.

---

13. St Paul remembers Rufus with special affection, calling Rufus' mother
his own, such is his love and veneration for her. It is possible that Rufus was
one of the sons of Simon of Cyrene (cf. Mk 15:21).

17-18. This is a reference to Judaizing preachers, like those with whom St
Paul had difficulties in many churches in the East (cf. 2 Cor 11:13-15; Gal
1:6-7; Phil 3:18-19). They sought to maintain the distinction between clean and
unclean food, and insisted on circumcision and the observance of Mosaic
precepts. This is why he says they serve not Christ but their own appetites, that
is, food. They used to worm their way into Christian communities by projecting
themselves as very religious people and by preaching what they argued was a
more perfect lifestyle (cf. 2 Cor 11:21-23; Gal 2:4; 3:1; Phil 3:2-3).

[z]Greek *their own belly* (Phil 3:19).

163

Gen 3:15

Acts 16:1; 13:1;
17:5; 19:22;
20:4
Phil 2:19
1 Cor 1:14

²⁰then the God of peace will soon crush Satan under your feet. The grace of our Lord Jesus Christ be with you.^a

²¹Timothy, my fellow worker, greets you; so do Lucius and Jason and Sosipater, my kinsmen.

²²I Tertius, the writer of this letter, greet you in the Lord.

²³Gaius, who is host to me and to the whole church, greets you. Erastus, the city treasurer, and our brother Quartus, greet you.^b

Doxology

Eph 1:9; 3:5, 9
Col 1:26

²⁵Now to him who is able to strengthen you according to my gospel and the preaching of Jesus Christ, according to the revelation of the mystery which was kept secret for long

---

²¹Salutat vos Timotheus adiutor meus et Lucius et Iason et Sosipater cognati mei. ²²Saluto vos ego Tertius, qui scripsi epistulam in Domino. ²³ Salutat vos Gaius hospes meus et universae ecclesiae. (24) Salutat vos Erastus arcarius civitatis et Quartus frater. ²⁵Ei autem, qui potens est vos confirmare iuxta

---

20. One of the effects of the Redemption wrought by Christ is victory over the devil. This had been foretold at the very beginning of the History of Salvation, when it was prophesied that the Messiah would crush the head of the serpent (cf. Gen 3:15). Those who, by being one with Christ, share in his power, also triumph over the snares of the devil.

It is true, of course, that the devil is powerful and that he never ceases to search for those whom he might devour (cf. 1 Pet 5:8); but we should always remember that he can only operate within the limits imposed on him by God. Furthermore, since we can count on the Lord's help, we should never be afraid of the devil: God is stronger than he is. Until this conviction becomes clearly rooted in us, we can feel threatened by the devil, but this conviction, once we have it, makes us feel quite safe. St Teresa of Avila gives us the benefit of her own experience in this regard: "I was left with a mastery over the demons, given me by the Master of all, which means I gave them no more importance than flies. They seem such cowards to me: as soon as they see that you give them little importance, they become powerless [. . .]. I do not understand these fears: Demon! demon! What we should be doing is saying: God! God!, and make them tremble. Yes, we should realize that they cannot even stir unless God allow it" (*Life*, 25).

23. Gaius, one of the very few Christians of Corinth whom St Paul himself baptized (cf. 1 Cor 1:14), had made his house available to the Apostle and let it be used for church assembly.

^aOr *slave*.
^bGreek *according to man*.

ages ²⁶but is now disclosed and through the prophetic writings is made known to all nations, according to the command of the eternal God, to bring about the obedience of faith – ²⁷to the only wise God be glory for evermore through Jesus Christ! Amen.

Rom 1:5
2 Tim 1:10

1 Tim 1:17
Jude 25

---

evangelium meum et praedicationem Iesu Christi secundum revelationem mysterii temporibus aeternis taciti, ²⁶manifestati autem nunc, et per scripturas prophetarum secundum praeceptum aeterni Dei ad oboeditionem fidei in cunctis gentibus patefacti, ²⁷soli sapienti Deo per Iesum Christum, cui gloria in saecula. Amen.

25-27. Unlike other letters, this one ends with an elaborate poem of praise, or doxology, addressed through Jesus Christ, to God almighty and wise.

The Epistle of St Paul to the Galatians

ENGLISH AND LATIN VERSIONS, WITH NOTES

1

INTRODUCTION

Greeting

¹Paul an apostle – not from men nor through man, but through Jesus Christ and God the Father, who raised him from the dead – ²and all the brethren who are with me,
   To the churches of Galatia:

Rom 1:1
Gal 1:11-12

Rom 1:7
Phil 1:2

---

¹Paulus apostolus, non ab hominibus neque per hominem, sed per Iesum Christum et Deum Patrem, qui suscitavit eum a mortuis, ²et qui mecum sunt

---

1-5. The epistle's opening salutation indicates the two main themes of the letter – St Paul's credentials, his apostolic authority (v. 1), dealt with in chapters 1-2, and the effectiveness of the Redemption of mankind achieved by Jesus Christ (v. 4), which is explored in the rest of the letter.

By beginning his letter as he does, the Apostle takes issue immediately with the errors being spread by Judaizers – who were denying his authority and were maintaining the need for circumcision and the other Mosaic observances.

1. St Paul begins this letter by recalling that it was God himself who made him an Apostle. True, unlike the Twelve, he had not been called by our Lord during his public life; he recognizes this: "Last of all, as to one untimely born, he appeared also to me. For I am the least of the apostles, unfit to be called an apostle" (1 Cor 15:8-9). That is why he stresses that his calling is a gift bestowed without merit – and the fruits of his apostolate are also due to God: "But by the grace of God I am what I am, and his grace toward me was not in vain. On the contrary, I worked harder than any of them, though it was not I, but the grace of God which is in me" (1 Cor 15:10; cf. 1 Cor 9:1-2; Gal 2:8). As St Augustine observes, Paul's late arrival on the scene was made up for by the fact that it was the glorified Christ himself who called him and therefore the authority of Paul's witness is on a par with that of the Twelve (cf. *Exp. in Gal*, 2).

The basis of Paul's apostolic authority, therefore, is the vocation he received directly from Jesus Christ (cf. Acts 9:1-18). This shows that he is an apostle "not from men nor through man" but "through Jesus Christ." By joining so closely, in the same phrase, the name of Christ and that of God the Father, the Apostle is defending his authority as being based on the will of Jesus Christ – as was the case with the Twelve – and on God the Father's salvific plans.

2. On who the Galatians were, and the particular circumstances of the church of Galatia, see "Introduction to St Paul's Epistles to the Galatians and the Romans", above, p. 52.

Gal 2:20
Mt 20:28
1 Tim 2:6
Tit 2:14
1 Jn 5:19

Rom 16:27

2 Thess 2:2

³Grace to you and peace from God the Father and our Lord Jesus Christ, ⁴who gave himself for our sins to deliver us from the present evil age, according to the will of our God and Father; ⁵to whom be the glory for ever and ever. Amen.

A warning

⁶I am astonished that you are so quickly deserting him

---

omnes fratres, ecclesiis Galatiae: ³gratia vobis et pax a Deo Patre nostro et Domino Iesu Christo, ⁴qui dedit semetipsum pro peccatis nostris, ut eriperet nos de praesenti saeculo nequam secundum voluntatem Dei et Patris nostri, ⁵cui

---

3. On the gifts of grace and peace, cf. note on Rom 1:7.

4. Christ's redemptive death is the efficient cause of atonement for our sins and, therefore, is what frees us from "the present evil age". This phase refers – as it does often in St John's Gospel – to sin and other forces opposed to God which are at work in history and which are manifest to us. Man is rescued from them by the redemptive action of Christ. The world in itself was created as something good, but its original goodness became tarnished, and, to the extent that it reflects the perverse will of man, it is an occasion of sin. Through Revelation there "has been revealed in a new and more wonderful way the fundamental truth concerning creation to which the Book of Genesis gives witness when it repeats several times: 'God saw that it was good' (cf. Gen 1) [. . .]. In Jesus Christ the visible world which God created for man (cf. Gen 1:26-30) – the world that, when sin entered, 'was subjected to futility' (Rom 8:20) – recovers again its original link with the divine source of Wisdom and Love (cf. Rom 8:19-22; Vatican II, *Gaudium et spes*, 2 and 13)" (John Paul II, *Redemptor hominis*, 8). Man then begins to glimpse the things of heaven.

To use St Jerome's comparison, man is like the fish, which is caught on the hook of the divine fisherman and drawn up to the word of God out of the abyss of this world. "But what happens in nature does not happen here: fish die when they are taken out of the sea, whereas the Apostles drew us out of the sea of this world; they fished us, in order to bring the dead to life [. . .]. We have begun to see the sun, to see the true light, and we are stirred with pure joy in the intimacy of our soul" (*Hom. to neophytes on Ps 41*). In this light man can look optimistically on the world which Christ has redeemed; he can discern its good aspects, can see it as something which can be sanctified and which can contribute to his own sanctification. "A Christian has to be ready, at all times, to sanctify society from within. He is fully present in the world, but without belonging to the world, when it denies God and opposes his lovable will of salvation, not because of its nature, but because of sin" (J. Escrivá, *Christ is passing by*, 125).

6-9. The Galatians had suddenly begun to go off course, for no sooner had

170

who called you in the grace of Christ and turning to a
different gospel – [7]not that there is another gospel, but there   Acts 15:24
are some who trouble you and want to pervert the gospel
of Christ. [8]But even if we, or an angel from heaven, should   1 Cor 16:22
preach to you a gospel contrary to that which we preached   2 Cor 11:4
to you, let him be accursed. [9]As we have said before, so   Rom 9:3
now I say again, If any one is preaching to you a gospel   1 Thess 2:4
contrary to that which you received, let him be accursed.

---

gloria in saecula saeculorum. Amen. [6]Miror quod tam cito transferimini ab eo,
qui vos vocavit in gratia Christi, in aliud evangelium; [7]quod non est aliud, nisi
sunt aliqui, qui vos conturbant et volunt convertere evangelium Christi. [8]Sed
licet nos aut angelus de caelo evangelizet vobis praeterquam quod
evangelizavimus vobis, anathema sit! [9]Sicut praediximus, et nunc iterum dico:
Si quis vobis evangelizaverit praeter id, quod accepistis, anathema sit! [10]Modo
enim hominibus suadeo aut Deo? Aut quaero hominibus placere? Si adhuc

---

St Paul preached to them during his second visit, than enemies of his appeared
on the scene seeking to undermine his authority and had won over the Galatians,
especially on the matter of circumcision.

In view of this, the Apostle clearly and forcefully spells out to the Galatians
that there is only one Gospel, only one way to attain salvation. "These people",
St Jerome explains, "wanted to change the Gospel, to twist it; but that is
something they cannot succeed in doing, for this Gospel is such that it cannot
be true if it is tampered with" (*Comm. in Gal*, 1, 7).

The content of Revelation – the deposit of faith – cannot be interfered with.
The Apostles, as their very title implies, were sent to pass on, in all its integrity,
what had been entrusted to them (cf. 1 Cor 11:23). That is why St Paul tells his
assistants in the government of the Church, Titus and Timothy, to guard very
carefully the truths he has taught them (cf. 1 Tim 6:20; 2 Tim 1:14; Tit 1:9; 2:1;
etc.).

St Paul is extremely insistent on the need to protect the deposit of faith, and
he reacts very forcefully against those who seek to adulterate it, as we can see
in this present text. Any attempt to replace the true Gospel of Jesus Christ with
a different teaching does indeed warrant the severe judgment which the Apostle
here delivers in God's name. In the same way, "the Church which received the
office of safeguarding the deposit of faith along with the apostolic duty of
teaching, likewise possesses the right and duty of proscribing [. . .] opinions
that are known to be opposed to the doctrine of the faith" (Vatican I, *Dei Filius*,
chap. 4).

There is, then, no "new Christianity" waiting to be discovered. "The
Christian economy, therefore, since it is the new and definitive covenant, will
never pass away; and no new public revelation is to be expected before the
glorious manifestation of our Lord Jesus Christ" (Vatican II, *Dei Verbum*, 5).

10Am I now seeking the favour of men, or of God? Or am I trying to please men? If I were still pleasing men, I should not be a servant[a] of Christ.

---

hominibus placerem, Christi servus non essem! 11Notum enim vobis facio, fratres, evangelium, quod evangelizatum est a me, quia non est secundum

---

10. One of the accusations directed against St Paul was that, in order to make it easier for people to become Christians, he tried to win them over by not requiring Gentiles to undergo circumcision. In fact the Apostle's only aim was to serve Christ; for him, as St John Chrysostom put it, "to love Christ was life, the world, heaven, present well-being, the kingdom, the promise, immeasurable good; outside of this he did not concern himself with classifying things as sorrowful or joyful, nor did he regard anything that one might have in this world as disagreeable or pleasant" (*Second hom. in praise of St Paul*).

St Paul can assert that he did not mind if there were people who did not understand him or even rejected his teaching. He had plenty of experience of opposition to the demands of the Gospel; and this never led him to play down the reality of the Cross in order to make more acceptable the truth he was proclaiming. In addition to lack of response from Gentiles, his faithfulness to Christ had also earned him enmity and persecution from Jews (cf. Acts 13:50).

We can learn a great deal from Paul to help us not to be cowed by "what people may think". Although Christian living does sometimes clash with the environment around us, we should not desist from trying to be faithful to the demands of the Gospel. "Therefore, when in our own life or in that of others we notice something that is not going well, something that requires the spiritual and human help which, as children of God, we can and ought to provide, then a clear sign of prudence is to apply the appropriate remedy by going to the root of the trouble, resolutely, lovingly and sincerely. There is no room here for inhibitions, for it is a great mistake to think that problems can be solved by inaction or procrastination" (J. Escrivá, *Friends of God* 157).

St Teresa, for her part, writes: "We are trying to attain union with God. We want to follow the counsels of Christ, on whom were showered insults and false witness. Are we, then, really so anxious to keep intact our own reputation and credit? We cannot do so and yet attain to union, for the two ways diverge" (*Life*, chap. 31). If we are truly to serve God we must be ready to face indifference and misunderstanding whenever it may arise. "You must indeed have purified your intention well when you said: From this moment on I renounce all human gratitude and reward" (J. Escrivá, *The Way*, 789).

11-12. "What shall I do, Lord?" (Acts 22:10), Paul asked at the moment of his conversion. Jesus replied, "Rise, and go into Damascus, and there you will be told all that is appointed for you to do" (*ibid.*). The former persecutor, now

[a] Or *slave*.

PAUL'S PERSONAL APOLOGIA

God's call

¹¹For I would have you know, brethren, that the gospel which was preached by me is not man's^b gospel. ¹²For I did not receive it from man, nor was I taught it, but it came through a revelation of Jesus Christ. ¹³For you have heard of my former life in Judaism, how I persecuted the church of God violently and tried to destroy it; ¹⁴and I advanced in Judaism beyond many of my own age among my people, so extremely zealous was I for the traditions of my fathers.

Mt 16:17

Eph 3:3

Acts 8:3; 9:21;
22:3-5; 26:9-11
Phil 3:4-6
2 Cor 11:22

---

hominem; ¹²neque enim ego ab homine accepi illud, neque didici, sed per revelationem Iesu Christi. ¹³Audistis enim conversationem meam aliquando in Iudaismo quoniam supra modum persequebar ecclesiam Dei et expugnabam illam ¹⁴et proficiebam in Iudaismo supra multos coaetaneos in genere meo, abundantius aemulator exsistens paternarum mearum traditionum. ¹⁵Cum

---

under the influence of grace, will receive instruction and Baptism through the ordinary course of divine Providence – from a man, Ananias. Thereby Jesus led him to humility, obedience and abandonment. The Gospel which St Paul preached was identical with that preached by the other Apostles, and already had the character of "tradition" in the nascent Church (cf. 1 Cor 15:3; Gal 2:2). This is compatible with Paul's claim – made in this passage – that his Gospel does not come from any man but through a revelation from Jesus Christ. Firstly, because on seeing the risen Christ he was given supernatural light to understand that Jesus was not only the Messiah but also the Son of God; and also because this first revelation was followed by many others to which he refers in his epistles (cf. 1 Cor 11:23; 13:3-8 and especially 2 Cor 12:1-4).

St Paul's was a unique case, because normally a person came to know the Gospel of Christ by receiving it or learning it from those who had seen Christ during his life on earth and listened to his teachings. This was what happened in St Luke's case, for example (cf. Lk 1:2). St Paul still felt the need to go to Jerusalem to hear the Apostles' preaching (cf. below 1:16-18), especially that of St Peter.

13-14. The Acts of the Apostles tell us about Paul's religious zeal; a Pharisee, he had studied under Gamaliel (cf. Acts 22:3; Phil 3:5) and had consented to and been present at the martyrdom of Stephen (cf. Acts 7:58; 8:1). Saul had stood out as a persecutor of Christians, so keen was he to seek them out and imprison them, even going beyond Judea to do so (cf. Acts 9:1-2). Clearly he had been a man convinced of his Jewish faith, a zealous keeper of the Law, and proud to be a Jew (cf. Rom 11:1; 2 Cor 11:22). Such was the fear

^bGreek *according to man.*

Jer 1:5
Jas 49:1
Lk 1:15
Acts 9:3-19
and par.

15But when he who had set me apart before I was born, and had called me through his grace, 16was pleased to reveal his Son to[c] me, in order that I might preach him among the

---

autem placuit Deo, qui me segregavit de utero matris meae et vocavit per gratiam suam, 16ut revelaret Filium suum in me, ut evangelizarem illum in

---

the early Christians had of him that they could not bring themselves to believe in his conversion (cf. Acts 9:26). However, this same fervour and passion, to use St Augustine's comparison (cf. *Contra Faustum*, XXII, 70) was like a dense jungle – a serious obstacle, and yet an indication of immensely fertile soil. Our Lord sowed the seed of the Gospel in that soil and it produced a very rich crop.

Everyone, no matter how irregular his life may have been, can produce good results like this – with the help of grace, which does not displace nature but heals and purifies it, and then raises and perfects it: "Courage! You . . . can! Don't you see what God's grace did with sleepy-headed Peter, the coward who had denied him . . ., and with Paul, his fierce and relentless persecutor?" (J. Escrivá, *The Way*, 483).

15-16. More than once in Scripture we read about God choosing certain people for special missions even when they were still in their mother's womb (cf. Jer 1:5; Is 49:1-5; Lk 1:15; etc.). This emphasizes the fact that God makes a gratuitous choice: there is no question of the person's previous merits contributing to God's decision. Vocation is a supernatural divine gift, which God has planned from all eternity. When God made his will known on the road to Damascus (cf. Acts 9:3-6), St Paul "did not confer with flesh and blood", that is, did not seek advice from anyone, because he was absolutely sure that God himself had called him. Nor did he consent to the prudence of the flesh, seeking to "play safe": his self-surrender was immediate, total and unconditional. When the Apostles heard Jesus inviting them to follow him, they "immediately left their nets" (Mt 4:20, 22; Mk 1:18) and followed the Master, leaving everything behind (cf. Lk 5:11). We see the same thing happening in Saul's case: he responds immediately. If he makes his way to Ananias, he does so on the explicit instructions of Jesus – in order to receive instruction and Baptism and to discover what his mission is to be (Acts 9:15-16).

God's call, therefore, should receive an immediate response. "Consider the faith and obedience of the Apostles", St John Chrysostom says. "They are in the midst of their work (and you know how attractive fishing is!). When they hear his command, they do not vacillate or lose any time: they do not say, 'Let's go home and say goodbye to our parents.' No, they leave everything and follow him [. . .]. That is the kind of obedience Christ asks of us – not to delay even a minute, no matter how important the things that might keep us" (*Hom. on St Matthew*, 14, 2). And St Cyril of Alexandria comments: "For Jesus also said,

[c]Greek *in*.

Gentiles, I did not confer with flesh and blood, [17]nor did I go up to Jerusalem to those who were apostles before me, but I went away into Arabia; and again I returned to Damascus.

[18]Then after three years I went up to Jerusalem to visit Cephas, and remained with him fifteen days. [19]But I saw none of the other apostles except James the Lord's brother. [20](In what I am writing to you, before God, I do not lie!)

Mt 16:17
Rom 1:1
Acts 9:22-25

Acts 9:26-30

Mt 13:55
Gal 2:9
Acts 12:17
Rom 1:9

gentibus, continuo non contuli cum carne et sanguine, [17] neque ascendi Hierosolymam ad antecessores meos apostolos, sed abii in Arabiam et iterum reversus sum Damascum. [18]Deinde post annos tres ascendi Hierosolymam videre Cepham et mansi apud eum diebus quindecim; [19] alium autem apostolorum non vidi nisi Iacobum fratrem Domini. [20]Quae autem scribo vobis, ecce

'No one who puts his hand to the plough and looks back is fit for the Kingdom of God', and he looked back who asked permission to return home and speak to his parents. But we see that the holy Apostles did not act in that way; rather, they followed Jesus, immediately leaving the boat and their parents behind. Paul also acted immediately. He 'did not confer with flesh and blood'. That is how those who want to follow Christ must act" (*Commentarium in Lucam*, 9).

A person has a duty to follow Christ even if his relatives are opposed to his doing so or want him to delay making a final decision, perhaps because they feel that would be the more (humanly) prudent course: "A person should honour his parents, but God he should obey. We should love the one who has begotten us, but the first place should be given to him who created us", St Augustine says, not mincing words (*Sermon 100*).

Even if we are unsure as to whether we are strong enough to persevere, this should not delay us or concern us: it should simply lead us to pray confidently for God's help, because, as Vatican II teaches, when God calls a person, he "must reply without taking counsel with flesh and blood and must give himself fully to the work of the Gospel. However, such an answer can only be given with the encouragement and help of the Holy Spirit [. . .]. Therefore, he must be prepared to remain faithful to his vocation for life, to renounce himself and everything that up to this he possessed as his own, and to make himself 'all things to all men' (1 Cor 9:22)" (*Ad gentes*, 24).

17-20. After a period of time devoted to penance and prayer, St Paul made his way to Jerusalem (cf. Acts 9:26-30) to see Cephas, that is, Peter. His stay of two weeks is an important indication of Paul's recognition of and veneration for Peter, chosen as he had been as the foundation stone of the Church.

In subsequent generations, right down the centuries, Christians have shown their love for Peter and his successors, travelling to Rome often at great personal effort and sometimes, even, risk. "Catholic, apostolic, *Roman!* I want you to be very Roman. And to be anxious to make your 'path to Rome', *videre Petrum*

Acts 9:30;
11:25-26
1 Thess 2:14
²¹Then I went into the regions of Syria and Cilicia. ²²And I was still not known by sight to the churches of Christ in Judea; ²³they only heard it said, "He who once persecuted us is now preaching the faith he once tried to destroy." ²⁴And they glorified God because of me.

2

Acts 11:30;
15:1-2
Acts 4:36
Phil 2:16
Visit to Jerusalem

¹Then after fourteen years I went up again to Jerusalem with

---

coram Deo quia non mentior. ²¹Deinde veni in partes Syriae et Ciliciae. ²²Eram autem ignotus facie ecclesiis Iudaeae, quae sunt in Christo, ²³tantum autem auditum habebant: "Qui persequebatur nos aliquando, nunc evangelizat fidem, quam aliquando expugnabat", ²⁴et in me glorificabant Deum.

¹Deinde post annos quattuordecim iterum ascendi Hierosolymam cum

---

– to see Peter" (J. Escrivá, *The Way*, 520). Solidarity with and veneration for the Pope is, then, a clear, practical sign of good Christian spirit.

"James the Lord's brother" (cf. notes on Mt 12:46-47 and 13:55) is, most commentators think, James the Less (cf. Mk 15:40), also called the son of Alphaeus (cf. Lk 6:15) and author of the letter which bears his name (cf. Jas 1:1).

1-10. St Paul had ended his first apostolic journey by returning to Antioch in Syria, from where he had set out. We know that the Christian community in that city, which was an important crossroads of race and culture, had developed as a providential result of the dispersal of Jerusalem Christians following on Stephen's matryrdom (cf. Acts 11:19-26). Some of these refugees had brought the new faith to Antioch but had confined themselves to preaching and converting Jews. Later, through the activity of other Christians, Jews of the Diaspora, that is, domiciled outside Palestine, and pagans also began to adopt the new religion. Barnabas had been commissioned by the Jerusalem church to organize the young Christian community in Antioch (cf. Acts 11:19-24). He later chose Paul, who had been living quietly in Tarsus, to act as his assistant (cf. Acts 11:25-26).

The disciples in Antioch, where the name "Christians" was first used to describe them, belonged to the whole gamut of social and ethnic backgrounds, as we can see from the short list of "prophets and teachers" of the church at Antioch (cf. Acts 13:1-3): some were of African origin, like Symeon "who was called Niger"; others came from the western Mediterranean, like Lucius of Cyrene; Manaen was from the household of Herod the tetrarch; and there were Jews from communities outside Palestine – for example, Barnabas and Saul themselves.

176

Barnabas, taking Titus along with me. ²I went up by revelation; and I laid before them (but privately before those who were of repute) the gospel which I preach among the Gentiles, lest somehow I should be running or had run in vain. ³But even Titus, who was with me, was not compelled

Acts 16:3

Barnaba, assumpto et Tito; ²ascendi autem secundum revelationem; et contuli cum illis evangelium, quod praedico in gentibus, seorsum autem his, qui observabantur, ne forte in vacuum currerem aut cucurrissem. ³Sed neque Titus,

---

Among these different types, we find some Christians of Jewish background who felt that pagan converts to Christianity should observe the prescriptions of the Mosaic Law (including the detailed precepts which Jewish tradition kept adding to that Law); these guardians of the gate of entry into the chosen people were requiring that pagan converts be circumcised, as all Jews were.

When these "Judaizers" from Jerusalem (cf. Acts 15:1) asserted that circumcision was necessary for salvation, they were raising an issue which went much deeper than simply conforming to the Law of Moses: was the Redemption wrought by Christ enough, of itself, for attaining salvation, or was it still necessary for people to become part of the people of Israel, conforming to all its ritual requirements?

Clearly, this question was a source of considerable division. Acts 15:2 refers to its causing "no small dissension". The present passage of Galatians shows that Paul, receiving a revelation from God, decided to grasp the nettle by stating unequivocally that Christ's redemption – on its own, and alone – brings salvation. In other words, circumcision was not necessary, nor did the elaborate ritual regulations of Judaism apply to Christians. In Jerusalem Paul expounded "the Gospel" he had been proclaiming to the Gentiles. He was accompanied by Barnabas, and by a young disciple, Titus, the son of pagan parents, quite possibly baptized by Paul himself (cf. Tit 1:4, where he calls him his "true child"), who would later became one of his most faithful co-workers.

1. Between his conversion and the date of his letter, St Paul had visited Jerusalem three times (cf. Acts 9:26; 11:29-30; 15:1-6). Of these three journeys he here mentions only two, omitting the time he and Barnabas went there (cf. Acts 11:29-30), because that visit was not particularly significant.

The Judaizers' demands were inadmissible and clearly dangerous. That was why Paul and Barnabas had opposed them openly at Antioch, and in fact it was their failure to achieve unity and peace on this point that had led them to go up to the Holy City to obtain a decision from the Apostles themselves and the priests living in Jerusalem.

3-5. These "false brethren" were certain Christians of Jewish background who saw circumcision and the other observances which had grown up around the Law as necessary for Gentile as well as Jewish converts.

Acts 15:1, 24-29
Rom 6:18, 22;
8:15, 21

Deut 10:17
Acts 10:34
Rom 2:11
1 Pet 1:17

to be circumcised, though he was a Greek. ⁴But because of false brethren secretly brought in, who slipped in to spy out our freedom which we have in Christ Jesus, that they might bring us into bondage – ⁵to them we did not yield submission even for a moment, that the truth of the gospel might be preserved for you. ⁶And from those who were

qui mecum erat, cum esset Graecus, compulsus est circumcidi. ⁴Sed propter subintroductos falsos fratres, qui subintroierunt explorare libertatem nostram, quam habemus in Christo Iesu, ut nos in servitutem redigerent; ⁵quibus neque ad horam cessimus subicientes nos, ut veritas evangelii permaneat apud vos. ⁶Ab his autem, qui videbantur esse aliquid – quales aliquando fuerint, nihil mea

St Paul saw the theories and practice of these "false brethren" as a very serious error in faith and as an equally serious danger to Christian living: acceptance of their position amounted to conditioning the redemptive value of Christ's Life, Death and Resurrection. Although the Judaizers did not realize it, their doctrines meant that people were in the same position now as they had been prior to the Redemption. They were arguing that, to become a Christian, a person first had to adopt the Jewish religion and keep all its observances: they thereby failed to grasp that Jesus Christ had set us free also from the slavery which the Old Law brought with it. Therefore, in this passage St Paul reminds the Galatians that there can be no compromise with these "false brethren" and that his own position is the correct one: there was no question of having Titus circumcised, when this whole question was put to the Apostles in Jerusalem.

6-9. The phrase "those who were reputed to be something" may seem somewhat sarcastic, but in the context it is evident that St Paul totally accepts the authority he refers to. It is as if he were saying: All authority comes from God, and if he chooses to put certain people, in positions of authority, he does so without "partiality". Human prestige, the apparent qualities of those in authority, carry no weight with him: they are to be obeyed simply because God has given them positions of authority.

Those who were in charge, the "pillars" of the Church, saw Paul's mission as a further expression of God's mercy. Just as Peter had been chosen to preach mainly to the Jews, so Paul had been designated to evangelize mainly the Gentiles.

This distinction does not mean that St Peter and St Paul had mutually exclusive areas of preaching. The fact is that they both could and did preach to pagans and Jews indiscriminately. The decision made here refers to the primary mission of each at the time.

6. "Added nothing to me": "imposed" no particular prescription or obligation; this can be read as meaning: those in authority did not impose any obligation on me or in any way require me to modify my teaching or policy.

reputed to be something (what they were makes no difference to me; God shows no partiality) — those, I say, who
were of repute added nothing to me; 7but on the contrary,
when they saw that I had been entrusted with the gospel to
the uncircumcised, just as Peter had been entrusted with the
gospel to the circumcised 8(for he who worked through
Peter for the mission to the circumcised worked through me
also for the Gentiles), 9and when they perceived the grace
that was given to me, James and Cephas and John, who
were reputed to be pillars, gave to me and Barnabas the right
hand of fellowship, that we should go to the Gentiles and
they to the circumcised;10only they would have us remember the poor, which very thing I was eager to do.

Acts 15:12
Rom 15:16-18

Acts 12:17
Rom 3:24-25

Act 11:27-30
1 Cor 16:1
2 Cor 8:14;
9:1, 12
Rom 15:25-28

Peter and Paul at Antioch
11But when Cephas came to Antioch I opposed him to his

interest; Deus personam hominis non accipit – mihi enim, qui observabantur,
nihil contulerunt, 7sed e contra, cum vidissent quod creditum est mihi evangelium praeputii, sicut Petro circumcisionis, 8– qui enim operatus est Petro in
apostolatum circumcisionis, operatus est et mihi inter gentes – 9et cum
cognovissent gratiam, quae data est mihi, Iacobus et Cephas et Ioannes, qui
videbantur columnae esse, dexteras dederunt mihi et Barnabae communionis,
ut nos in gentes, ipsi autem in circumcisionem; 10tantum ut pauperum memores
essemus, quod etiam sollicitus fui hoc ipsum facere. 11Cum autem venisset

10. The Acts of the Apostles show us how concerned the early Church was
about looking after the material needs of its members. We can see this, for
example, when it tells us about "serving tables", which refers to the work of
giving help to the needy: this began to take up more and more time, with the
result that the seven deacons were appointed to allow the Apostles to
concentrate on their own specific work – prayer and the ministry of the word
or preaching (cf. Acts 6:1-6).
St Paul was faithful to this charge about not forgetting the poor, as we can
see from many references in his letters to collections for the poor (cf. 1 Cor
16:1-3; 2 Cor 8:1-15; 9:15; etc.). Indeed, one of the reasons for his last visit to
Jerusalem was to hand over the monies collected in the Christian communities
of Greece and Asia Minor.

11-14. In his dealing with Jews, St Paul sometimes gave way in secondary
matters, provided that this did not take from the essence of the Gospel: he had
Timothy, whose mother was Jewish, circumcised "because of the Jews that
were in those places" (Acts 16:3), and he himself kept to Jewish practices in
order to allay suspicion and jealousy (cf. Acts 21:22-26). Similarly, he

Acts 10:13-17;
11:1-19
face, because he stood condemned. ¹²For before certain men came from James, he ate with the Gentiles; but when they came he drew back and separated himself, fearing the circumcision party. ¹³And with him the rest of the Jews acted insincerely, so that even Barnabas was carried away by their insincerity. ¹⁴But when I saw that they were not

---

Cephas Antiochiam, in faciem ei restiti, quia reprehensibilis erat. ¹²Prius enim quam venirent quidam ab Iacobo, cum gentibus comedebat; cum autem venissent, subtrahebat et segregabat se, timens eos, qui ex circumcisione erant. ¹³Et simulationi eius consenserunt ceteri Iudaei, ita ut et Barnabas simul abduceretur illorum simulatione. ¹⁴Sed cum vidissem quod non recte ambu- larent ad veritatem evangelii, dixi Cephae coram omnibus: "Si tu, cum Iudaeus sis, gentiliter et non Iudaice vivis, quomodo gentes cogis iudaizare?" ¹⁵Nos natura Iudaei et non ex gentibus peccatores, ¹⁶scientes autem quod non

---

recommends patience and certain understanding towards those "weak" in the faith, that is, Christians of Jewish origin who held on to some Jewish obser- vances connected with fast days, clean and unclean food and abstinence from the flesh of animals sacrificed to idols (cf. Rom 14:2-6; 1 Cor 10:23-30). But on the key issue of Christians' freedom from the Mosaic Law, the Apostle was always firm and unambiguous, relying on the decisions of the Council of Jerusalem.

Paul's correction of Peter did not go against the latter's authority. On the contrary, if it had been just anyone, the Teacher of the Gentiles might have let the matter pass; but because it was Cephas, that is, the "rock" of the Church, he had to take action in order to avoid the impression being given that Christians of Gentile origin were obliged to adopt a Jewish lifestyle.

Far from undermining the holiness and unity of the Church, this episode demonstrated the great spiritual solidarity among the Apostles, St Paul's regard for the visible head of the Church, and Peter's humility in correcting his behaviour. St Augustine comments: "He who was rebuked was worthier of admiration and more difficult to imitate than he who made the rebuke [. . .]. This episode serves as a fine example of humility, the greatest of Christian teachings, because it is through humility that charity is maintained" (*Exp. in Gal*, 15).

12. When he speaks of these Judaizers as coming "from James", this does not mean that they had been sent by that Apostle. It is, rather, a reference to their coming from Jerusalem, where, after the persecution organized by Herod Agrippa and the forced flight of St Peter (cf. Acts 12-17), St James the Less remained as bishop. But what is probable is that these Christians, who had not given up the Mosaic Law and Jewish observances, made use of that Apostle's name: as "the brother of the Lord", he enjoyed universal veneration and respect.

straightforward about the truth of the gospel, I said to
Cephas before them all, "If you, though a Jew, live like a
Gentile and not like a Jew, how can you compel the Gentiles
to live like Jews?" ¹⁵We ourselves, who are Jews by birth
and not Gentile sinners, ¹⁶yet who know that a man is not
justified^d by works of the law but through faith in Jesus
Christ, even we have believed in Christ Jesus, in order to
be justified by faith in Christ, and not by works of the law,

Acts 15:7-11
Rom 3:20-28;
4:5; 11:6
Eph 2:8
Ps 143:2

iustificatur homo ex operibus legis nisi per fidem Iesu Christi, et nos in
Christum Iesum credidimus, ut iustificemur ex fide Christi et non ex operibus
legis, quoniam ex operibus legis *non iustificabitur omnis* caro. ¹⁷Quodsi

15. St Peter, St Paul and the other Apostles were of Jewish race and
therefore belonged to the holy people of God. In spite of this, they held that
salvation was not attainable through observance of the Mosaic Law "because
by works of the law shall no one be justified" (v. 16; cf. Rom 3:21-26).

16. "All that shadowy observance", St Augustine comments, "had to cease
in an unnoticed way, gradually, as the pace grew of the wholesome preaching
of the grace of Christ [. . .], during the lifetime of that generation of Jews who
had experienced the physical presence of our Lord and had lived through the
apostolic times. This sufficed to make it clear that those practices were not to
be deemed hateful or idolatrous. But neither were they to be kept up any longer
than that, in case people might hold them to be necessary, as if salvation came
from them or could not be obtained without them" (*Letter 82*, II, 15).

We might say that there are three periods in observance of the prescriptions
of the Law. In the first period, prior to Christ's Passion, the precepts of the Law
were "alive", that is, it was obligatory to keep them. A second period was
between the Passion and the spread of apostolic preaching: the Law's precepts
were already "dead", no longer obligatory, but they were not "lethal": Jewish
converts could keep them provided that they did not rely on them, for Christ
was already the basis of their hope. In the third stage, in which we find
ourselves, observance of Jewish precepts as a means of salvation amounts to
denying the redemptive power of Christ and therefore they could be termed
"lethal" (cf. St Thomas Aquinas, *Commentary on Gal, ad loc.*).

St Augustine uses a very interesting comparison: with the arrival of faith in
Christ the old "sacraments" of the Law come to resemble the dead – who merit
respect and honour. They should be interred with all the necessary ritual,
religiously, reverently. They should not be thrown out, to be devoured by
predators. But if a Christian now wants to keep them in force "disturbing the
ashes which lie at rest, he would not be a pious son or a relative who keeps vigil
at the grave, but an impious profaner of tombs" (*Letter 82, ibid.*).

^dOr *reckoned righteous*, and so elsewhere.

Rom 6:11;
7:6, 13
Jn 17:21, 23
Rom 8:10-11
Phil 1:21
Col 3:3-4
1 Jn 3:16, 24
Eph 5:2
2 Cor 5:14-15

because by works of the law shall no one be justified. ¹⁷But if, in our endeavour to be justified in Christ, we ourselves were found to be sinners, is Christ then an agent of sin? Certainly not! ¹⁸But if I build up again those things which I tore down, then I prove myself a transgressor. ¹⁹For I through the law died to the law, that I might live to God. ²⁰I

quaerentes iustificari in Christo, inventi sumus et ipsi peccatores, numquid Christus peccati minister est? absit! ¹⁸Si enim, quae destruxi, haec iterum aedifico, praevaricatorem me constituo. ¹⁹Ego enim per legem legi mortuus sum, ut Deo vivam. Christo confixus sum cruci: ²⁰vivo autem iam non ego, vivit vero in me Christus; quod autem nunc vivo in carne, in fide vivo Filii Dei, qui

17-18. In order to lay even more stress on the fact that justification comes only through faith in Jesus Christ and not through adherence to the Law, St Paul poses a false objection, which he immediately refutes. He is saying in effect: If we Christians of Jewish background, convinced that only faith in Christ can justify us, are not keeping the Mosaic Law, it might be argued that we now find ourselves in the same situation as sinful Gentiles. And that would mean that faith in Christ had led us into sin. In which case we might ask: Is Christ then an agent of sin? The Apostle energetically rejects this absurd line of reasoning. If we were to return to observance of the Mosaic Law – St Paul argues – we would be saying that our abandonment of the Law to embrace faith in Christ has made sinners of us, and that Christ would have been the cause, the agent, of sin.

19-20. Through the sacrament of Baptism we have been united to Christ in a union which far exceeds mere solidarity of feeling: we have been crucified with him, dying with him to sin, so as to rise reborn into a new life (cf. note on Rom 6:3-8). This new life requires us to live in a new, supernatural way, which with the help of grace gradually becomes stronger and stronger and acts to perfect man's behaviour: he is no longer living on a purely natural level. "That is why a Christian should live as Christ lived, making the affections of Christ his own, so that he can exclaim with St Paul: 'It is now no longer I who live, but Christ lives in me' [. . .], to such an extent that each Christian is not simply *alter Christus*: another Christ, but *ipse Christus*: Christ himself!" (J. Escrivá, *Christ is passing by*, 103 and 104).

The life in Christ which the Apostle is speaking about here is not a matter of feelings: it is something real which grace brings about: "Paul's soul was in between God and his body: his body was alive, and moved, thanks to the action of Paul's soul, but his soul drew *its* life from Christ's action. Therefore, in referring to the life of the flesh, which he was living, St Paul speaks of 'the life I now live in the flesh'; but as far as his relationship with God was concerned, Christ it was who was living in Paul, and therefore he says, 'I live by faith in the Son of God': it is he who lives in me and makes me act" (St Thomas

P: Paul's ; Paul's
Soul ; Body

have been crucified with Christ; it is no longer I who live, but Christ who lives in me; and the life I now live in the flesh I live by faith in the Son of God, who loved me and gave himself for me. [21]I do not nullify the grace of God; for if justification[e] were through the law, then Christ died to no purpose.

---

dilexit me et tradidit seipsum pro me. [21]Non irritam facio gratiam Dei; si enim per legem iustitia, ergo Christus gratis mortuus est.

Aquinas, *Commentary on Gal, ad loc.*). This is why the Apostle goes as far as to say elsewhere, "to me to live is Christ" (Phil 1:21).

All this is a consequence of Christ's love: he freely gave himself up to death out of love for each and every one of us. We, like St Paul, can come to appreciate, through faith, that Christ's Passion affects us personally. From this faith will arise that love which "has the power to effect union [. . .], which inspires those who love to leave where they are, and which does not allow them to stay the way they are, but rather transforms them into the object of their love" (Pseudo-Dionysius, *De divinis nominibis*, 4). People who are very keen on academic pursuits or on hunting often refer to these things as being "their life". Similarly, if someone pursues only his own interest, he is living for himself. If, on the contrary, he seeks the good of others, we say that he "lives for others". Therefore, if we love Jesus and are united to him, we will live "for" him, "by" him, "through" him. "Do you love the earth?", St Augustine exclaims. "You will be earth. Do you love God? What am I to say? That you will be God? I almost don't dare to say it, but Scripture says it, 'You are gods, sons of the Most High' (Ps 82:6)" (*In Epist. Ioann. ad Parthos*, II, 14).

This profound truth should move us to devote ourselves to an asceticism motivated by love: "Let us hasten, therefore, full of spirit, to the fight, fixing our gaze on the crucified Jesus, who from the Cross offers us his help and promises us victory and laurels. If we happened to stumble in the past, it was because we did not keep before our eyes the wounds and disgrace which our Redeemer suffered and because we did not seek his help. For the future, let us not cease to keep before our eyes him who suffered on our account and who is ever-ready to come to our aid [. . .]; if we do so, we shall surely emerge victorious over our enemies" (St Alphonsus Mary Liguori, *The love of Jesus Christ reduced to practice*, 3).

[e]Or *righteousness.*

183

3

DOCTRINAL MATTERS

1 Cor 1:23-24;
2:2
Justification by faith

Rom 1:16-17;
10:17; 5:5;
8:5-14
[1]O foolish Galatians! Who has bewitched you, before whose eyes Jesus Christ was publicly portrayed as cruci-

---

[1]O insensati Galatae, quis vos fascinavit, ante quorum oculos Iesus Christus

1-14. It is his love for the Galatians, rather than indignation at their behaviour, that causes the Apostle to call them "foolish". His love causes him suffering because they have forgotten that only Jesus, and not the Law, brings salvation. The Galatians should know very well that they received justification without even having heard mention of the Law, for the Holy Spirit came upon them prior to the arrival of the people from Jerusalem (vv. 1-5). All they have to do is remember the charisms which they received – the "so many things", the "miracles", which are manifestations of the Spirit (cf. 1 Cor 12-14).

Besides, there is the example of Abraham (vv. 6-9; cf. Rom 4). The Lord promised him that his descendants would be blessed; he established a covenant with him and justified him not by the works of the Law, which had not yet been promulgated, but through his faith. In the same way, all who have believed and who will in the future believe in God as Abraham did will be his true descendants and will also receive God's blessing.

Finally, the Mosaic Law, far from bringing salvation, is rather a cause of spiritual death, insofar as every precept involves a penalty if it is not obeyed (vv. 10-14; cf. Rom 7:7-12). Our Lord freed us from the curse of the Law by voluntarily taking on himself the punishment merited by man's sin (cf. Is 53:4; Mt 8:17; Rom 3:21-26; 5:6-10). By reverting and submitting to the Law they would in effect be saying that our Redeemer's sacrifice was unnecessary and ineffective.

1. St Paul boasted that he preached Christ crucified, even though he fully realized that it was a stumbling-block to Jews and folly to pagans (cf. 1 Cor 1:23). The mystery of the Passion, Death and Resurrection of Christ was in fact the very essence of the Apostles' teaching (cf. Acts 2:22-24; 3:13-15; etc.), for it was these mysteries that contained all hope of eternal life and salvation. That is why Paul adds that, for believers, Christ crucified, far from being folly, is the power of God and the wisdom of God (cf. 1 Cor 1:24).

Paul had probably described our Lord's Sacrifice with such force and effect that it had been deeply engraved in their memory – and now these Judaizers, these deceivers, were hypnotizing the naive Galatians and causing them to lose sight of Christ: they had switched their attention from Christ on the Cross to the actions of the interlopers.

fied? ²Let me ask you only this: Did you receive the Spirit by works of the law, or by hearing with faith? ³Are you so foolish? Having begun with the Spirit, are you now ending with the flesh? ⁴Did you experience so many things in vain? – if it really is in vain. ⁵Does he who supplies the Spirit to you and works miracles among you do so by works of the law, or by hearing with faith?
⁶Thus Abraham "believed God, and it was reckoned to

Jn 20:21-23
Acts 1:8
Mk 16:20

Rom 4:3
Gen 12:1; 15:6
Jas 2:20-24

---

descriptus est crucifixus? ²Hoc solum volo a vobis discere: Ex operibus legis Spiritum accepistis an ex auditu fidei? ³Sic stulti estis? Cum Spiritu coeperitis, nunc carne consummamini? ⁴Tanta passi estis sine causa? Si tamen et sine causa! ⁵Qui ergo tribuit vobis Spiritum et operatur virtutes in vobis, ex operibus legis an ex auditu fidei? ⁶Sicut Abraham *credidit Dei, et reputatum est ei ad*

St Paul's warning is an invitation to fix one's gaze once more on that sign which, as it were, sums up all Christianity – the image of Christ on the Cross, which ever since apostolic times presides over altars and altarpieces, and places of work and leisure.

2-5. St Paul reminds the Galatians that in Baptism they received the Holy Spirit and his gifts. Since their Baptism, and not prior to it, they had experienced the action of the Spirit who, although he is in all ages a source of joy in the Church, was even more evident in the apostolic age in which the Galatians were living. So, how did this life of the Spirit reach the Galatians – through faith in Christ and through Baptism, or through the works of the Law? The Apostle poses the question without providing an answer, surely because it is obvious that it came through Christ. The Mosaic Law played no part at all. How, then, can they be so foolish as to change the Gospel which Paul had preached to them?

6-9. The Apostle recalls the figure of Abraham in order to show that man's justification is not the result of the material works prescribed by the Mosaic Law, but rather the result of faith in God's word. According to Gen 15:6, when God promised Abraham that he would have a son even though he was already an old man and his wife Sarah was barren, Abraham immediately took God at his word. It was this faith that justified Abraham: God had not yet established circumcision or given the Law. Therefore, St Paul argues, "it is men of faith who are the sons of Abraham".

God had given the Patriarch a promise whose implications were universal: "In you shall *all the nations* be blessed." That promise is now being kept through the entry of the Gentiles, through faith, into the new people of God. Abraham is in effect the father of those who believe, for in him all those who would believe in Jesus Christ were already blessed.

185

Gen 12:3; 18:18
Acts 3:25
Rom 4:16
him as righteousness." [7]So you see that it is men of faith who are the sons of Abraham. [8]And the scripture, foreseeing that God would justify the Gentiles by faith, preached the gospel beforehand to Abraham, saying, "In you shall all the nations be blessed." [9]So then, those who are men of faith are blessed with Abraham who had faith.

Rom 7:7-10
Deut 27:26
Mt 5:18-19
Jas 2:10
[10]For all who rely on works of the law are under a curse; for it is written, "Cursed be every one who does not abide by all things written in the book of the law, and do them."

Hab 2:4
Rom 1:17
Heb 10:38
Lev 18:5
Rom 10:5
[11]Now it is evident that no man is justified before God by the law; for "He who through faith is righteous shall live";[f] [12]but the law does not rest on faith, for "He who does them

---

iustitiam. [7]Cognoscitis ergo quia qui ex fide sunt, hi sunt filii Abrahae. [8]Providens autem Scriptura quia ex fide iustificat gentes Deus, praenuntiavit Abrahae: *"Benedicentur in te omnes gentes."* [9]Igitur, qui ex fide sunt, benedicuntur cum fideli Abraham. [10]Quicumque enim ex operibus legis sunt, sub maledicto sunt; scriptum est enim: *"Maledictus omnis, qui non permanserit in omnibus, quae scripta sunt in libro Legis, ut faciat ea."* [11]Quoniam autem in lege nemo iustificatur apud Deum manifestum est, quia *iustus ex fide vivet*; [12]lex autem non est ex fide, sed *qui fecerit ea, vivet in illis.* [13]Christus nos

---

In the same way as he justified Abrahram, God justifies every man – through faith (cf. Gen 15:6; Rom 4:2ff; Jas 2:21ff). Thus, people do not become sons of the Kingdom simply because they are descendants of Abraham according to the flesh: no, they must become like him by being men of faith like him. Therefore, man's greatness in God's eyes is not a matter of blood or descent, as the Jews believed, but of divine grace, which makes us children of the blessing, children of God (cf. Jn 1:12-13).

God grants the gift of justification by faith to all who believe in his word, as Abraham did. The true imitators of Abraham, St John of Avila says, are "those who believe with loving faith, with firm and constant faith, who are so well grounded in faith that nothing, no adversity, no temptation, no ill-treatment can disconsole them or dismay them" (*Lecciones sobre Gal, ad loc.*).

10-12. In what is called the Council of Jerusalem, St Peter had said, "Why do you make trial of God by putting a yoke upon the neck of the disciples which neither our fathers nor we have been able to bear?" (Acts 15:10): the Jews could not, despite their efforts, keep the Mosaic Law – the Law which they thought justified them in God's sight. Therefore, those who place their hope of salvation in the Law are subject to the curse which the Law itself places on those who infringe it: "Cursed be he who does not confirm the words of the Law by doing them" (Deut 27:26).

[f]Or *the righteous shall live by faith.*

shall live by them." [13]Christ redeemed us from the curse of
the law, having become a curse for us – for it is written,
"Cursed be every one who hangs on a tree" – [14]that in
Christ Jesus the blessing of Abraham might come upon the
Gentiles, that we might receive the promise of the Spirit
through faith.

Deut 21:23
Acts 5:30-31

Rom 8:3
2 Cor 5:21
Eph 2:14-15
Col 2:13-14

The Law and the promise

[15]To give a human example, brethren: no one annuls even

---

redemit de maledicto legis factus pro nobis maledictum, quia scriptum est:
"Maledictus omnis, qui pendet in ligno", [14]ut in gentes benedictio Abrahae
fieret in Christo Iesu, ut promissionem Spiritus accipiamus per fidem. [15]Fratres,
secundum hominem dico, tamen hominis confirmatum testamentum nemo

---

The curse of the Law falls on anyone who fails to keep it, given that every
commandment involves a penalty for its transgressor. That is why the Apostle
argues that those who rely only on the Law are subject to the risk of being
cursed, of being punished – "are under a curse". He then goes on to recall once
more the passage in Habakkuk which says that "the righteous shall live by his
faith" (2:4; cf. note on Rom 1:17). If the righteous or justified man lives by
faith, the Apostle concludes, he does not live by the Law, for the Law does not
call for faith but for fulfilment of its precepts.

13-14. Christ, who was innocent, wished to offer the Father perfect
atonement and thereby blot out our sin. To this end he voluntarily turned upon
himself the curse which the Law laid on its transgressors. He bore the curse of
the Law on our behalf and thereby set us free from the curse. What was for our
Lord punishment was for men salvation. As St Jerome puts it, "the injury
suffered by the Lord is our glory. He died so that we might live; he descended
into hell so that we might ascend into heaven. He became folly so that we might
be reaffirmed in wisdom. He emptied himself of the fulness and form of God,
taking the form of a slave, so that this divine fulness might dwell in us and we
might be changed from slaves into lords. He was nailed on the Cross so that
the sin committed at the tree of the knowledge of good and evil might be blotted
out, once he was hung on the tree of the Cross" (*Comm. in Gal, ad loc.*).

With our Lord's death, the world's redemption is achieved, God's promise
is fulfilled and the blessing he gave to Abraham multiplies his posterity, making
them more numerous than the stars of heaven or the sand of the seashore (cf.
Gen 15:5-6; 22:17).

15-29. God is merciful and faithful; he keeps the promises he makes. His
will is as fixed and unalterable as that contained in a last will and testament.
Therefore the promise which he made to Abraham could not have been revoked

Gen 12:7;
13:15; 17:7;
22:18; 24:7
a man's will,[g] or adds to it, once it has been ratified. [16]Now the promises were made to Abraham and to his offspring. It does not say, "And to offsprings," referring to many; but, referring to one, "And to your offspring," which is Christ.

Ex 12:40
[17]This is what I mean: the law, which came four hundred and thirty years afterward, does not annul a covenant previously ratified by God, so as to make the promise void.

Rom 4:13-18;
11:6
[18]For if the inheritance is by the law, it is no longer by promise; but God gave it to Abraham by a promise.

---

irritum facit aut superordinat. [16]Abrahae autem dictae sunt promissiones *et semini eius*. Non dicit: "*Et seminibus*" quasi in multis, sed quasi in uno: "*Et semini tuo*", qui est Christus. [17]Hoc autem dico: Testamentum confirmatum a Deo, quae post quadringentos et triginta annos facta est lex, non irritum facit, ad evacuandam promissionem. [18]Nam si ex lege hereditas, iam non ex

---

by the Mosaic Law, which was promulgated much later (cf. Rom 4:13-17). What then is the function of the Law, if everything is due to the promise? Firstly, the Law was given in order to punish transgressions committed prior to the coming of Christ (v.19a). This does not go against the promise of salvation made to Abraham; on the contrary, by identifying what is sin, the Law is at the same time showing that sin can and must be redeemed. Secondly (vv. 23-25), God gave the Law in order to protect and guide men towards Christ, in the same kind of way as, in the Greco-Roman world in which St Paul lived, the tutor ("custodian" v. 24) was a servant whose task it was to look after the children and bring them to school; but once they reached their majority, the tutor had no further role.

With the coming of the Redemption wrought by Christ (v. 26b), man attains his majority and with it his freedom. Through faith in Christ and through Baptism he becomes a son of God and puts on Christ (v. 27). From this moment onwards all differences between men disappear (v. 28): all become descendants of Abraham and sharers in the promises made to him.

15-18. In communicating his Revelation God speaks through men and uses images and examples taken from ordinary life in order to make more intelligible what he wants to reveal about himself; these examples are helps, but they are only analogies and bring us only a certain distance. Here God's promise is compared to someone's last will and testament, in order to convey the idea that God does not change his mind. Scripture often speaks about God making a "covenant" or "pact" with men (for example, Gen 9:8f; Ex 24:3ff; etc.). Here it is described in more detail, as a legally ratified will, a will so sacred that the things promised in it cannot be added to or subtracted from. No one has the right to change them in any way whatsoever. Therefore, the Law does not condition nor can it alter the promises "previously ratified".

[g]Or *covenant* (as in verse 17).

19Why then the law? It was added because of trans- Rom 3:20; 4:14;
gressions till the offspring should come to whom the 5:13, 20; 7:7-13
promise had been made; and it was ordained by angels Acts 7:38, 53
through an intermediary. 20Now an intermediary implies Heb 2:2
more than one; but God is one.

21Is the law then against the promises of God? Certainly
not; for if a law had been given which could make alive,

---

promissione; Abrahae autem per promissionem donavit Deus. 19Quid igitur
lex? Propter transgressiones apposita est, donec veniret semen, cui promissum
est, ordinata per angelos in manu mediatoris. 20Mediator autem unius non est,
Deus autem unus est. 21Lex ergo adversus promissa Dei? Absit. Si enim data

---

The simile of the will also contains the notion of the absolute freedom of the
testator, in this case God, who has taken the initiative and freely decided to save
man through Christ – called here "the offspring of Abraham". In Gen 12:7 this
offspring has a plural, collective meaning; but St Paul interprets it in an
individual sense. In fact there is no contradiction, given that Christ is the Head
of the Church and forms one single Body with it (cf. 1 Cor 12:12; Col 1:18).
That is why St Irenaeus says that the Church is the offspring of Abraham (cf.
Against heresies, 32, 2), and St Augustine adds that by presenting Christ as the
offspring of Abraham, all Christians are being included in him (cf. *Exp. in Gal*,
ad loc.).

19-20. With the coming of Christ, God has fulfilled his promise to
Abraham. This is a much more important event than the giving of the Law to
Moses on Mount Sinai, as can be seen from the form in which the promise was
made and the way the Law was delivered: according to Jewish traditions, the
Law was promulgated on Mount Sinai through angels (cf. Acts 7:53). These
traditions thus emphasized two significant things – the sacred and sublime
character of the Law, and the transcendence of God, who had made his will
known, not directly but through angels. The promise, on the other hand had
been made already by God to Abraham – which puts it on a higher level than
the Law. Also, the Law had been delivered in the context of a covenant in which
there were two parties – God and the chosen people. Hence the need for a
mediator – Moses (cf. Deut 5:5); whereas the promise is not dependent on the
will of the two parties: it issues from one only – from the merciful will of God,
who makes the promise to Abraham and fulfils it in a totally gratuitous manner
through Jesus Christ – another indication that the promise is superior to the
Law.

21-25. "But the scripture consigned all things to sin": it is not easy to
understand this phrase but its meaning becomes clearer in the context of the
whole passage: God reveals that all men are under the power of sin, Jews as
well as Gentiles, despite the Jews having received the Law (cf. Rom 3:10-18).

Ps 14:1-3
Rom 3:9-20, 23;
11:32

Jn 1:12
Rom 8:14-15;
8:29

then righteousness would indeed be by the law. ²²But the scripture consigned all things to sin, that what was promised to faith in Jesus Christ might be given to those who believe.

²³Now before faith came, we were confined under the law, kept under restraint until faith should be revealed. ²⁴So that

esset lex, quae posset vivificare, vere ex lege esset iustitia. ²²Sed conclusit Scriptura omnia sub peccato, ut promissio ex fide Iesu Christi daretur credentibus. ²³Prius autem quam veniret fides, sub lege custodiebamur conclusi in eam fidem, quae revelanda erat. ²⁴Itaque lex paedagogus noster fuit in

The reason this is so is, again, the inability of the Law to confer justification; the Law had no power to free us from the devil, sin or death. But now, in the fulness of time, God's purpose in giving the Law is made manifest – namely, to protect and guide mankind during its minority, rather as a governess or tutor looks after a child until he has grown up. The tutor keeps an eye on the child: the child cannot do whatever he likes but must be guided by his teacher. And so it is with mankind: it was a minor, of whom the Law was the custodian, so to speak; but when the fulness of time came God sent his son Jesus Christ, who set us free from sin, from death and from the Law itself, our tutor. That is why the Apostle says, "Now that faith has come, we are no longer under a custodian." This faith is the new life which has taken over from the harsh discipline of the Law.

To us, centuries later, these arguments and teachings of St Paul's may seem irrelevant. We need to put ourselves in the position of a Jew of his time – a zealous upholder of the Law, and yet unable to cope with the sheer weight of all its precepts and accretions – who, now that he has converted to faith in Christ, has a real sense of liberation: he has been freed from all his old shackles and is now eager to show his former Jewish brothers that they too can attain the same freedom in Christ Jesus.

24. The Law, like the whole of the Old Testament, had this function in relation to the New – to prepare the way for its promulgation. Everything in the books of the Old Testament refers directly or indirectly to our Lord Jesus Christ and his work of redemption: the two Testaments are intimately connected, as Tradition teaches and the Second Vatican Council reminds us: "God, the inspirer and author of the books of both Testaments, in his wisdom has so brought it about that the New should be hidden in the Old and that the Old should be made manifest in the New. For, although Christ founded the New Covenant in his blood (cf. Lk 22:20; 1 Cor 11:25), still the books of the Old Testament, all of them caught up into the Gospel message, attain and show forth their full meaning in the New Testament (cf. Mt 5:17; Lk 24:27; Rom 16:25-26; 2 Cor 3:14-16) and, in their turn, shed light on it and explain it" (*Dei Verbum*, 16).

the law was our custodian until Christ came, that we might
be justified by faith. ²⁵But now that faith has come, we are
no longer under a custodian; ²⁶for in Christ Jesus you are
all sons of God, through faith. ²⁷For as many of you as were
baptized into Christ have put on Christ. ²⁸There is neither

Rom 6:3-4;
13:14
Eph 4:24
Rom 10:12
1 Cor 12:13
Col 3:11
Jn 17:21-22
Rom 12:5

Christum, ut ex fide iustificemur; ²⁵at ubi venit fides, iam non sumus sub
paedagogo. ²⁶Omnes enim filii Dei estis per fidem in Christo Iesu. ²⁷Quicumque
enim in Christo baptizati estis, Christum induistis; ²⁸non est Iudaeus neque

---

27.   St John of Avila, commenting on this passage, says, "The Holy Spirit
was not content with saying that we are bathed and anointed: here he says that
we are clothed, and the clothing we are given is not just something beautiful
and costly: it is Jesus Christ himself, who is the sum total of all beauty, all value,
all richness, etc. What he means is that the beauty of Jesus Christ, his justice,
his grace, his riches, his splendour, shine out from us with the splendour of the
sun and is reflected as in the purest of mirrors" (*Lecciones sobre Gal, ad loc.*).
   St Paul uses this metaphor of our being decked out in Christ in many other
passages (cf. Rom 13:14; 1 Cor 15:43; Eph 4:24; 6:11; Col 3:10; etc.) to
describe the intimate union between the baptized person and Christ, a union so
intense that the Christian can be said to be "another Christ".

28.   In the order of nature, it may be said, all men are radically equal: as
descendants of Adam, we are born in the image and likeness of God (cf. Gen
1:26-27). The different functions which people have in the life of society do
not alter this basic, natural equality. From this point of view there is no real
difference, nor should there be, between one person and another, no difference
even between man and woman: both are made in the image and likeness of
God.
   In the order of grace, which the Redemption inaugurates, this essential,
original equality was restored by Christ, who became man and died on the Cross
to save all. John Paul II points out that this true meaning of the dignity of man
is enhanced by the Redemption: "In the mystery of the Redemption man
becomes newly 'expressed' and, in a way, is newly created. He is newly
created! 'There is neither Jew nor Greek, there is neither slave nor free, there
is neither male nor female; for you are all one in Christ Jesus' (Gal 3:28). The
man who wishes to understand himself thoroughly – and not just in accordance
with immediate, partial, often superficial, and even illusory standards and
measures of his being – must with his unrest, uncertainty and even his weakness
and sinfulness, with his life and death, draw near to Christ. He must, so to speak,
enter into him with all his own self, he must 'appropriate' and assimilate the
whole of the reality of the Incarnation and Redemption in order to find himself"
(*Redemptor hominis*, 10).
   From this radical equality of all men is derived that universal fraternity which
should govern human relations: "Our Lord has come to bring peace, good news

Jew nor Greek, there is neither slave nor free, there is neither male nor female; for you are all one in Christ Jesus. [Rom 9:6-8] 29And if you are Christ's, then you are Abraham's offspring, heirs according to promise.

4

Divine sonship

1I mean that the heir, as long as he is a child, is not better than a slave, though he is the owner of all the estate; 2but

---

Graecus, non est servus neque liber, non est masculus et femina: omnes enim vos unus estis in Christo Iesu. 29Si autem vos Christi, ergo Abrahae semen estis, secundum promissionem heredes.

1Dico autem: Quanto tempore heres parvulus est, nihil differt a servo, cum sit dominus omnium, 2sed sub tutoribus est et actoribus usque ad praefinitum

---

and life to all. Not only to the rich, nor only to the poor. Not only to the wise, nor only to the simple. To everyone. To the brethen, for brothers we are, children of the same Father, God. So there is only one race, the race of the children of God. There is only one colour, the colour of the children of God. And there is only one language, the language which speaks to the heart and to the mind, without the noise of words, making us know God and love one another" (J. Escrivá, *Christ is passing by*, 106).

1-11. St Paul here gives a summary of human history from the point of view of the salvation which God offers men. As a consequence of Adam's sin man was in a state of sin, a slave of the devil. This long period of darkness caused by sin was lit by God's aboriginal promise of a Redeemer (cf. Gen 3:15), but it was a period in which God's justice was meting out to man the punishment due to sin (cf. Gen 6-7; 19:1-29; etc.). However, the Lord's mercy never faltered; his abiding love prevented him from wiping out the human race despite its evildoing (cf. Gen 9:9-11; Hos 11:8; etc.). Often, and in many different ways, he sought man out and spoke to him to show him the way of salvation. We might say that God did everything he could to help man. Finally, "when the time had fully come", God decided to bring to an end this period of tutelage; as the supreme expression of his love he sent his Only-begotten Son, who became man in order to end mankind's alienation from God. "Jesus Christ, the Word made Flesh, sent as 'a man among men' (*Letter to Diognetus*, 7, 4), 'speaks the words of God' (Jn 3:34), and accomplishes the saving work which the Father gave him to do (cf. Jn 5:36; 17:4) [...] (and) completed and perfected Revelation and confirmed it with divine guarantees [...]. He revealed that God was with us, to deliver us from the darkness of sin and death, and to raise us up to eternal life" (Vatican II, *Dei Verbum*, 4).

he is under guardians and trustees until the date set by the father. ³So with us; when we were children, we were slaves to the elemental spirits of the universe. ⁴But when the time

Gal 3:23; 5:1
Eph 1:10
Gen 3:15
Rom 1:3

tempus a patre. ³Ita et nos, cum essemus parvuli, sub elementis mundi eramus servientes; ⁴at ubi venit plenitudo temporis, misit Deus Filium suum, factum

The original text (v. 4) says literally that he "was made from woman": St Paul, who so often speaks of Jesus' divinity, here emphasizes that he was truly man: Jesus did not suddenly appear on earth in a kind of heavenly apparition; he really became man in the way he did, taking on human nature in the pure womb of a woman. This distinguishes his eternal generation (his divine condition, his pre-existence as the Word) from his birth in time: Jesus, as God, is mysteriously begotten, not made, by the Father from all eternity; as man, however, he is born, "was made", of the Virgin Mary.

St Gregory Nazianzen comments on this by saying that "the Son of God in person, he who exists from all eternity, he who is invisible, incomprehensible, incorporeal, light from light, source of life and immortality, expression of the supreme archetype, immutable seal, most faithful image, term and measure of the Father: he it is who comes to the aid of his image; out of love for man he became man, out of love for my soul he unites himself to an intellectual soul, to purify those like unto whom he has become, taking on human nature – except for sin; conceived by the Virgin, whose body and soul the Holy Spirit had earlier purified" (*Sermon 45*, 9).

Thus, the Blessed Virgin Mary, by becoming the Mother of Jesus Christ, who is God, is truly the Mother of God, as the Council of Ephesus later defined: "If anyone does not profess that Emmanuel is truly God and that the Holy Virgin is, therefore, Mother of God (for she gave birth in the flesh to the Word of God made flesh): let him be anathema" (*Dz-Sch*, 252).

This mystery has been beautifully described by Monsignor Escrivá in these terms: "When the Blessed Virgin said Yes, freely, to the plans revealed to her by the Creator, the divine Word assumed a human nature – a rational soul and a body, which was formed in the pure womb of Mary. The divine nature and the human were united in a single Person – Jesus Christ, true God and, thenceforth, true Man; the only-begotten and eternal Son of the Father and, from that moment on, as Man, the true Son of Mary. This is why our Lady is the Mother of the Incarnate Word, the second Person of the Blessed Trinity who has united our human nature to himself for ever, without any confusion of the two natures. The greatest praise we can give to the Blessed Virgin is to address her loud and clear by the name that expresses her very highest dignity – Mother of God" (*Friends of God*, 274).

3. "The elemental spirits of the universe": this refers, firstly, to the rites and practices of pagan religions and, more specifically, to idolatrous concepts and superstitions which saw the stars and occult forces as custodians of the

Mk 14:36
Rom 8:15-17

Jn 15:15
Rom 8:28-30
Rev 21:7

had fully come, God sent forth his Son, born of woman, born under the law, [5]to redeem those who were under the law, so that we might receive adoption as sons. [6]And because you are sons, God has sent the Spirit of his Son into our hearts, crying, "Abba! Father!" [7]So through God you are no longer a slave but a son, and if a son then an heir.

---

ex muliere, factum sub lege, [5]ut eos, qui sub lege erant, redimeret, ut adoptionem filiorum reciperemus. [6]Quoniam autem estis filii, misit Deus Spiritum Filii sui in corda nostra clamantem: "Abba, Pater!" [7]Itaque iam non

universe and of human history. Also, by including himself among the slaves of these elements St Paul seems to be referring to certain ritual precepts of the Mosaic religion. In both cases, the "elemental spirits" subjected man to a slavery of observance of "days, and months, and seasons, and years" (Gal 4:10; cf. Rom 14:5; Col 2:16).

The Gentiles superstitiously sought to placate the gods and the powers of nature. The Jews, on the other hand, observed an explicit precept of God, but this was now no longer in force. The Galatians had lived as slaves to these "elemental spirits" until "when the time had fully come" they were liberated by Christ, in the same kind of way as a child, once he has reached maturity, finds himself free from tutors and custodians.

6   *Abba* is an Aramaic word which has come down to us with its translation "Father" As can be deduced from Mt 14:36 (cf. note on Lk 11:1), this is the same word as our Lord used in his personal prayer. However, it is not a word ever used by Jews to address God, probably because it contains the kind of trust and tenderness that small children have in their dealings with their father. Jesus, however, did not hesitate to use it and to encourage his followers to use it. In this way he invites us to relate to God with the trust and tenderness of a child towards its father – as well he might, because by redeeming us Christ not only freed us from the yoke of the Law but enabled us to have a new relationship to God, to be God's sons and daughters. St Paul echoes this teaching (cf. also Rom 8:16-17) and attributes to the Holy Spirit that movement in man's heart which impels him to cry out, full of love and hope, "Abba! Father!"

This all means that "if we have a constant relationship with the Holy Spirit, we shall become spiritual ourselves, we shall realize that we are Christ's brothers and children of God, and we shall not hesitate to call upon our Father [. . .]. Words cannot go so far as the heart, which is moved by God's goodness. He says to us, 'You are my son.' Not a stranger, not a well-treated servant, not a friend – that would be a lot already. A son! He gives us free access to treat him as sons, with a son's piety and I would even say with the boldness and daring of a son whose Father cannot deny him anything" (J. Escrivá, *Christ is passing by*, 136 and 185).

pietà

A lot of people
said the minivan
just couldn't
get any better.

(We took that as a challenge.)

When we designed the new Plymouth Grand Voyager, we followed one simple rule: Make it absolutely, positively, as good as it can be. Then make it better. We looked at everything anew. What we'd been doing. What competitors were doing. What our customers wanted us to do. We improved, reengineered, invented, reinvented. And now we introduce the new Plymouth Grand Voyager. Inside, there's a new kind of rear bench seat—Easy Out Roller Seats™— that glides on wheels, making it a cinch to move and roll away. It's an industry exclusive. There's also more cargo space than any other minivan. And visibility is improved by a windshield that's 32 percent larger than before. Outside, Grand Voyager is aerodynamically streamlined to cheat the wind. (And please the eye.)

Introducing the new Plymouth Grand Voyager. The Next Generation of the Minivan.

†Always wear your seat belt.

1 Cor 12:2
1 Cor 8:4-6
1 Thess 1:9

Rom 14:5
Col 2:16

Phil 2:16

⁸Formerly, when you did not know God, you were in bondage to beings that by nature are no gods; ⁹but now that you have come to know God, or rather to be known by God, how can you turn back again to the weak and beggarly elemental spirits, whose slaves you want to be once more? ¹⁰You observe days, and months and seasons, and years! ¹¹I am afraid I have laboured over you in vain.

---

es servus sed filius; quod si filius, et heres per Deum. ⁸Sed tunc quidem ignorantes Deum, his, qui natura non sunt dii, servistis; ⁹nunc autem, cum cognoveritis Deum, immo cogniti sitis a Deo, quomodo convertimini iterum ad infirma et egena elementa, quibus rursus ut antea servire vultis? ¹⁰Dies observatis et menses et tempora et annos! ¹¹Timeo vos, ne forte sine causa

---

In this verse we can see the roles of the three divine Persons in man's supernatural life. The Father sends the Holy Spirit, here called "the Spirit of his Son", to help us activate our gift of divine sonship.

8-10. St Paul reminds his readers of the sad situation they were in when they did not know God and adored false gods. They were at the mercy of their passions, slaves of sin (cf. Rom 1:18-33; Eph 2:11-12; 4:17ff). Now that they do know God they cannot but love him: it is not possible to know Supreme Goodness and not love him with one's whole soul. The Apostle corrects himself, pointing out that in fact it is not they who have come to know God, but God who has recognized them; even then, with the initiative coming entirely from God, knowing is also the same as loving. That is, God has loved us. See also note on Gal 4:3.

10. St Paul reproaches the Galatians for continuing to keep these observances which no longer apply (cf. note on Gal 4:3).

From antiquity God chose to establish, through a revealed precept, a rule of the natural and moral order, by specifying days to be consecrated to divine worship. In addition to the sabbath he instituted other festivals, to commemorate mercies and wonders he had worked for his people (cf. Lev 23; Num 28 and 29).

Just as the New Testament revelation is more perfect than the Old, so the form of worship – both private and public – laid down by Christ is on a much higher level. The rites laid down in connexion with the third commandment of the Mosaic Law must give way to those established by the Gospel, which has a new form of worship and special festivals of its own. Thus, "by a tradition handed down from the Apostles, which took its origin from the very day of Christ's Resurrection, the Church celebrates the paschal mystery every seventh day, which day is appropriately called the Lord's Day or Sunday. For on this day Christ's faithful are bound to come together into one place. They should

A fatherly appeal

1 Cor 9:19-23
2 Thess 3:7-10
Acts 16:6
1 Cor 2:3-5
Mt 10:40-42

¹²Brethren, I beseech you, become as I am, for I also have become as you are. You did me no wrong; ¹³you know it was because of a bodily ailment that I preached the gospel to you at first; ¹⁴and though my condition was a trial to you, you did not scorn or despise me, but received me as an angel of God, as Christ Jesus. ¹⁵What has become of the satisfaction you felt? For I bear you witness that, if possible, you would have plucked out your eyes and given them to me.

---

laboraverim in vobis. ¹²Estote sicut ego, quia et ego sicut vos, fratres, obsecro vos. Nihil me laesistis; ¹³scitis autem quia per infirmitatem carnis pridem vobis evangelizavi, ¹⁴et tentationem vestram in carne mea non sprevistis, neque respuistis, sed sicut angelum Dei excepistis me, sicut Christum Iesum. ¹⁵Ubi est ergo beatitudo vestra? Testimonium enim perhibeo vobis, quia si fieri posset

---

listen to the word of God and take part in the Eucharist, thus calling to mind the Passion, Resurrection and glory of the Lord Jesus, and giving thanks to God who has begotten them anew 'through the resurrection of Jesus Christ from the dead [. . .] into a living hope' (1 Pet 1:3). The Lord's Day is the original feast day, and it should be proposed to the faithful and taught to them so that it may become in fact a day of joy and of freedom from work" (Vatican II, *Sacrosanctum Concilium*, 106).

The obligation attaching to Sunday rest and attendance at Mass on Sundays and other holydays is contained in the Code of Canon Law (can. 1246-1248). This is a Church law which specifies the natural law concerning worship of God and the divine-positive law on the sanctification of feast-days. These regulations are made by the Church, which is entrusted with the deposit of Christ's teaching and which, being a fully-fledged society, is endowed with the authority to make laws for the benefit of its subjects.

The Church also has made regulations about days of penance on which the faithful should practise the virtue of penance through fasting and abstinence from meat or alternatively by doing certain works of charity and devotion laid down by Church authorities (cf. *ibid.*, can. 1249-1253). Cf. note on Gal 4:3.

12. Paul reminds the Galatians of the time he spent among them preaching the Gospel. His tone becomes more tender at this point. They know that he left the way of the works of the Law once he met the Gospel. For doing so he was persecuted and harassed by his former co-religionists. Paul had lived among the Galatians, trying his best not to be different from them (unless it meant going against the Gospel). He has a perfect right to say that he became as they were, so much so that the Jews regarded him as a renegade, an unclean Gentile.

Paul gave up his previous Jewish observances: the Galatians, also, if they are to follow the Gospel, should give up their old pagan practices (the "days and months, and seasons, and years": v. 10). Paul can see that it would be dangerous

¹⁶Have I then become your enemy by telling you the truth?ʰ
¹⁷They make much of you, but for no good purpose; they
want to shut you out, that you may make much of them.
¹⁸For a good purpose it is always good to be made much of,
and not only when I am present with you. ¹⁹My little
children, with whom I am again in travail until Christ be
formed in you! ²⁰I could wish to be present with you now
and to change my tone, for I am perplexed about you.

1 Cor 4:14-15
2 Cor 6:13
1 Thess 2:7-8
Philem 10
1 Jn 2:1, 12, 18;
3:7, 18

oculos vestros eruissetis et dedissetis mihi. ¹⁶Ergo inimicus vobis factus sum
verum dicens vobis? ¹⁷Aemulantur vos non bene, sed excludere vos volunt, ut
illos aemulemini. ¹⁸Bonum est autem aemulari in bono semper, et non tantum
cum praesens sum apud vos, ¹⁹filioli mei, quos iterum parturio, donec formetur
Christus in vobis! ²⁰Vellem autem esse apud vos modo et mutare vocem meam,

for the integrity of the Christian religion if the Galatians were to revert to
observing those pagan practices: and it would also be dangerous if they now
started, as apparently they had, to adopt Jewish practices. They must stop this
completely. To explain what he means, he gives them a simple rule, one they
can easily apply – to follow his example. He has already explained his teaching
to them: now he provides a living example of how that teaching works in
practice.

19. St Paul speaks full of affection: they are running the risk of cutting
themselves off from faith in Christ, which he had brought to them; and this
makes him feel birth-pains all over again, because he has to start to re-confirm
their faith. He cannot go in person, because he is too far away. So he is speaking
to them from his heart, like a mother or father: he will continue to suffer, because
they need to hear the Gospel again "until Christ be formed" in them, just as a
child takes shape in its mother's womb.

Jesus taught us to call no one on earth our Father but God our Lord (cf. Mt
23:9), because only from God the Father does all fatherhood in heaven and on
earth take its origin (cf. Eph 3:15). Obviously we cannot interpret our Lord's
words as meaning that we are forbidden to describe our mother and father by
these terms.

Similarly, the Church sees as fathers those who give us life in the faith,
through preaching and Baptism (cf. *St Pius V Catechism*, III, 5, 8). It is to that
kind of spiritual fatherhood St Paul refers here, and elsewhere (cf. 1 Cor 4:15).
"It is good to give glory to God, without seeking foretastes (wife, children,
honours...) of that glory, which we will enjoy fully with him in the next Life.

"Besides, he is generous. He returns a hundredfold: and he does so even in
children. Many give them up for the sake of his glory, and they have thousands
of children of their spirit. Children, as we are children of our Father who is in
heaven" (J. Escrivá, *The Way*, 779).

ʰOr *by dealing truly with you.*

The two covenants: Hagar and Sarah

²¹Tell me, you who desire to be under law, do you not hear the law? ²²For it is written that Abraham had two sons, one by a slave and one by a free woman. ²³But the son of the slave was born according to the flesh, the son of the free

---

quoniam incertus sum in vobis. ²¹Dicite mihi, qui sub lege vultis esse: Legem non auditis? ²²Scriptum est enim quoniam Abraham duos filios habuit, unum de ancilla et unum de libera. ²³Sed qui de ancilla, secundum carnem natus est,

---

The Church teaches that the Virgin Mary is the Mother of all Christians (cf. Vatican II, *Lumen gentium*, 61). She is an example we should all follow: "May the soul of Mary be in each of you, to praise the Lord; may the Spirit of Mary be in each of you, to rejoice in God," St Ambrose writes. And this Father of the Church goes on in a vein which may at first seem rather daring, but which has a clear spiritual meaning for the life of the Christian. "According to the flesh there is only one Mother of Christ; according to faith, Christ is the fruit of all of us" (*Expositio Evangelii sec. Lucam*, II, 26).

"If we become identified with Mary and imitate her virtues, we shall be able to bring Christ to life, through grace, in the souls of many who will in turn become identified with him through the action of the Holy Spirit. If we imitate Mary, we shall share in some way in her spiritual motherhood. And all this silently, like our Lady; without being noticed, almost without words, through the true and genuine witness of our lives as Christians, and the generosity of ceaselessly repeating her *fiat* – Let it be done unto me – which we renew as an intimate link between ourselves and God" (J. Escrivá, *Friends of God*, 281).

21-31. The entire Old Testament narrative contains lessons for Christians. The Apostle says as much when he declares that these things have a symbolic meaning and "were written down for your instruction, upon whom the end of the ages has come" (1 Cor 10:11). However, certain episodes and people have particular significance, and this passage cites one (cf. Gen chaps. 16, 17 and 21). Abraham had been given a promise by God that he would have a son (Gen 15:4) by his wife Sarah (cf. Gen 17:19). However, both of them were quite old, and Sarah, besides, was barren; so, in keeping with the ancestral customs of the tribe, Sarah made Abraham take Hagar, her slave-girl, and Hagar had a son, Ishmael. However, God told Abraham that this son was not the son of the promise (cf. Gen 17:19). The promise was fulfilled sometime later when, through a miracle of God, Sarah gave birth to a son. St Paul speaks to us about the allegorical meaning of this episode: two women – Sarah, Abraham's wife and the mother of Isaac, and Hagar, her slave and the mother of Ishmael – stand for two stages in Salvation History. Hagar symbolizes the stage of the Old Covenant made on Mount Sinai, while Sarah represents the New Covenant, sealed forever by the blood of Christ, the covenant which frees us from the yoke of the Law and from sin.

woman through promise. ²⁴Now this is an allegory: these women are two covenants. One is from Mount Sinai, bearing children for slavery; she is Hagar. ²⁵Now Hagar is Mount Sinai in Arabia;ⁱ she corresponds to the present Jerusalem, for she is in slavery with her children. ²⁶But the Jerusalem above is free, and she is our mother. ²⁷For it is written,

"Rejoice, O barren one that dost not bear;
break forth and shout, thou who art not in travail;
for the desolate hath more children
than she who hath a husband."

1 Cor 10:6
Heb 12:18-24
Jn 8:32-33
Rev 21:2

Is 54:1
1 Sam 2:5
Ps 113:9

---

qui autem de libera, per promissionem. ²⁴Quae sunt per allegoriam dicta; ipsae enim sunt duo Testamenta, unum quidem a monte Sinai, in servitutem generans, quod est Agar. ²⁵Illud vero Agar mons est Sinai in Arabia, respondet autem Ierusalem, quae nunc est; servit enim cum filiis suis. ²⁶Illa autem, quae sursum est Ierusalem, libera est, quae est mater nostra; ²⁷scriptum est enim: *"Laetare, sterilis, quae non paris, erumpe et exclama, quae non parturis, quia multi filii*

Paul's conclusion from this is that Christians are brothers of Isaac, born of the free woman, and therefore they are heirs of the promise made to Abraham and his descendants.

24-26. The sacred writer wants to stress that if one continues to be subject to the Mosaic Law it is equivalent to remaining a slave, to being a son of Hagar. People in that position constitute the present Jerusalem, who is "in slavery with her children". Against this there is the heavenly Jerusalem, a metaphor also used in the Apocalypse to describe the Church triumphant in glory (cf. Rev 21:2, 10). This metaphor also conveys the idea of the transcendent, supernatural character of the Church.

Undoubtedly St Paul's Jewish contemporaries would have regarded this comparison of Jerusalem with Hagar as virtually blasphemous. However, we do know that the rabbis of his time did make a distinction between the earthly Jerusalem and the heavenly Jerusalem, the former being only a pale shadow of the latter. The Apostle uses these teachings, which can be deduced from Sacred Scripture, to explain that those who believe in Christ are the true descendants – spiritual descendants – of the lawful wife, Sarah, who prefigures the heavenly Jerusalem; whereas those who do not believe in Christ, although they belong racially to the people of Israel, are no longer true descendants of the lawful wife, but rather are children of Hagar.

St Paul then makes a play on words, in typical rabbinal style: since Hagar is one of the names of the mountainous region of Sinai, to which, according to the geographical notions of the time, Mount Sion also belongs (Sion being the

ⁱOther ancient authorities read *For Sinai is a mountain in Arabia.*

Gen 21:9
1 Thess 2:14-15

Gen 21:10

²⁸Now we,ʲ brethren, like Isaac, are children of promise. ²⁹But as at that time he who was born according to the flesh persecuted him who was born according to the Spirit, so it is now. ³⁰But what does the scripture say? "Cast out the slave and her son; for the son of the slave shall not inherit with the son of the free woman." ³¹So, brethren, we are not children of the slave but of the free woman.

---

desertae magis quam eius, quae habet virum." ²⁸Vos autem, fratres, secundum Isaac promissionis filii estis. ²⁹Sed quomodo tunc, qui secundum carnem natus fuerat, persequebatur eum, qui secundum spiritum, ita et nunc. ³⁰Sed quid dicit Scriptura? "*Ecce ancillam et filium eius; non enim heres erit filius ancillae cum filio liberae.*" ³¹Itaque, fratres, non sumus ancillae filii sed liberae.

---

hill on which Jerusalem is built), this earthly Jerusalem is connected with Hagar, the slave, to whom the divine promise was not made. This whole passage, while we may find it very odd, does reveal St Paul's earlier training as a rabbi, a training which divine Providence uses to show us the inner meaning of one of the most important episodes in Old Testament history.

29. A rabbinical tradition, recounted in the Talmud (*Sota*, 6, 6), glossed the passage of Gen 21:9, in which we are told that Ishmael was playing with Isaac, as meaning that Ishmael felt a certain animosity towards Isaac and was ill-treating him during play. According to this Jewish tradition, and in the light of Ishmael symbolizing the Jews and Isaac the Christians, St Paul points out that, in the same way as then, the children born according to the flesh (the Jews) are persecuting those born according to the Spirit (the Christians); and, similarly, those who have been set free from the Law through Christ's death are suffering oppression from those who remain subject to the Law, that is, those Judaizers who are bent on imposing the yoke of the Mosaic Law on Christians of pagan background.

ʲOther ancient authorities read *you.*

EXHORTATION

Christian liberty

¹For freedom Christ has set us free; stand fast therefore, and do not submit again to a yoke of slavery.

²Now I, Paul, say to you that if you receive circumcision, Christ will be of no advantage to you. ³I testify again to every man who receives circumcision that he is bound to keep the whole law. ⁴You are severed from Christ, you who would be justified by the law; you have fallen away from grace. ⁵For through the Spirit, by faith, we wait for the hope

Rom 6:17-22
Jn 8:36
Acts 15:10

Gal 2:21; 3:10
Jas 2:10
Rom 2:25

Rom 3:24-26

Rom 8:23-25

---

¹Hac libertate nos Christus liberavit; state igitur et nolite iterum iugo servitutis detineri. ²Ecce ego Paulus dico vobis quoniam, si circumcidamini, Christus vobis nihil proderit. ³Testificor autem rursum omni homini circumcidenti se quoniam debitor est universae legis faciendae. ⁴Evacuati estis a Christo, qui in lege iustificamini, a gratia excidistis. ⁵Nos enim spiritu ex fide spem iustitiae

---

1-3. The Law of Moses, which was divinely revealed, was something good; it suited the circumstances of the time. Christ came to bring this Law to perfection (cf. notes on Mt 5:17-19 and Gal 5:14-15). All the elaborate legal and ritual prescriptions in the Mosaic Law were laid down by God for a specific stage in Salvation History, that is, the stage which ended with the coming of Christ. Christians are under no obligation to follow the letter of that Law (cf. St Thomas Aquinas, *Summa theologiae*, I-II, q.108, a.3 ad 3).

Although in this letter to the Galatians the Apostle is emphasizing, as we have seen, freedom from the Law of Moses, obviously this liberation cannot be entirely disconnected from freedom in general. If someone submits to circumcision after being baptized, it amounts to subjecting oneself to a series of practices which have now no value and to depriving oneself of the fruits of Christ's Redemption. In other words, subjection to the Law brings with it a loss of freedom in general. Paul is using the full might of his apostolic authority when he says, "If you receive circumcision, Christ will be of no advantage to you." Christ's Redemption alone is effective; it has no need of the rites of the Old Testament.

4-5. There is now not just a clear distinction but actual opposition between following Christ and the observance of the Law, with the result that if anyone tries to live by the Law only he is cutting himself off from Christ. Baptism is the sacrament whereby we are inserted into Jesus Christ, becoming members of his Body and branches of the vine (cf. Jn 15:5). If we cut ourselves off from Christ, the true vine and source of life, we cannot bear fruit. Nor can we do so

1 Cor 7:19
Gal 6:15
Jas 2:14
1 Cor 13:13
of righteousness. ⁶For in Christ Jesus neither circumcision nor uncircumcision is of any avail, but faith working through love. ⁷You were running well; who hindered you from obeying the truth? ⁸This persuasion is not from him

---

exspectamus. ⁶Nam in Christo Iesu neque circumcisio aliquid valet neque praeputium, sed fides, quae per caritatem operatur. ⁷Currebatis bene; quis vos impedivit veritati non oboedire? ⁸Haec persuasio non est ex eo, qui vocat vos.

---

by going back and submitting to the Old Law, for that Law is now out of date and no longer operates.

On the other hand, if we remain in the grace which Christ has won for us, we shall produce the "hope of righteousness", which is not simply what we have now – the life of grace – but its perfect fulfilment in eternal life: this is really what we "wait" for, what we yearn for.

6. In the stage of Salvation History which begins with Christ, the fact that a person is Jewish or Gentile, circumcised or uncircumcised, counts for nothing as far as salvation is concerned. What does matter is truly believing that only Christ Jesus can save us: true faith, genuine faith, moves us to love Christ and, as a consequence of this, to love everyone without exception. The faith to which St Paul is referring can be described, as the Apostle St James implies (Jas 2:17), as "living faith", that is, faith which is translated into a profound conviction which motivates us to love: this is "faith working through love".

St Paul is obviously speaking about the supernatural virtue of faith in its proper sense, that is, "living faith". In the Christian tradition, stemming from St James, "dead faith" is a caricature of faith which is incapable of expressing itself in words.

The Magisterium of the Church teaches that "faith, unless it be joined to hope and charity, neither makes us one with Christ nor loving members of his Body. That is why it is rightly said that 'faith by itself, if it has no works, is dead' (Jas 2:17) and idle, and that 'in Christ Jesus neither circumcision nor uncircumcision is of any avail, but faith working through love' (Gal 5:6; 6:15)" (Council of Trent, *De iustificatione*, chap. 7).

Therefore, a person who has faith but does not live in the grace of God is really a kind of dead person: charity is as it were the soul of all the virtues, it is what gives them life: "it must be remembered that if someone had all the gifts of the Holy Spirit with the exception of the first gift, charity, he could not be supernaturally alive [. . .]. He would be like a dead body: however much he deck himself out in gold and precious stones, he continues to be a dead body" (St Thomas, *On the two commandments . . .*, intro. 3).

Our Lord said that his disciples would be recognized by their charity (cf. Jn 13:35), because faith begets hope, and hope leads on to love. "When one asks if someone is good," St Augustine says, "one does not check to see what he believes or what he hopes for, but what it is he loves. For someone who loves

who called you. ⁹A little leaven leavens the whole lump. ¹⁰I
have confidence in the Lord that you will take no other view
than mine; and he who is troubling you will bear his
judgment, whoever he is. ¹¹But if I, brethren, still preach
circumcision, why am I still persecuted? In that case the
stumbling block of the cross has been removed. ¹²I wish
those who unsettle you would mutilate themselves!

1 Cor 5:6

Gal 1:7
Phil 2:3

1 Cor 1:23

Phil 3:2

---

⁹Modicum fermentum totam massam corrumpit. ¹⁰Ego confido in vobis in
Domino quod nihil aliud sapietis; qui autem conturbat vos, portabit iudicium,
quicumque est ille. ¹¹Ego autem, fratres, si circumcisionem adhuc praedico,
quid adhuc persecutionem patior? Ergo evacuatum est scandalum crucis.

---

rightly certainly also believes and hopes rightly; but he who does not love
believes in vain, even if what he believes in is true [. . .]. Therefore, this is the
faith in Christ, which the Apostle extols – 'faith which works through love'"
(*Enchiridion*, chap. 117).

9. This sentence, a kind of adage, indicates that a few people can corrupt
all the rest, which was what was happening with these false preachers who were
leading the Galatians astray. But it can be applied also in a positive sense, as
we know from the parable of the leaven which leavens all the dough (cf. Mt
13:33 and par.): that is, a handful of apostles of Christ can lead crowds of people
in the right direction.

"It is true; we are few, in comparison with the rest of mankind, and of
ourselves we are worth nothing. But our Master's affirmation resounds with
full authority: Christians are the light, the salt, the leaven of the world and 'a
little leaven leavens the whole lump' (Gal 5:9). [. . .] Jesus has redeemed us all,
and he wishes to make use of a few of us, despite our personal nothingness, to
make his salvation known to all" (J. Escrivá, *Friends of God*, 9).

11-12. St Paul now answers one of the calumnies which the Judaizers were
using in their case against him. They said he was two-faced on the matter of
circumcision: in Judea, they said, he was preaching that it was obligatory, in
order to ingratiate himself with the Jews; whereas among the Gentiles – the
Galatians, for instance – he was saying that it was not necessary.

Moreover, since circumcision was only a sign or symbol of the Old Covenant,
it was designed to disappear once that Covenant ended. Now that the
Redemption has come about and a New Covenant is in place, circumcision no
longer has any meaning: it is simply a physical incision. Commenting on this
passage, St Thomas interprets it as high sarcasm: "If they are so keen on
circumcision, then let them not just circumcise themselves, but also castrate
themselves" (*Commentary on Gal. ad loc.*). Actually, in those times, fanatical
worshippers of Cybele did castrate themselves in honour of that goddess.

The fruit of the Spirit and the works of the flesh

Rom 6:19
1 Pet 2:16

13For you were called to freedom, brethren; only do not use your freedom as an opportunity for the flesh, but

Lev 19:18
Mt 22:39
Rom 13:8-10
Col 3:14

through love be servants of one another. 14For the whole law is fulfilled in one word, "You shall love your neighbour as yourself." 15But if you bite and devour one another take heed that you are not consumed by one another.

Rom 8:1-4
Rom 7:14-23
1 Pet 2:11

16But I say, walk by the Spirit, and do not gratify the desires of the flesh. 17For the desires of the flesh are against

---

12Utinam et abscidantur, qui vos conturbant! 13Vos enim in libertatem vocati estis, fratres; tantum ne libertatem in occasionem detis carni, sed per caritatem servite invicem. 14Omnis enim lex in uno sermone impletur, in hoc: *Diliges proximum tuum sicut teipsum.* 15Quod si invicem mordetis et devoratis, videte, ne ab invicem consumamini! 16Dico autem: Spiritu ambulate et concupiscentiam carnis ne perfeceritis. 17Caro enim concupiscit adversus spiritum, spiritus autem adversus carnem; haec enim invicem adversantur, ut non,

---

14-15. To prepare the way for the coming of the Redeemer, God revealed to the chosen people the fundamental principles of the natural law, because, as a result of original sin and personal sins, mankind's knowledge of these principles had been obscured and weakened. The ten commandments which he revealed to Moses (Ex 20:1-21; Deut 5:6-22) traced out very clearly the way to follow to please God and be saved (cf. Lev 18:5; Neh 9:29; etc.).

When the Saviour came, the Decalogue continued in force, because it was part of the natural law. Indeed, Christ reinforced it and showed that the key to and essence of the ten commandments is Love – love of God, which necessarily brings with it love of neighbour (cf. notes on Mt 22:34-40 and Jn 13:34-35).

"It might also be asked", St Augustine comments, "why the Apostle here speaks only of love of neighbour, saying that this way the whole Law is fulfilled [. . .], when in fact charity is perfect only if one practises the two precepts of love of God and love of neighbour [. . .]. But who can love his neighbour, that is, all men, as himself, if he does not love God, since it is only by God's precept and gift that one can love one's neighbour? So, since neither precept can be kept unless the other be kept, it is enough to mention one of them" (*Exp. in Gal*, 45). See also the note on Rom 13:8-10.

17-21. The fall of Adam and Eve left us with a tendency to seek created things for our own pleasure, instead of using them to lead us to God. The desires of the flesh make their appearance, urges which are at odds with God and with all that is noble in our personality. But when grace enters our soul and justifies us, we share in the fruits of the Redemption wrought by Christ and we are enabled to conquer our concupiscence and life according to the flesh.

The vices referred to in vv. 19-21 have their roots in something much deeper

the Spirit, and the desires of the Spirit are against the flesh; for these are opposed to each other, to prevent you from doing what you would. [18]But if you are led by the Spirit you are not under the law. [19]Now the works of the flesh are plain: immorality, impurity, licentiousness, [20]idolatry, sorcery, enmity, strife, jealousy, anger, selfishness, dissension, party spirit, [21]envy,[k] drunkenness, carousing, and the like. I warn you, as I warned you before, that those who do such things shall not inherit the kingdom of God. [22]But the fruit

Rom 8:14
Rom 1:29-32
1 Cor 6:9-10
Eph 5:5
Col 3:5, 8
Rev 22:15

Eph 5:9
2 Cor 6:6-10

---

quaecumque vultis, illa faciatis. [18]Quod si Spiritu ducimini, non estis sub lege. [19]Manifesta autem sunt opera carnis, quae sunt fornicatio, immunditia, luxuria, [20]idolorum servitus, veneficia, inimicitiae, contentiones, aemulationes, irae, rixae, dissensiones, sectae, [21]invidiae, ebrietates, comissationes et his similia, quae praedico vobis, sicut praedixi, quoniam, qui talia agunt, regnum Dei non consequentur. [22]Fructus autem Spiritus est caritas, gaudium, pax, longanimitas,

---

– life "of the flesh". And, St Augustine asserts, "it is said that someone lives according to the flesh when he lives for himself. Therefore, in this case, by 'flesh' is meant the whole person. For everything which stems from a disordered love of oneself is called work of the flesh" (*The City of God*, 14, 2).

This is why we find included in the "works of the flesh" not only sins of impurity (v. 19) and faults of temperance (v. 21) but also sins against the virtues of religion and fraternal charity (v. 20).

"Significantly, when speaking of 'the works of the flesh' Paul mentions not only 'immorality [fornication], impurity, licentiousness [. . .], drunkenness, carousing' – all of which objectively speaking are connected with the flesh; he also names other sins which we do not usually put in the 'carnal' or 'sexual' category – 'idolatry, sorcery , enmity, strife, jealousy, anger, envy' [. . .]. All these sins are the outcome of 'life according to the flesh', which is the opposite to 'life according to the spirit'" (John Paul II, *Address*, 7 January 1981).

Therefore, as the Apostle says, anyone who in one way or other obstinately persists in his sin will not be able to enter the Kingdom of heaven (cf. 1 Cor 6:9-10; Eph 5:5).

22-25. When someone lets himself be led by his instincts he is said to be leading an "animal life"; whereas, if he acts as his reason advises, he is leading a rational, human, life. Similarly, when one allows the Holy Spirit to act, one's life becomes life according to the Spirit – a supernatural life, a life which is no longer simply human but divine. This is what happens when a person is in the state of grace and is mindful of the treasure he bears within.

"Alone! You are not alone. We are keeping you close company from afar. Besides . . . , the Holy Spirit, living in your soul in grace – God with you – is

[k]Other ancient authorities add *murder*.

of the Spirit is love, joy, peace, patience, kindness, goodness, faithfulness, [23]gentleness, self-control; against such
there is no law. [24]And those who belong to Christ Jesus have
crucified the flesh with its passions and desires.
    [25]If we live by the Spirit, let us also walk by the Spirit.
[26]Let us have no self-conceit, no provoking of one another,
no envy of one another.

6

Sir 8:6
Mt 18:15
1 Cor 10:12
2 Thess 3:15
2 Tim 2:25
Jas 5:19-20

Fraternal charity

[1]Brethren, if a man is overtaken in any trespass, you who
are spiritual should restore him in a spirit of gentleness.
Look to yourself, lest you too be tempted. [2]Bear one

---

benignitas, bonitas, fides, [23]mansuetudo, continentia; adversus huiusmodi non
est lex. [24]Qui autem sunt Christi Iesu, carnem crucifixerunt cum vitiis et
concupiscentiis. [25]Si vivimus Spiritu, Spiritu et ambulemus. [26]Non efficiamur
inanis gloriae cupidi, invicem provocantes, invicem invidentes.

[1]Fratres, et si praeoccupatus fuerit homo in aliquo delicto, vos, qui spiritales
estis, huiusmodi instruite in spiritu lenitatis, considerans teipsum, ne et tu
tenteris. [2]Alter alterius onera portate et sic adimplebitis Legem Christi. [3]Nam

---

giving a supernatural tone to all your thoughts, desires and actions" (J. Escrivá,
The Way, 273).

    The soul then becomes a good tree which is known by its fruits. Its actions
reveal the presence of the Paraclete, and because of the spiritual delight they
give the soul, these actions are called fruits of the Holy Spirit (cf. St Thomas
Aquinas, *Summa theologiae*, I-II, q. 70, a. 1).

    "Those blessed fruits enumerated by the Apostle (Gal 5:22) the Spirit
produces and shows forth in the just, even in this mortal life – fruits replete
with all sweetness and joy. Such must, indeed, be from the Spirit 'who in the
Trinity is the love of the Father and the Son, filling all creatures with immeasurable sweetness' (St Augustine, *De Trinitate*, 6, 9)" (Leo XIII, *Divinum
illud munus*, 12).

    1-2. By loving others one keeps the Law of Christ. Earlier on the Apostle
said that "the whole law is fulfilled in one word, 'You shall love your neighbour
as yourself'" (5:14). This doctrine is to be found in many places in the New
Testament (cf. Mt 22:40; Rom 13:8-10; Col 3:14; etc.), because mutual love is
the "New Commandment" of Christ (cf. Jn 13:34). "The Messiah's words are
quite clear. He stresses, once and for all, 'by this you will be known, by the
love you have for one another!' This is why I feel I must remind people

another's burdens, and so fulfil the law of Christ. ³For if any one thinks he is something, when he is nothing, he deceives himself. ⁴But let each one test his own work, and then his reason to boast will be in himself alone and not in his neighbour. ⁵For each man will have to bear his own load.

Jn 13:14, 34
Rom 15:1
1 Cor 8:9-13

2 Cor 13:5

Rom 14:12
1 Cor 3:8

si quis existimat se aliquid esse, cum sit nihil, ipse se seducit; ⁴opus autem suum probet unusquisque et sic in semetipso tantum gloriationem habebit et non in altero. ⁵Unusquisque enim onus suum portabit. ⁶Communicet autem is, qui

constantly about these words of our Lord. St Paul adds, 'Bear one another's burdens; and so fulfil the law of Christ' (Gal 6:2) [. . .]. And yet you have so many brothers, your friends about you, who are overworked! Help them unobtrusively, with kindness, with a smile on your lips, in such a way that it will be practically impossible for them to notice what you are doing for them. Thus they will not even be able to express their gratitude, because the discreet refinement of your charity will have made your help pass undetected" (J. Escrivá, *Friends of God*, 44).

A first logical consequence of love for others is that fraternal correction, which a Christian offers another, gently and humbly, seeking only his brother or sister's good, and conscious at the same time of his own weakness and personal shortcomings. "We should never take issue with another's sin", St Augustine comments, "without first examining our own conscience by inner questioning and by then replying, before God, without ambiguity, that we are acting out of love" (*Exp. in Gal*, 57).

The other expression of charity which this passage draws to our attention is that of bearing the burdens of others, while not neglecting our own.

3-5. Because they subjected themselves to Jewish legal prescriptions some Galatians considered themselves better than the rest. This is reminiscent of the boastfulness of the Pharisee who stood in the Temple praying and thanking God for all his qualities (cf. Lk 18:11). As our Lord says, that foolish man left the Temple as he entered it – his soul stained by pride and estranged from the love of God, who rejoices in those who are humble and rewards them with his grace (cf. Lk 1:51-53).

Like the Pharisee, the Judaizers' pride stemmed from lack of self-knowledge. Hence the Apostle's exhortation to everyone to examine himself sincerely, in the sight of God, who sees everything. "Man on his own", St John of Avila teaches, "is nothing but vanity, and if he be anything more than that, it is because the Lord God makes him so" (*Audi, filia*, II, 66). St Augustine exclaims, "No good man can boast in your presence, nor is any living man justified; for if there be any good in him, small or great, it is by your grace" (*Sermon 99*, 6).

Self-knowledge leads us, therefore, to humility, to distrusting ourselves and

Lk 10:7
1 Cor 9:14
Rom 15:27

Job 13:9

Jn 3:6; 6:63
Rom 6:22;
8:12-13
1 Cor 15:44-49

1 Thess 5:15
2 Thess 3:13
2 Pet 1:5-7

⁶Let him who is taught the word share all good things with him who teaches.

⁷Do not be deceived; God is not mocked, for whatever a man sows, that he will also reap. ⁸For he who sows to his own flesh will from the flesh reap corruption; but he who sows to the Spirit will from the Spirit reap eternal life. ⁹And let us not grow weary in well-doing, for in due season we shall reap, if we do not lose heart. ¹⁰So then, as we have opportunity, let us do good to all men, and especially to those who are of the household of faith.

---

catechizatur, verbum ei, qui se catechizat in omnibus bonis. ⁷Nolite errare: Deus non irridetur. Quae enim seminaverit homo, haec et metet; ⁸quoniam, qui seminat in carne sua, de carne metet corruptionem, qui autem seminat in spiritu, de spiritu metet vitam aeternam. ⁹Bonum autem facientes infatigabiles, tempore enim suo metemus non deficientes. ¹⁰Ergo dum tempus habemus, operemur

---

abandoning ourselves totally in God's hands: he can do everything. St Paul recommends that we examine our conscience, in order to discover what really motivates our actions and our moods. "Self-knowledge leads us by the hand, as it were, to humility" (J. Escrivá, *The Way*, 609).

6. Our Lord instructed his Apostles to give without pay what they had received without charge (Mt 10:8); but he also said that a worker deserves his food (Mt 10:10), that is, that the preachers of the Gospel have a right to live by that work. We find the same idea in the life and teachings of St Paul. For, although he normally supported himself by working (cf. Acts 18:3; 1 Thess 2:6-9; 2 Cor 11:7-15), sometimes he did accept material help (cf. Phil 4:10-20). In the present passage he expounds a general rule, making it quite clear that a disciple should share what he has with his teacher. "If we have sown spiritual good among you, is it too much if we reap your material benefits? [. . .] Nevertheless, we have not made use of that right" (1 Cor 9:11-12).

In the teaching of the Second Vatican Council the Church reminds us of this: "Completely devoted as they are to the service of God in the fulfilment of the office entrusted to them, priests are entitled to receive a just remuneration. For 'the labourer deserves his wages' (Lk 10:7) and 'the Lord commanded that those who proclaim the Gospel should get their living by the Gospel' (1 Cor 9:14). For this reason, insofar as provision is not made from some other source for the just remuneration of priests, the faithful are bound by a real obligation of seeing to it that the necessary provision for a decent and fitting livelihood is made available to priests" (*Presbyterorum ordinis*, 20).

7-10. There are some who live as if the Lord were not going to ask them to render an account some day – as if they could deceive God. St Paul's words contain a truth which the Church also reminds us about (cf. *Dz-Sch*, 1000-1001,

CONCLUSION

^{2 Thess 3:17}
^{1 Cor 16:21}
^{Col 4:18}

^{Phil 3:18}

^{Rom 2:21-24}

^{Gal 5:11}
^{1 Cor 1:31; 2:2}

¹¹See with what large letters I am writing to you with my own hand. ¹²It is those who want to make a good showing in the flesh that would compel you to be circumcised, and only in order that they may not be persecuted for the cross of Christ. ¹³For even those who receive circumcision do not themselves keep the law, but they desire to have you circumcised that they may glory in your flesh. ¹⁴But far be

---

bonum ad omnes, maxime autem ad domesticos fidei. ¹¹Videte qualibus litteris scripsi vobis mea manu. ¹²Quicumque volunt placere in carne, hi cogunt vos circumcidi, tantum ut crucis Christi persecutionem non patiantur; ¹³neque enim, qui circumciduntur, legem custodiunt, sed volunt vos circumcidi, ut in carne vestra glorientur. ¹⁴Mihi autem absit gloriari nisi in cruce Domini nostri Iesu

---

1304, 1488): when death comes the time for meriting is over. That is why the Apostle stresses the need to strive actively to behave in an upright way, "for whatever a man sows, that he will also reap".

The simile of sowing, which is often to be found in the Bible, is rich in content (cf. Ps 107:37; 126:5; Prov 6:19; 22:8; Hos 8:7; 10:12; Jer 12:13; Mt 13:27; 25:24-26; Jn 4:37; 1 Cor 9:11; Jas 5:7; etc.). St John of Avila, commenting on this passage, says: "He had said that to do good was to sow; and when one sows, at first there is nothing but loss: the sower divests himself of what he has for the sake of what he hopes to gain. He is referring to the same metaphor, and says that we should not grow weary, we should not give up doing good, we should put our hope in God" (*Lecciones sobre Gal, ad loc.*)

11. Here, as on other occasions and at greater length (cf. 1 Cor 16:21; Col 4:18; 2 Thess 3:17; Philem 19), St Paul refers to some words written in his own hand. We know that, in line with the custom of his time, the Apostle did not actually write his letters himself, but instead usually used a scribe. For example, in Rom 16:22 the scribe sends a personal greeting of his own to the people Paul is addressing. St Peter used this same method for his first letter, in which we are actually told the scribe's name, Silvanus (cf. 1 Pet 5:12).

14. Those who had been circumcised – both Gentiles and Jews – used to boast about bearing on their body the sign of the Old Covenant, circumcision. St Paul points out to them that to his mind there is only one ground for boasting – the Cross of our Lord Jesus Christ, by which the New Covenant has been sealed and the Redemption brought about and which therefore has come to be the sign of the Christian. This was the core of his preaching – the power and the wisdom of God (cf. 1 Cor 1:23-24). The Apostle's assertion has been echoed by Christians down the ages and has inspired pages of singular piety. For example, here is something from an Easter homily (preacher unknown) of the

it from me to glory except in the cross of our Lord Jesus Christ, by which[1] the world has been crucified to me, and I to the world. [15]For neither circumcision counts for anything, nor uncircumcision, but a new creation. [16]Peace and mercy be upon all who walk by this rule, upon the Israel of God.

Christi, per quem mihi mundus crucifixus est, et ego mundo. [15]Neque enim circumcisio aliquid est, neque praeputium, sed nova creatura. [16]Et quicumque hanc regulam secuti fuerint, pax super illos et misericordia et super Israel Dei.

---

second century: "When I am overtaken by fear of God, the Cross is my protection; when I stumble, it is my help and my support; when I engage in combat, my prize; when I conquer, my crown. The Cross is for me a narrow path, a narrow way – Jacob's ladder, which angels ascend and descend, at the top of which the Lord is to be found."

From the Holy Cross our salvation comes, for it was there that Jesus died for our sins. St John Chrysostom, therefore, praises it: "The Cross is the sign of victory displayed to fend off demons, the sword to use against sin, the sword with which Christ ran the serpent through; the Cross is the will of the Father, the glory of his Only Son, the joy of the Holy Spirit, the ornament of the angels, the assurance of the Church; it is what Paul glories in, it protects the saints and lights up the whole universe" (*De coemeterio et de cruce*, 2).

For his part St Anselm is so moved that he exclaims: "O Cross, chosen and designed to do such ineffable good: you are praised and exalted not so much by the minds and tongues of men, or even angels, as by the works that have been done thanks to you. O Cross, in whom and by whom salvation and life have come to me, in whom and by whom all good things come to me: God would not have me glory unless it be in you (cf. Gal 6:14)" (*Prayers and Meditations*, 4).

In the Cross, therefore, every Christian should be able to find support and strength for his daily life: "When you see a poor wooden Cross, alone, uncared-for, and of no value . . . and without its Crucified, don't forget that that Cross is your Cross: the Cross of each day, the hidden Cross, without splendour or consolation . . . , the Cross which is waiting the Crucified it lacks: and that Crucified must be you" (J. Escrivá, *The Way*, 178).

15. The expression "new creation" is full of theological content. It points to the fact that supernatural grace operates at a much higher level than any mere human action: just as God in creating the world made everything out of nothing, so too grace is granted without there being any previous merits. The phrase also indicates that, in regard to salvation, the only thing which matters as far as God is concerned is grace: just as things exist because they have been created, so

[1]Or *through whom.*

210

¹⁷Henceforth let no man trouble me; for I bear on my body the marks of Jesus.

¹⁸The grace of our Lord Jesus Christ be with your spirit, brethren. Amen.

---

¹⁷De cetero nemo mihi molestus sit; ego enim stigmata Iesu in corpore meo porto. ¹⁸Gratia Domini nostri Iesu Christi cum spiritu vestro, fratres. Amen.

---

man exists on the supernatural plane because he has been "created again". Finally, "new creation" gives us a glimpse into the mystery of grace: thus, when we were originally created we were given existence, and a nature, and certain faculties: in a similar way, on being created anew we are made to share in God's nature, we are given a new nature (super-nature) and a whole supernatural biology (the infused virtues and gifts of the Holy Spirit).

The nature which God gave man through creation was damaged by the sin of Adam, becoming thereby an "old creation", the old man. Our new life or new creation is in brilliant contrast with the dark background of sin and death caused by that original fall. "We have been created," St Thomas comments, "and we have received our natural being through Adam; but that creature grew old, and died, and therefore the Lord, by constituting us in the state of grace, worked a kind of new creation, 'that we should be a kind of first fruits of his creatures' (Jas 1:18). And he adds 'new' because we are renewed by him, given a new life; and by the Holy Spirit also. 'When thou sendest forth thy Spirit, they are created, and thou renewest the face of the earth' (Ps 104:30); and by the Cross of Christ [. . .]. Thus, by means of the new creation, that is, through faith in Christ and through the love of God, which has been poured into our hearts, we are renewed and we are united to Christ" (*Commentary on Gal, ad loc.*).

We find this parallelism between creation and the new creation (re-creation) in a number of places in the New Testament. The new life which is attained through union with Christ is called a "new creation" (cf. 2 Cor 5:17). This new creation is the new man, who is born not of blood nor of the will of the flesh nor of the will of man, but of God (cf. Jn 1:12-13), man raised up to the supernatural state of grace, created in Christ (cf. Eph 2:10, 15) for a life of righteousness and holiness (cf. Rom 6:4; Col 3:9-10), man, God's adoptive son and heir (cf. Rom 8:16), in whom Christ's own life is definitively manifested (cf. Gal 2:20).

17. A reference to the sign or brand put on livestock to show which herd it belongs to. In ancient times slaves were also branded – to show which family they belonged to – as were the adherents of some religions. St Paul alludes to these customs by declaring that he is metaphorically a servant of Christ.

Headings added to the text of the Epistles for this edition